SELECTED CL

NORTHEAST

SELECTED CLIMBS IN THE
NORTHEAST

ROCK, ALPINE, AND ICE ROUTES FROM THE GUNKS TO ACADIA

S. PETER LEWIS
DAVE HOROWITZ

THE MOUNTAINEERS BOOKS

For my faithful dog, Blackfoot.
—*D.H.*

For my wonderful wife, Karen.
—*S.P.L.*

Published by
The Mountaineers Books
1001 SW Klickitat Way, Suite 201
Seattle, WA 98134

First edition, 2003

Published simultaneously in Great Britain by Cordee, 3a DeMontfort Street, Leicester, England, LE1 7HD

Manufactured in the United States of America

Acquiring Editors: Margaret Foster, Christine Ummel Hosler
Project Editor and Copyeditor: Kris Fulsaas
Cover and book design: The Mountaineers Books
Layout: Mayumi Thompson
Cartographer: Moore Creative Designs and Jim Miller/Fennana Design

Cover photograph: *Dave Horowitz on Shockleys Ceiling in the Trapps at New York's Shawangunks.* Photo by Phil Wolin
Frontispiece: *Steve Nichipor and Alden Strong on the seaside classic Morning Glory at Great Head in Acadia National Park, Maine.* Photo by S. Peter Lewis

Library of Congress Cataloging-in-Publication Data
Lewis, S. Peter.
  Selected climbs in the Northeast : rock, alpine, and ice routes from
the Gunks to Acadia / S. Peter Lewis and Dave Horowitz.— 1st ed.
    p. cm.
Includes bibliographical references and index.
  ISBN 0-89886-857-2 (pbk.)
  1. Mountaineering—Northeastern states—Guidebooks. 2. Northeastern
states—Guidebooks. I. Horowitz, Dave, 1970- II. Title.
  GV199.42.N68L49 2003
  796.52'0974—dc21
                              2003013290

CONTENTS

MAP LEGEND

🌲	Tree	**1**	Ranger station	●	City, town
‖‖‖	Cliff	─91─	Interstate highway	★	Climbing area
〰	River	─86─	U.S. highway	57-60	Climb number(s)
🟤	Lake	─15─	State route	△	Camping
▲	Mountain	------	Boundary line	■	Building
		··········	Trail	Ⓟ	Parking

MAP 1

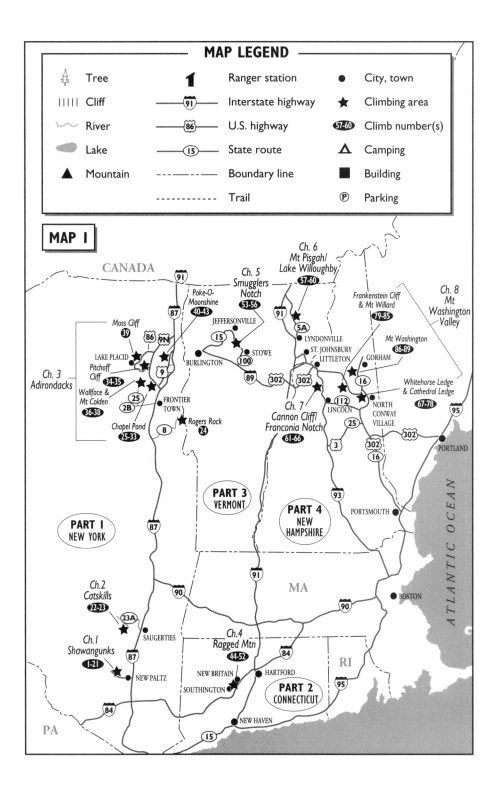

CANADA

Ch. 5 Smugglers Notch 53-56

Ch. 6 Mt Pisgah/ Lake Willoughby 57-60

Poke-O-Moonshine 40-43

Frankenstein Cliff & Mt Willard 79-85

Ch. 8 Mt Washington Valley

Moss Cliff 39

JEFFERSONVILLE

5A

LYNDONVILLE

Mt Washington 86-89

Ch. 3 Adirondacks

LAKE PLACID

Pitchoff Cliff 34-35

Wallface & Mt Colden 36-38

Chapel Pond 25-33

STOWE

BURLINGTON

FRONTIER TOWN

Rogers Rock 24

ST. JOHNSBURY

LITTLETON

GORHAM

Whitehorse Ledge & Cathedral Ledge 67-78

Ch. 7 Cannon Cliff/ Franconia Notch 61-66

LINCOLN

NORTH CONWAY VILLAGE

PORTLAND

PART 3 VERMONT

PART 4 NEW HAMPSHIRE

PORTSMOUTH

PART 1 NEW YORK

ATLANTIC OCEAN

MA

BOSTON

Ch.2 Catskills 22-23

23A

SAUGERTIES

Ch.1 Shawangunks 1-21

NEW PALTZ

Ch.4 Ragged Mtn 44-52

NEW BRITAIN

SOUTHINGTON

HARTFORD

RI

PART 2 CONNECTICUT

NEW HAVEN

PA

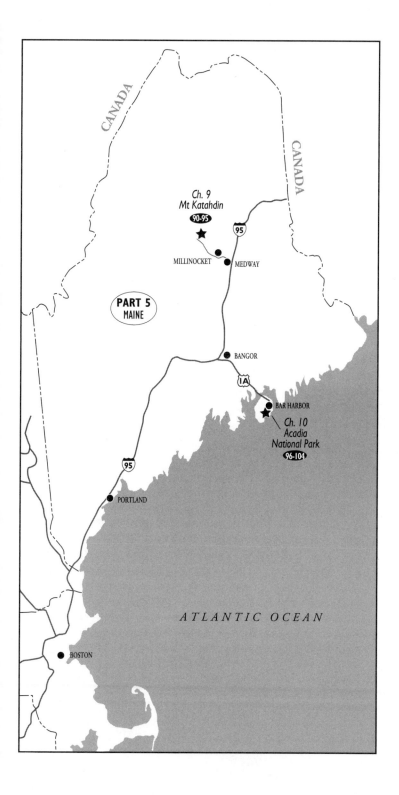

CANADA

CANADA

Ch. 9
Mt Katahdin
90-95

95

MILLINOCKET ● ● MEDWAY

PART 5
MAINE

● BANGOR

1A

● BAR HARBOR
Ch. 10
Acadia
National Park
96-104

95

● PORTLAND

ATLANTIC OCEAN

● BOSTON

ACKNOWLEDGMENTS

Dave wishes to thank everyone who was so generous with their time, knowledge, and help in contributing to this book. Special thanks to Jennifer East; without her, I would have been lost. Thanks to Phil Wolin, longtime climbing partner, friend, and world-class photographer. Thank you for the expert input, Marty Molitoris and Mike Cross. Thanks to Billy "B," Matt Calardo, Bill Cramer, Teegan Delli-Bovi, Tylor Durand, Justin Ferren, Fixx, Sheldon Fogelman, Steve Goldman, Rich Gottlieb, Ken Horowitz, Tor Jacobson, Leif Johansson, Jim Ianora, Anissa Kapsales, Beth and Donald Kimmel, Rit Picone, Bill Rosner, Christopher Ross, Randy Ross, Marc Roussel, Karina Sampson, Craig Shaw, Gene Simmons, Kim Tischler, Matt Wade, David Weeks, Marcia Wernick, Evangeline Wolfe, and everyone at Alpine Endeavors, the Eastern Mountain Sports Climbing School, and *Rock and Snow*. Thanks to my family.

Peter wishes to thank his many friends who have given such enthusiastic support and help to this project (and many others) over the last two decades. Thanks to the following folks for their generous help with route information or photos for this book: Mark Arsenault, Henry Barber, Bob Baribeau, the folks at Baxter State Park, John Bouchard, Jeff Butterfield, Marc Chauvin, Peter Cole, Jason Huckaby, John Imbrie, Bernie Mailhot, Doug Millen, Alden Pellett, John Peterson, Brian Post, Jim Shimberg, Tyler Stableford, David Stone, Jon Sykes, Joe Terravecchia, Pat Viljanen, Ed Webster, Rick Wilcox, Kurt Winkler, and a special thank-you to Laura and the late Guy Waterman for both their friendship and their diligent chronicling of Northeast climbing history—their research added immeasurably to this book. A special thank-you also to Brad White for all the hours he spent poring over the manuscript. Thanks also to the many friends who have cheerfully put up with me over the last twenty years, either at the other end of the climbing rope or when I was hanging over their heads with a camera: Steve Arsenault, Brad Beaurhinger, Dave Breashears, Kitty Calhoun, Polly DeConto, Gabe Flanders, Blair Foltz, George Hurley, Brian Johnston, Dave Kelly, Mike Levasseur, Jeremiah Lewis, Bruce Luetters, Claude Muff, Steve Nichipor, Ray Omerza, Alison Osius, Bill Pelkey, Dave Rose, Louise Shepherd, Sam Streibert, Alden Strong, Jim Surette, Craig Taylor, Jennifer Tennica, John Tremblay, Tom Vinson, Conrad Yager, and Nick Yardley.

INTRODUCTION

It may seem that our intent in *Selected Climbs in the Northeast* is to document the finest climbs in the land so that you can find them and do them enjoyably and safely. If that were precisely true, then this book will have fallen far short. Is the information here as accurate as possible? Yes. If followed, will the instructions in this book help you find the climbs, ascend and descend them safely, and enjoy them along the way? Absolutely. Are these the finest routes in the land? Now there is the sticking point—the answer is both yes and no.

While we are confident that the routes in this book will bring a smile and nod of consent from those who know this region and its climbs, we are also certain that each critic will take but a few seconds to say, "Hey, but what about? . . ." The Northeast has too much history and is simply too big, too diverse, and too overflowing with wonderful climbing to try to melt it down into just a handful of routes. It is like boiling maple sap to make maple candy, that intensely sugary delight for which the Northeast is so well known. Long before the sap has been rendered into hard candy, it becomes maple syrup—in itself so wonderful that it cannot be passed up. So here is our list—the maple syrup, if you will—of the sweetest climbing that the Northeast has to offer. But be advised: for every treat you read about, there is candy

Maple syrup buckets are part of Vermont's winter scenery. Photo by S. Peter Lewis

just as sweet only a few yards down the cliff, over the next hill, or coming into shape next month. We struggled hard to pare down our list, shedding a few tears along the way, but we are proud of the result. Even if we had been limited to 300 routes instead of the 104 listed here, we still would have found ourselves saying, "Hey, but what about? . . ."

This book covers all of New England, plus the eastern third of New York. This is not an arbitrary demarcation. Climbing in the Northeast is defined more by history and culture than geography and political boundaries. Since the early part of the twentieth century, climbers have flitted over this region, exploring, climbing, mixing with each other, and sharing adventures with little regard to governing boundaries or regional labels. Traveling through Connecticut on Interstate 84 today, it would not be unusual to see a carload of Boston climbers heading west to New York's Shawangunks pass a bunch of New Yorkers heading east for New Hampshire. Meanwhile, the Connecticut folks have beat it to Maine, while a group of Vermont climbers have decided to spend the weekend in New York's Adirondacks. As far as Northeastern climbers are concerned, the borders just do not exist. Sure, we could have limited this book to routes in just New England and it would have seemed geographically tidy, but historically and culturally it would have been insensitive and nowhere near as much fun. Imagine having a potluck supper but not inviting anyone who would bring dessert—not only would you offend some dear friends, it would also mean you would not eat any pie.

Our definition of "Northeast," eastern New York plus New England, is a region with such a diversity of climbing types and styles as well as cultural and climatic conditions that a person could spend a lifetime here and not sample the best of everything. Faced with such abundance, we had to make some tough decisions about what to include. In the end, we concluded that it was the rich history of Northeastern climbing and its heritage of adventure that would be the most important criteria. Thus you will find, for the most part, multipitch, traditional climbs (both rock and ice), including many that have contributed to the rich history of climbing in this region (and the country as a whole). In some instances where only short routes prevail (for example, Connecticut's Ragged Mountain or Maine's Acadia National Park), we have given you a quiver full of short routes to choose from and link together into a longer adventure. Alas, we have not included any bouldering or sport climbing—though the region has much to offer in both these arenas; nor is there anything from Massachusetts or Rhode Island (both of which have quality climbing). But what we have chosen should give everyone something to cheer about. And we are also confident that even those who have climbed here for decades will find reasons to earmark many pages.

The Northeast

You could fit the area covered in this guide—the eastern third of New York and all of New England—into Colorado and still have enough room for just about all of West Virginia. But we will stick our necks out and bet that in our little corner of the United States lies a greater diversity of climbing than in many of the western states that are much touted for their climbing.

Mount Katahdin's Armadillo in winter, one of the most impressive alpine rock routes in the Northeast. Photo by Peter Cole

The Northeast climbing experience is one of diversity and extremes set in a simply charming countryside. Rolling hills, snowy mountains, hardwood forests in the south, towering pines in the north, rivers and lakes everywhere, four real seasons (and oh, what gorgeous autumns), tiny towns (village green, bandstand, steepled church, and 200-year-old, white Cape-style homes), huge tracts of wildland full of silence, and . . . well, you get the idea.

For many years now, the Northeast has had to defend its geography and its climbing:

"New York? Just a big city."

Tell that to folks who live upstate in the six-million-acre Adirondack State Park, which is bigger than Yosemite, Yellowstone, Grand Teton, Zion, Rocky Mountain, North Cascades, Sequoia/Kings Canyon, and Black Canyon of the Gunnison National Parks combined. And northern Maine could swallow the Adirondacks without even chewing.

"There are no real mountains in the East."

If a lump of geography that rises more than 5,000 feet above its surrounding valleys, extends well above timberline, is snow covered at least eight months of the year, gets more than 250 inches of snow annually, and is home to the highest wind speed ever recorded on the surface of the earth is considered a "real" mountain, then we have one—Mount Washington in New Hampshire's White Mountains (there's Katahdin in Maine and the High Peaks of the Adirondacks too).

"The Northeast is too congested."

The cities are, but that is true everywhere—however, the wild areas are not. Peter's father, a very experienced woodsman who never got lost, admitted that he was once "confused for upward of four days" in the Adirondacks. And the northern 20,000 square miles of Maine is so sparsely populated that the region is divided into dozens of unincorporated townships—they do not even have names.

"All the climbing is just short stuff."

We have some of the best rock cragging and short ice climbing in the country. But we also have big-wall routes more than twelve pitches long, 500-foot frozen waterfalls, and 1,500-foot alpine climbs above timberline. It is not all short.

If there is one thing the Northeast is known for, it is diversity. Say you live in central Massachusetts and you want to plan nine 3-day climbing weekends over the course of a year. In May you drive south to Ragged Mountain in Connecticut to sample some steep trad crack climbing and then head west to the Gunks for some multipitch quartzite overhangs. In late June you beat the bugs by heading to Maine for a day of climbing over the ocean in Acadia. In July you are off to the Adirondacks for some backcountry rock. In August you do the alpine circuit with a marathon trip to Katahdin and a quick one-day hit of the rock above timberline on Mount Washington. September is pure gold on the great granite crags of the White Mountains (including a 1-day trip up a Grade V on Cannon Cliff). Come December, it is early season ice on the alpine crags of New Hampshire. It is too cold in January to head north, so head south to the Catskills for some banana-belt ice. February is perfect in the Adirondacks, with deep snow and thick ice; and then you grab a day climbing endless pillars at Lake Willoughby in Vermont. And March, with its longer days and moderating temperatures, is the perfect time to head back to rugged Katahdin to tick some of the longest snow and ice climbs in the region.

Now to be able to do all this, you have to have a lot of diverse skills. If living and climbing in the Northeast has one outstanding characteristic, it is that it helps climbers build a wide skill base. If you climb here year-round and push yourself, you can get very good at a lot of different types of climbing. You will learn to crank hard moves (up to 5.14 if you want); get comfortable on slabs, faces, cracks, and overhangs; build bowling-ball calves on long ice pillars; get those lungs in shape on long slogs up steep snow chutes; and learn how to move fast on alpine rock.

Ever hear of Robert Underhill, Ken Henderson, Fritz Wiessner, Brad Washburn, Jim McCarthy, George Hurley, Jimmy Dunn, Henry Barber, John Bragg, Steve Wunsch, Ed Webster, John Bouchard, Mark Richey, Rick Wilcox, Hugh Herr, Russ Clune, Randy Rackcliff, Jim Surrette, Lynn Hill, Joe Terravecchia, Kevin Mahoney, Mark Synnott, or Dave Breashears? They are all Northeast folks who have distinguished themselves around the world on every type of climbing terrain imaginable. And these are just the folks you have heard of.

Northeast climbing is magical. Climbing in and around these old hills will bring you back to the roots of American climbing. Climb Cannon's Whitney-Gilman Ridge and you will be repeating the hardest climb in the country from 1929. Swing your tools into the blue ice in Keene Valley, New York, and you may be cutting into the same drip that Yvon Chouinard used to usher in the ice revolution back in 1969. Crank the overhanging Yellow Wall in the Gunks, and you may be following in the chalk dabs of Lynn Hill. On a perfect winter day, with an undercast of clouds below your feet, step out of the top of Pinnacle Gully on Mount Washington and gaze out at the Atlantic Ocean 90 miles away, and you will understand why so many climbers have fallen under the spell of the Northeast.

How to Use This Book

The format of this book is simple. We start with New York and take that state south to north, then head east into Connecticut, and then cross northern New England from Vermont through New Hampshire, and finish in Maine, north to south. The New York chapters were written by Dave Horowitz; Peter Lewis wrote all the other chapters.

Each climbing area has an introduction in which we give an overview (including types of climbing, type of rock, general elevation, and number of routes in the area), describe any special considerations (fees, locked gates, etc.), provide emergency contact information, discuss the weather and climbing seasons, give a list of standard equipment for the area, and provide directions to the place (driving directions are under Getting There; hiking directions are under Approach).

After that, we describe each route (both summer and winter) for that area. Route descriptions contain historical data, any unusual information not covered in the area description (for example, an additional Equipment list tells you to bring huge cams in addition to the standard rack for the area), specific start and descent information, and a pitch-by-pitch route description. Route photos, cliff photos with route lines, and topos help you stay on route. For most routes, we also include a personal anecdote or some history—something to convey the flavor of the climb, to give it a hook, to make you nod in appreciation, wince, or chuckle. We hope to make you lie awake at night thinking about your next road trip.

In the back of the book there are appendixes on ratings and resources (climbing shops, supplies, camping, and websites) for each area, plus a bibliography. Throughout the book we use the standard rating systems used in North America. For each route you will find a commitment grade (i.e., how long the route should take) and the appropriate overall technical rating for the rock, aid, ice, or mixed climbing. Each pitch also gets a separate technical rating. If you are unfamiliar with any of these systems, please see Appendix A, Ratings.

TOPO LEGEND

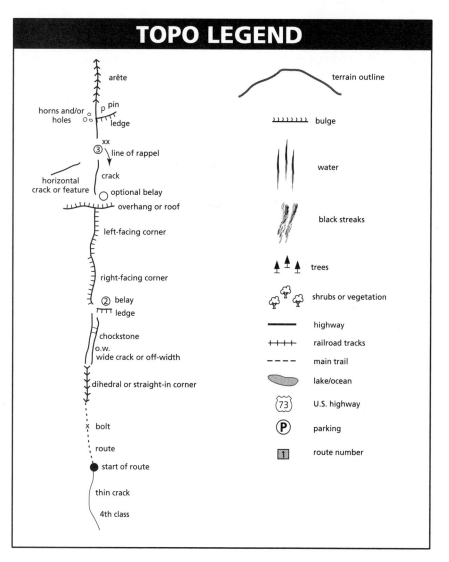

arête

horns and/or holes

pin

ledge

xx

③ line of rappel

horizontal crack or feature

crack

optional belay

overhang or roof

left-facing corner

right-facing corner

② belay

ledge

chockstone

o.w. wide crack or off-width

dihedral or straight-in corner

x bolt

route

start of route

thin crack

4th class

terrain outline

bulge

water

black streaks

trees

shrubs or vegetation

highway

railroad tracks

main trail

lake/ocean

(73) U.S. highway

(P) parking

1 route number

Access and Land-Use Regulations

We have made every effort to research the access to the areas and routes we describe, and to our knowledge all the climbs in this book were legally accessible at the time of publication via the routes and methods we describe. As climbing has become more popular, access issues have become more and more common. It is the responsibility of each climber to adhere to the laws regarding access to public lands and to honor the wishes of those landowners who allow climbing on their private land. Ask permission—private land is often open to climbers; help keep it that way by checking with landowners if you have any doubt about access privileges. Follow regulations and respect closures (for example, for nesting raptors). Please take the time to make sure that you access land legally and comply with any changes in status that have occurred since we wrote this book—even if it means you will not be able to tick off one of the wonderful routes described here. Get involved in solving access problems; consider joining the Access Fund (see Appendix B, Resources), a climber advocacy group that works to keep climbing areas open.

Environmental Concerns

Just as important is climbing responsibly and ethically. Climbers are one of the most environmentally friendly user groups. We are usually conscientious, follow the rules, and pack out our trash. Keep up the good reputation by following the general principles established by Leave No Trace, a national nonprofit organization committed to minimizing environmental impacts by recreationalists:

- Plan ahead and prepare.
- Camp and travel on durable surfaces.
- Pack it in, pack it out.
- Properly dispose of what you cannot pack out.
- Leave what you find.
- Minimize use and impact from fires.

   In addition, follow these specific principles when climbing:

- Do not chip or drill holds.
- Use removable protection. Bolts and pitons permanently change the rock.
- Do not use motorized drills in wilderness areas. Placing bolts is a privilege; follow the rules (and local tradition).
- Consider the overall environmental impacts of developing a new area or route. Traffic, trails, and disturbance to wildlife may follow.
- Leave anchors that blend in. If you place bolts on a new route, leave a fixed anchor at the belay or leave a dull-colored sling and make it as visually unobtrusive as possible.
- Do not rappel directly from trees. Use slings and rappel rings instead; trees can die if they are rappelled from repeatedly.
- Consider using a chalk color that blends in with the rock—or using none at all.
- If mixed climbing at a rock climbing area, take extra care not to scratch, mar, or otherwise make obvious your passage with tools and crampons.
- Clean up after yourself. Spend a few minutes cleaning up before you leave—even if it is not your trash.
- Keep the noise down, especially in urban areas. Be sensitive to the solitude enjoyed by residents and other users.
- Park where allowed, and keep a low profile along the road too.

Climbing Ethics

College degrees are offered in ethics, but here we do not need to get that deep. For climbers, it is common sense to:

- Be kind to climbers, landowners, and other users. Be sensitive, not a nuisance.
- Do not hog routes.

- Do not pass people on a route without their permission, and consider never passing anyone on an ice climb.
- Do not pressure other climbers to hurry up with your favorite climb; do something else while you wait.
- Do not mislead others about the characteristics of a route. "Sandbagging" can be dangerous.
- Be cautious about sharing routes. Be certain of the safety system's security before climbing on anyone else's rope.
- Be quick to help in an emergency. Keep your eyes open, step in if you see a life-threatening situation developing, help if you can if there is an accident, and let the person with the most medical experience take charge.

Safety Issues

Climbing is really dangerous, and anyone who says otherwise is trying to sell you something. Though we have made every effort to be accurate and complete, routes change and errors creep in. All climbers should take responsibility for their own safety and use common sense—even if it means going left when the guidebook says to go right.

So here you have it: 104 routes, 325-plus pitches, more than 30,000 feet of the best climbing anywhere, described so you can find the bottom, get up the middle, and get down from the top. Collectively we have spent more than three decades on these and other great routes in the Northeast and are as excited about climbing today as the day we first tied in. We hope this book and these routes get your juices flowing too.

A Note About Safety

Safety is an important concern in all outdoor activities. No guidebook can alert you to every hazard or anticipate the limitations of every reader. Therefore, the descriptions of roads, trails, routes, and natural features in this book are not representations that a particular place or excursion will be safe for your party. When you follow any of the routes described in this book, you assume responsibility for your own safety. Under normal conditions, such excursions require the usual attention to traffic, road and trail conditions, weather, terrain, the capabilities of your party, and other factors. Because many of the lands in this book are subject to development and/or change of ownership, conditions may have changed since this book was written that make your use of some of these routes unwise. Always check for current conditions, obey posted private property signs, and avoid confrontations with property owners or managers. Keeping informed on current conditions and exercising common sense are the keys to a safe, enjoyable outing.

The Mountaineers Books

PART I

NEW YORK _____

Opposite: *A climber on the Trapps in New York's Shawangunks.* Photo by Dave Horowitz

Many New Yorkers believe New York City is the center of the universe. We even refer to it as "the city," as if there could be another. Of course, we climbers realize that it is not entirely true. The actual center of the universe lies 100 miles northwest of the city at the Gunks.

If you can handle a little of this sort of attitude, you will be fine here. New Yorkers actually make some of the friendliest climbers you will meet. Used to tight spaces, they are often happy to share a top rope or some beta. Just watch where you toss your rope, or you might hear, "Hey, I'm frickin' climbin' here!"

Fritz Wiessner (pronounced VEES-ner) wrote in *Appalachia* in 1960, "It is rare in our days of overexploitation of the land to find, near a large city, country which is still unspoiled by man and as beautiful as when it was created." All things being relative, this quote is still, for the most part, true. Although the crowds have grown exponentially, and the trails and rock are feeling the effects, the Shawangunk ridge still seems to resist its place in time. One of traditional climbing's final bastions, the Gunks are still as inviting and imposing as ever.

To the north are the Catskills. Legend has it that it was in the Catskills where Rip Van Winkle encountered a band of strange little men at the base of a secluded ravine. They offered up a brew that put him to sleep for more than a hundred years. Ice climbers should mind their Thermos lest they miss all the fun.

If you crave remote, New York has that too. Less than a day's drive from the city are the Adirondacks. Rugged and immense, the region is home to a wealth of climbing accessible to those willing to bust out a map and scratch their chins.

I ♥ NY.

CHAPTER 1. THE SHAWANGUNKS ———————

Climbing type ▲ Traditional
Rock type ▲ Quartzite conglomerate
Elevation ▲ 1,000 feet
Number of routes ▲ 21 in this book

Among the rolling farmland of New York's Hudson Valley, four dramatic cliffs stand high above the peaceful landscape . . . and then there are the weekends.

Yes, the Shawangunks are crowded. One visit, however, and it is clear why. The Gunks are a playground of world-class rock climbing a mere 100 miles from New York City. A network of trails, built in the late 1800s as part of the carriage roads to the still-operating Mohonk Mountain House, link the cliffs, making access to the thousand or so routes incredibly simple.

The Gunks offer traditional climbing like it was meant to be. The Gunks is where 5.6 can still put your heart in your throat and some of the pitons are older than, well, me.

The rock, a very solid quartzite conglomerate, provides unique climbing. The walls are steep and the roofs are big. The horizontal fractures that ripple the cliffs typically offer ample protection and perfectly in-cut "thank God" holds right where you want them. Not only are the Gunks renowned for hard routes (read pumpy, sandbaggy, exposed), but at the same time it is home to the world's best moderate climbing. In most climbing areas, 5.3s are dirty, gnarly gullies. At the Gunks, because of the nature of the rock and its magnificent setting, 5.3 can be as spectacular and worthwhile as any test piece.

Although there are numerous other cliffs and outcrops in the Gunks, all the climbs described in this guidebook are on the two major escarpments: the Trapps and Near Trapps. (Climbing at Skytop is illegal.) The Trapps is the long, impressive wall that dominates the horizon as you approach from the interstate. This is the most popular cliff by far. On the opposite (south) side of US 44/55 is the Near Trapps, with colorful rock and soaring corners.

Special Considerations
The cliffs are on private property, owned by the Mohonk Preserve. Day-use and yearly passes are available from rangers at points of entry, the Überfall, or the visitor center (845-255-0919) located just below the hairpin turn on US 44/55 on the way up to the mountain.

Emergency Information
Accidents should be reported to a Mohonk Preserve ranger if possible. With a cell phone, during business hours call the preserve (845-255-0919); any other time, call the Mohonk Mountain House (845-255-1000). As a last resort, call local police and fire departments (911).

Weather and Seasons
April through early November; middle of October is best. Summers can be uncomfortably hot.

Standard Equipment
A good selection of nuts and cams up to a number 3 Camalot (3-inch); Tricams; long slings to avoid rope drag on the many roofs and corners. Sixty-meter ropes for linking pitches and for rappels. The Gunks are heavily trafficked; helmets are advisable.

Getting There
From the New York State Thruway (I-87), take exit 18 (New Paltz), then make a left onto Route 299 at the light after the toll. Follow Route 299 (aka Main Street) through New Paltz and stay on it until its end at the intersection with US 44/55. Make a right on US 44/55 and head up the mountain. At the apex of the hill, Trapps Bridge (a steel footbridge) crosses US 44/55. Continue under the bridge and head down the other side of the mountain; 0.1 mile down on the right is the West Trapps parking lot (the largest). (Another parking option is described in Approach, below.)

The Trapps
The Trapps has the majority of quality climbing here and therefore sees the most traffic. Most of the climbs on the Trapps are two to three pitches long. The cliff, like the entire ridgeline, runs north-south. A carriage trail (Undercliff Road) runs under and parallel to the cliff. A large horizontal ledge runs almost unbroken across the whole

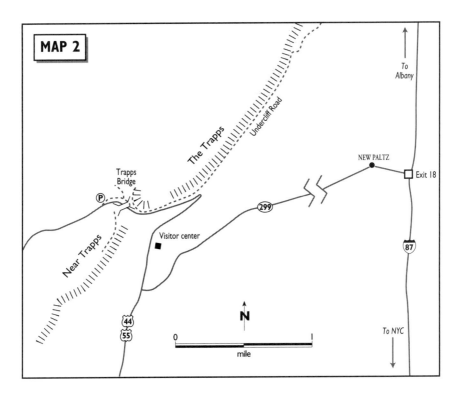

MAP 2

The Trapps

Undercliff Road

To Albany

NEW PALTZ

Exit 18

Trapps Bridge

P

299

87

Visitor center

Near Trapps

N

44
55

To NYC

0   1
mile

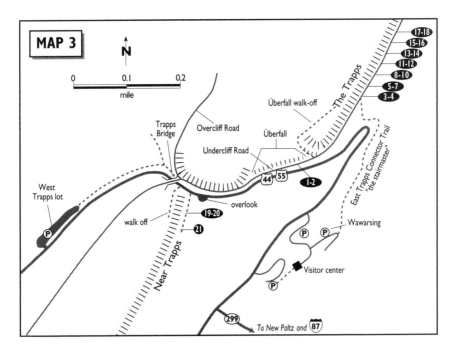

MAP 3

N

0   0.1   0.2
mile

The Trapps

17-18
15-16
13-14
11-12
8-10
5-7
3-4

Überfall walk-off

Overcliff Road

Überfall

Trapps Bridge

Undercliff Road

44 55

1-2

East Trapps Connector Trail "the stairmaster"

West Trapps lot

P

overlook

19-20

walk off

21

Wawarsing

P   P

Near Trapps

P

Visitor center

P

299   To New Paltz and   87

cliff. Conveniently traversing at about two-thirds height, this "Grand Traverse" (GT) Ledge offers frequently comfortable belays.

The Überfall (German for "packed with too many people," I think) is the name given to the 4th-class scramble/descent route near the southern end of the Trapps; it has also become the popular name for the whole area near this section of cliff. Throughout the Überfall, the carriage trail runs directly along the base of the cliff. The cliff is still short enough in some parts that top-roping is possible. It is an obvious meeting place, a common ranger hangout, and a bouldering playground. The Überfall is where most climbers congregate and peanut galleries gather.

Approach

From the north end of the West Trapps parking lot, walk the path up to Trapps Bridge. Take the steps up and walk away from the bridge (north), without crossing it, to reach the Trapps. Walking north (left, after you have climbed the steps) from Trapps Bridge, you reach the Überfall in a minute or two. Just past a large rectangular buttress (the Hurdy-Gurdy Block), just feet from the carriage trail, is the beginning of the Überfall. A big roof (Dougs Roof) literally hangs over the trail, and you can see the improbable corner up on Horseman (5.5). The Überfall extends for another minute's walk or so, until the cliff gets tall again just after the information kiosk.

A few minutes beyond the Überfall is a junction with the East Trapps Connector Trail (often rangers hang out here collecting fees). This trail, aka "the stairmaster," begins at the Wawarsing parking area (just uphill of the visitor center on US 44/55) and is another way to reach the Undercliff carriage trail.

1. Retribution   I, 5.10a

Nosedive and Retribution are great sister climbs that share the same anchors. Typically, climbers climb one and top-rope the other. Which you prefer is a matter of taste. I find the balancey finale on Nosedive superior to the early thuggish crux of Retribution. But hey, since you have the rope up, decide for yourself.

First ascent: Art Gran and Peter Himot, 1958; first free climb: Jim McCarthy, 1961.

Start: At the Überfall, just to the right of the Hurdy-Gurdy Block and a few feet right of the signs concerning slope restoration are a pair of parallel vertical corners/cracks with a large square roof between them about 35 feet up. The left-hand route is Retribution (the crack on the right is Nosedive, climb 2). Begin at the right-facing corner 8 feet left of Nosedive.

Route: Pitch 1 (90 feet, 5.10a): Climb the corner to the roof. Climb out around left and up. Follow the shallow inside corner to the anchors in the alcove above.

Descent: Belay and/or rappel.

2. Nosedive   I, 5.10b

I usually avoid Gunks climbs with fatalistic names like Crash and Burn, Talus Food, or Sudden Death, but I make an exception for the elegant Nosedive. Even its location in the often chaotic Überfall cannot detract from the quality of this short but sweet natural line.

Nosedive may be a single 5.10 pitch with good gear, but make no mistake: it is

Bolts
XX

1
Retribution

2
Nosedive

Two of the first climbs encountered at the Trapps in New York's Shawangunks.
Photo by Dave Horowitz

Chad Lewis starting the crux of Retribution in New York's Shawangunks. Photo by Bill Cramer

no giveaway. Interesting moves lead to the final rest stance before a long, committing crux. Once you have left that stance, it is pass or flail—30 feet of real rock climbing stands between you and victory. The longer you hesitate, the more hecklers will show up, so get going while the going is good.

There is really no trick to it; just climb efficiently and do not dawdle. After the rest, you move around left to below the final crack. There is an obvious slot for gear. But from your balancey position, defying a barn-door swing, can you place that gear? You had better hope so. Many have instead chosen to just keep going, only to learn that the horizontal above does not provide the obvious rest it looked like it would from below.

If this is your predicament, fighting the pump from this slopey ledge, fiddling with gear that just will not fit right, you have three choices: (1) suck it up and go for it; (2) scurry around and retreat like a cockroach startled by the kitchen light; or (3) take the horrifying Nosedive and get it over with.

First ascent: Ted Church and Krist Raubenheimer, 1956; first free ascent: Jim McCarthy, 1961.

Start: At the Überfall, just to the right of the Hurdy-Gurdy Block and a few feet right of the signs concerning slope restoration are a pair of parallel vertical corners/cracks with a large square roof between them about 35 feet up. The crack on the right is Nosedive (the left-hand route is Retribution, climb 1).

Route: Pitch 1 (90 feet, 5.10b): Climb the crack up to a stance below the bulge. Gather your courage and technique and follow the crack up and left to its end at a not-so-positive horizontal handshelf. Move left to a bolted anchor in the alcove above Retribution.

Descent: Belay and/or rappel.

3. Strictly from Nowhere   I, 5.7

With an exciting crux section and pleasant finish, Strictly from Nowhere is a fun climb by itself. It is possible, though, to climb the crux of Strictly and then diagonal over to link the crux pitch of Shockleys Ceiling (climb 4). This is highly recommended.

First ascent: Art Gran and Jim Andress, 1959.

Start: Walk a few minutes past the Überfall on the carriage trail to a signpost on the left for the East Trapps Connector Trail. A few feet right of the signpost is a yellow-blazed connector trail; follow this up to the cliff to a 20-foot-wide toe of rock. Strictly from Nowhere begins just left of the end of the trail.

Route: Pitch 1 (50 feet, 5.6): Climb the toe of rock about in its center, past a double overhang. Continue to gain the ledge atop the "pedestal." Belay near the slings in the big right-facing corner.

Pitch 2 (100 feet, 5.7): Climb up into the left-facing corner above and then out right onto the face with a prominent tree and a bolted rap station. This is a popular belay. (**Note:** If you plan to link with Shockleys Ceiling, from this belay, traverse out right and diagonally up to the belay alcove under Shockley's big roof [80 feet, 5.5]. Finish as for pitch 3 of Shockleys Ceiling.) To continue up Strictly from Nowhere, angle left past a small overhang and then back right past another overhang to a good belay ledge.

Pitch 3 (50 feet, 5.4): Climb the obvious left-facing corner and the face to the top.

Descent: It is possible to rappel the route. However, you are close enough to the Überfall that walking off (take the trail to the left) is easier and usually faster than rappelling.

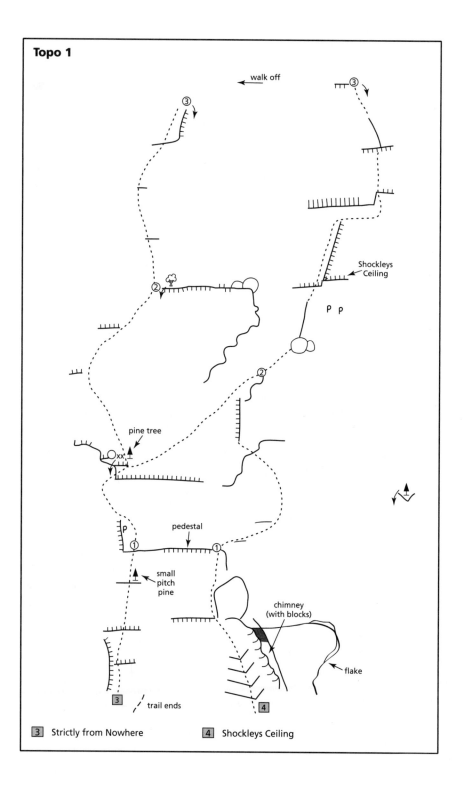

Topo 1

walk off

Shockleys Ceiling

pine tree

pedestal

small pitch pine

chimney (with blocks)

flake

trail ends

3 Strictly from Nowhere   **4** Shockleys Ceiling

Marty Molitoris belaying a client on Strictly from Nowhere in the Gunks, New York.
Photo by Dave Horowitz

THE SHAWANGUNKS ▲ 31

4. Shockleys Ceiling   I, 5.6+

With its imposing ceiling and clean, exposed corners, Shockleys Ceiling is a superclassic that transcends its rating. Besides following a bold natural line, Shockleys has three other things going for it: location, location, location. Highly visible from the hairpin turn in the road below, it has become the natural choice for Gunks climbers making a statement. In the 1960s, Dick Williams began a rare but still practiced tradition of shocking the tourists below by climbing the route naked. In the dark autumn of 2001, climbers chose this prominent location to fix a large American flag that lauded our unity and bespoke our loss. At the hairpin turn below, gapers frequently loiter with binoculars to watch the show.

When you are the one on display, though, it is not so entertaining. Like juggling or spinning a hula hoop, climbing a ceiling like Shockleys is one of those things you can only do perfectly if no one is watching. But unless it is a Tuesday in January, there will be someone watching. The pressure is on; so make it look good.

My debut performance on Shockleys was indeed a crowd pleaser. Getting my arms and torso past the roof was easy. I hung off the ceiling and felt the audience go silent. "Now what?" I thought. Somehow I had to get my legs up past the giant roof. I could not see my feet, let alone where I might put them. Out to the right, the ceiling comes to a prominent point. "What do I do with that?" I wondered. "Do I stem out there with my foot or step left?" My arms were melting. I wished I had placed some gear above the old pins.

Eventually my mind contrived the most cowardly of moves. With all the strength I could muster, I hauled myself as high as I could and straddled the point. There I huddled, with a leg dangling off each side of the protrusion, hugging the rock in front of me for dear life. So ridiculous was my position, I nearly laughed myself off my perch, totally aware the gapers below were getting what they came for.

First ascent: Bill Shockley (Nobel Prize–winning inventor of the transistor) and Doug Kerr, 1953.

Start: Walk a few minutes past the Überfall on the carriage trail to a signpost on the left for the East Trapps Connector Trail. A few feet right of the signpost is a yellow-blazed connector trail; follow this up to the cliff to a 20-foot-wide toe of rock. Begin either on the toe's right arête or a few feet right of it, uphill around the corner in the inside corner with blocks. A large flake to the right of the start lets you know you are in the right spot.

Route: Pitch 1 (60 feet, 5.4): Gain the first ledge about 15 feet up. Then climb around the blocks and up the chimney and flake to gain the right side of the pedestal. Belay here.

Pitch 2 (130 feet, 5.5): Step off the pedestal onto the face to the right. Diagonal up and right to climb through the small overhang. Step left and up the airy right-facing corner. When you reach the top of this corner, head for the ledge above you. (You can move over to nice holds on the flake to the right, which arches back to the ledge.) This small ledge is a possible belay. Continue up the short right-facing corner. Then traverse and angle up and right to an alcove with large blocks 25 feet below the beautiful white ceiling split by a right-leaning crack. Belay here.

Pitch 3 (90 feet, 5.6+): Have a conversation about what you will do when you cannot hear "on belay, off belay," etc. This will probably be the case when the leader tops out. If your second is not confident, you would be wise to break this pitch in two, so you can watch your second at the ceiling. Climb the inside corner past pitons to Shockleys Ceiling. Tell yourself it is only 5.6 and crank it. Follow the gorgeous inside corner above to its top. Move around the corner on good holds to the right. Then climb up the next small yet awkward overhang. Keep following the crack past slopey holds to the top.

Descent: It is possible to rappel to the right of the route. However, you are close enough to the Überfall that walking off (take the trail to the left) is easier and usually faster than rappelling.

5. The Climb Formerly Known as Three Pines   I, 5.3+

Sadly, in November 2002, an early season ice storm reminded us how small we are. This route's landmark second pine, once visible from the hairpin turn in the road below, now lies in pieces among the talus. This noble tree probably began pushing through the rocky Grand Traverse (GT) Ledge as the Declaration of Independence was being considered. Indeed, hundreds of us have "bellied" around or belayed off its mighty girth in the centuries since. A tree could not be more missed. Pay your respects as you climb this, the best route of its rating on the planet.

Many climbers cut their multipitch teeth on the Climb Formerly Known as Three Pines. It is a great choice. Take the first belay ledge; you can anchor off the mightiest tree in the county while nestled in a rock bathtub. On pitch 2, all of a sudden you are way up there, and the ledge is huge. Then classic Gunks: "The route goes out where?" It could not possibly go out around that nose, way up there, hanging out in space like that. Oh, but it does, and it is a touch balancey. But fear not, the gear is good and just around the corner is another fantastic belay ledge, of course. You are now perched on a corner so far from the cliff and so high up the wall that you are committed to the top. But again, the climbing to the top is quite easy. Usually. . . .

I was at that third belay early last autumn with a very pleasant older gentleman; maybe his name was George. He still had his EBs and ancient flat-tape harness. He also had not climbed in more than fifteen years, so Three Pines was the perfect route for getting his climbing legs back. Rain clouds had been building all morning, but we were moving fast and George was enthusiastic. When I pointed out the coming weather, he just smiled and said, "No problem." We were at the described point of no return when it started to drizzle.

"None of the climbing above is hard," I assured George. "But the last few feet is a slab. I want to get there before it really starts coming down."

"No problem," he smiled.

I took a few steps up to gain the next ledge. And right there, just inches from my face, was a 6-foot black snake. It was not moving, I was not going anywhere, and

Opposite: *"Westfield" Dave under Shockleys Ceiling in the Gunks, New York.* Photo by Phil Wolin

Topo 2

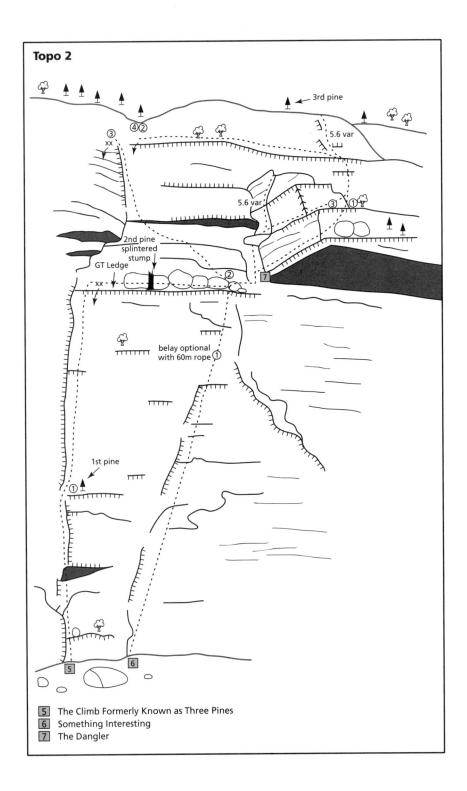

3rd pine

5.6 var

③
xx

④②

5.6 var

③ ①

2nd pine
splintered
stump

GT Ledge

xx

②

7

belay optional
with 60m rope ①

1st pine

①

5

6

5 The Climb Formerly Known as Three Pines
6 Something Interesting
7 The Dangler

the rock was not getting drier. The sky eventually opened up with all its fury. The rain did convince the snake to slither on, but not without drenching us and the final slab of rock too.

First ascent: Hans Kraus, Roger Wolcott, and Del Wilde, 1941.

Start: From the Überfall, walk the Undercliff carriage trail to the junction with "the stairmaster"; not very far past here, look up at the cliff to spot the large right-facing corner with a massive pine tree growing off a ledge about 70 feet up. Easier to spot is the obvious right-leaning crack system of Something Interesting (climb 6), especially when the leaves are in. A long stump of a recently cut maple tree leans out of the woods at a 45-degree angle toward the carriage trail. At this point you are just below the climb. Follow the yellow-blazed connecting trail up, and at the top of the trail go left about 50 feet to the large rock scooped perfectly for a belayer. Look for the huge pine tree about 70 feet up in the corner.

Route: Pitch 1 (65 feet, 5.3+): Climb up 8 feet to a ledge with a boulder and a tree. From atop the boulder, ease left into a V-notch, then move up right to a ledge sprouting grass. Lieback up and onto the face above and right. Climb up to a great handrail under a roof. Move up and left to the base of the left-facing corner. Stem up the incredible corner to a ledge. Climb up to belay at the grand pine tree.

Pitch 2 (90 feet, 5.3): Climb the right-facing corner up to the GT Ledge. Walk right across the ledge to belay at or past the second huge pine tree (now a splintered stump); be sure to protect your second at the top of the corner and across the traverse.

Pitch 3 (50 feet, 5.3+): Continue across the GT Ledge to just below the base of an impressive left-facing corner that juts into space at the far right side of the ledge. Make the awkward move up into the right-most of two inside corners before the base of the roof. Climb up to a ledge with a piton. Now get ready for some fun. Step onto the "diving board" to the right. Inch your way across the foot ledge to the blocks on the corner. (Alternatively, you can follow the cracks in the steep rock above, 5.6.) Climb up to the ledge above and belay on the left by a piton on some boulders.

Pitch 4 (70 feet, 5.2): Climb the crack behind the small tree to a ledge at the base of some clean white rock. (You can go up this white rock past the piton and flakes to the top of the cliff, 5.6; some say the pine atop this variation is the "third" pine.) Traverse left 15–20 feet past some brush. Move down a step and then up the short slab to a tree with rap slings.

Descent: Rappel with one rope from this final belay tree. Head over some roofs toward the splintered stump on the GT Ledge. When you reach the GT Ledge, scramble/tension left. Behind the boulders above the second pitch corner is a bolted rappel anchor. **Note:** With so many climbs crisscrossing this popular section of rock, this anchor spot has become the "Hillary Step" of the Shawangunks. The Mohonk Preserve has started bolting anchors both to save trees that were being overused and to keep rappellers from interfering with other climbers. If you must belay from a bolted anchor, please leave room for parties that wish to descend past you. Two 60-meter ropes from this anchor get you to the ground. With one rope, rappel to the first pine, then rappel off the first pine to the ground.

6. Something Interesting   I, 5.8-

A crack climb in the Gunks? That *is* Something Interesting.

I remember David Letterman once saying something interesting, or at least something humorous. I am paraphrasing his advice for happiness: "Folks," he began sincerely, "if you can, if it is at all possible," he paused to appreciate himself, "do yourself a favor—get your own talk show." Cue Anton Fig.

For years climbers have bellyached that Something Interesting should be a 5.8, though all the guidebooks insist it is 5.7. Not even 5.7+. How demoralizing. Well, if you can, if it is at all possible, do yourself a favor and write a guidebook. Because this is the first area guidebook written by authors under 5 feet 10 inches and we recommend linking the first two pitches for a long and varied climb, Something Interesting is now, at long last, rated 5.8—okay, let us not push it: 5.8-.

First ascent: Hans Kraus, Ken Prestrud, and Bonnie Prudden, 1946; first free ascent: Art Gran, 1950s.

Start: From the Überfall, walk the Undercliff carriage trail to the junction with "the stairmaster"; just past here, look up at the cliff to spot the large right-facing corner with a massive pine tree growing off a ledge about 70 feet up. Easier to spot is the obvious right-leaning crack system of Something Interesting. Where a long stump of a recently cut maple tree leans out of the woods at a 45-degree angle toward the carriage trail, you are just below the climb. Follow the yellow-blazed connecting trail up to the base of the cliff.

Route: Pitches 1–2 (140 feet, 5.8-): Twenty-five feet to the right of the Climb Formerly Known as Three Pines (climb 5) is an obvious corner and crack system, which leans right. Climb it past some "interesting" things. A small ledge partway up can be used for a belay. Continue to the GT Ledge.

Pitch 3 (70 feet, 5.7): Climb the left-facing corner behind what is left of the GT Ledge pine tree until you can get on the face to the right. Move up a bit and then traverse left to the prominent right-facing corner. Climb this to the top.

Descent: If you moved left up the last corner, you will find bolts. Rap from these to the GT Ledge, then descend same as for the Climb Formerly Known as Three Pines (climb 5). Or you can just make the descent the same as for Three Pines, from the tree at the top.

7. The Dangler   I, 5.9+

Although the Dangler is technically just a variation to the preceding climbs, it is so much fun that it deserves special mention. No matter which route you climb, this obvious hand traverse will catch your eye. One look and you will understand exactly why it is named the Dangler. Historically, this climb has been rated everything from 5.8 to 5.10a; it is really impossible to say. Have a look and you can tell whether you should do it. Sure, it is juggy and positive the whole way, but be cautioned: at the lip where you need to cut loose from the wall, the gravity has been turned up to 15.

First ascent: Kevin Bein, 1978.

Start: Climb either the Climb Formerly Known as Three Pines (climb 5) or Something Interesting (climb 6) to the GT Ledge. Belay near or to the right of what is left of the huge pine tree.

This is why they call it the Dangler, in the Shawangunks, New York. The massive pine in the foreground no longer exists. Photo from the Dave Horowitz collection

Route: Pitch 1 (40 feet, 5.9+): From the GT Ledge, climb up to the horizontal hand crack at the base of the roof that juts out from the wall above the right edge of the GT. Dangle out to the diving board at the end of the lip. Then, as my friend Rit Picone is fond of saying, "Go big and don't bail!" Crank up to gain the diving board on the corner. Then continue up the face and finish on the Climb Formerly Known as Three Pines (climb 5).

Descent: Same as for the Climb Formerly Known as Three Pines (climb 5).

8. Three Doves   I, 5.9

Three Doves is a real hidden gem. Looking at this part of the cliff, especially when comparing it to the neighboring climbs, you may not believe me. But if you like face climbing and you are too rad or too trad for Arrow (climb 10), the last pitch of Three Doves is for you.

First ascent: Dave Ingalls, Al Rubin, and Richie Petrowich, 1968.

Start: From the Überfall, walk the Undercliff carriage road for some 10 minutes. On the right you will see an opening in the trees below the carriage road, from which you have a good view of the valley and New Paltz. On the left, large white rocks and boulders have tumbled through the trees and almost onto the road. Follow the yellow-blazed trail up the talus to the cliff. Forty feet left of the start of Limelight (climb 9), three stacked blocks lean against the cliff; 120 feet above is the massive "Annie-Oh!" pine tree.

Route: Pitch 1 (120 feet, 5.8): Climb the right side of the stacked blocks and

Topo 3

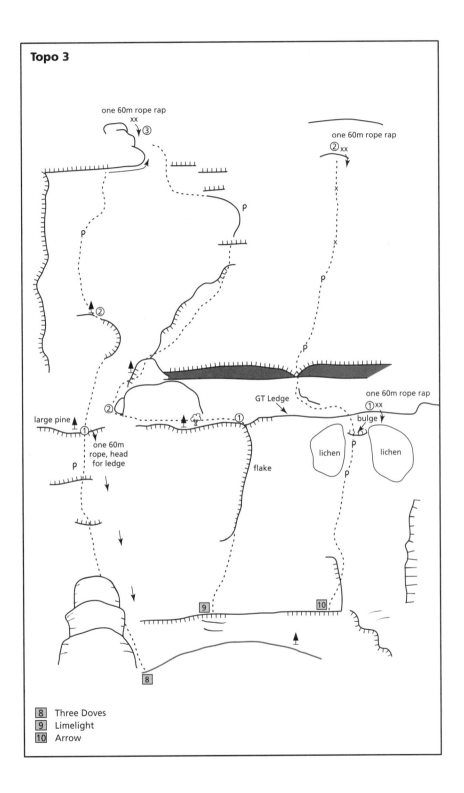

one 60m rope rap
xx ③

one 60m rope rap
② xx

P

x

x

P

② P

P

GT Ledge

one 60m rope rap
① xx

large pine
①

② bulge

one 60m rope, head for ledge

P

P

P

lichen

lichen

flake

① ①

🌲

9

10

8

8 Three Doves
9 Limelight
10 Arrow

the face above toward old pitons. Make the intricate moves through the bulge and up to the pine and belay.

Pitch 2 (40 feet, 5.6): Scramble up the blocks above and right. Diagonal up the face and left toward a small pine and belay. You can link this pitch with the third, but beware of rope drag.

Pitch 3 (75 feet, 5.9): Climb straight up the face, passing a faint left-facing corner and old pin. Keep dancing up to the crack in the long roof above. Traverse right to the end of the roof and up the crack to the bolted anchor atop Limelight. Dang, that was exciting, huh?!

Descent: A rappel with one 60-meter rope just barely gets you back to the big pine tree rappel station. If you are not heavy enough to max out the rope stretch, you may actually need to 4th-class over to it. Not a big deal, though.

A second rap with one 60-meter gets you down, but if you attempt to go straight down the face, you will run out of rope. Instead, when you rappel off the big pine, make your way slightly right to the obvious ledge, from which you can then scramble off right.

9. Limelight   I, 5.7

If not for the belly-scraping second pitch, Limelight would be the best 5.7 route at the Gunks. The route described here is not the original line; it avoids the offending second "pitch." The first pitch, a committing lieback up a huge flake system, is unique and exciting; the final pitch is airy and technical. It follows a stunning, arching crack through brilliant, exposed white rock, demanding a cool head and good footwork.

A climber in the Limelight in New York's Shawangunks. Photo by Dave Horowitz

Whether we like it or not, the Gunks have finally been dragged kicking and scream-ing into the twenty-first century. Five years ago you could count the number of bolts on the entire cliff without taking your socks off. Today this section of cliff alone has eight bolts. The new bolts are at "rappel" anchors, not protecting the climbs themselves. Nevertheless, these "convenient" anchors now speckling the cliffs have become so com-monplace that new leaders have almost come to expect a good anchor at every belay.

But this is still the Gunks. Most of the trees on the GT Ledge above the first pitch on Limelight are dead, and the few good spots for gear are pretty spread out. Building a belay anchor here reminds even the laziest tree-slinging bolt-clippers that creativity is a must when trad climbing. Often leading the pitch is the easy part; it is the stuff that happens between the pitches that separates the rock climbers from the gumbies.

While guiding a pair of first-timers on the nearby Easy Verschneidung, I wit-nessed a party on Limelight who illustrated that no matter how many perils technol-ogy may seem to remove from climbing, some people really ought to just stay on the ground. The leader had just reached the GT Ledge, about 70 feet to my left. He said very loudly, "Jane, I'm at the anchor," followed by the digital chirp of his walkie-talkie, *bleeooop*. Now this pitch is straight up and the belayer is in plain sight.

After a moment, "Okay . . . off belay" *bleeooop*.

I shook my head and felt old.

"*No!*" the leader bellowed into his technically advanced communication tool, "I said I was at the anchor! Not off belay! *On belay! On* belay!" *bleeooop*.

"Well, then you shouldn't say anything . . . until you are off belay" *bleeooop*.

"Listen! When you lead . . . you can do it your way!" *bleeooop*.

This bickering went on and on. During a lull, I leaned out from the ledge and looked straight at my belayer. "Off belay, Rob," I said plainly. And Rob, 100 feet below, who until that morning had never even seen a belay device, took me off belay.

"Uh . . . Jane? . . ." the leader's tone was now less ornery. "Um . . . does the guidebook say where the anchor is?" *bleeooop*.

First ascent: Dick Williams and Art Gran, 1965.

Start: From the Überfall, walk the Undercliff carriage trail for some 10 minutes. On the right there is an opening in the trees below with a good view of the valley and New Paltz. On the left, large white rocks and boulders have tumbled through the trees and almost onto the carriage trail. Follow the yellow-blazed connector trail up the ta-lus to the cliff. At the left side of the prominent face, about 60 feet up is an enormous flake. Start on a ledge 15 feet above the ground, directly below this flake.

Route: Pitch 1 (100 feet, 5.6): Climb the face as it grows steeper to gain the bottom of the flake. Climb the flake and face above to the broken ledges and GT Ledge. With mostly dead trees and only a few good pockets on the ledge, anchor-building savvy is a must.

Pitch 2 (40 feet, 2nd class): Walk left on the GT Ledge about 40 feet, toward the massive pine tree with a rappel station. Belay on the nice ledge just above and before the big pine.

Pitch 3 (100 feet, 5.7): Scramble up and right toward the thin tree growing out of the left side of a broken, blocky pillar about 25 feet up. Continue diagonaling up and right on the easy face to a small overhang below a groove in the pretty white face above. Pull the small roof and follow the arching crack up and left past fixed wires and a piton. Traverse left 8 feet to a crack. Easily climb this to a nice ledge, where a few feet to the left is a bolted anchor.

Descent: Same as for Three Doves (climb 8).

10. Arrow   1, 5.8+

Arrow is a particularly sweet line up this section of flawless white rock. The clean face up top is so sparse, you can almost understand how it happened that a classic Gunks route was first rehearsed on a top rope and rap-bolted before being led. Whatever old-school notions they may cling to, though, most climbers do not complain

Evangeline Wolfe on the clean upper face of Arrow in New York's Gunks. Photo by Dave Horowitz

when they clip the shiny (spinner) bolt protecting the very height-related crux.

First ascent: Willie Crowther and Gardiner Perry, 1960.

Start: From the Überfall, walk the Undercliff carriage trail for some 10 minutes. On the right there is an opening in the trees below the carriage road with a good view of the valley and New Paltz. On the left, large white rocks and boulders have tumbled almost onto the road. Follow the yellow-blazed connector trail up the talus to the cliff. To the right of Limelight (climb 9) 40 feet, left of the large left-facing corner, scramble up to the blocky ledge 15 feet up. You could belay from the ground, but this ledge makes a better starting point.

Route: Pitch 1 (100 feet, 5.6): Climb up the face above to a small right-facing corner. Continue up the face, trending a bit left through a bulge and passing two pitons, and head up to the GT Ledge. You can belay at the bolted rap-station, but be conscientious of other parties that may wish to rappel through.

Pitch 2 (100 feet, 5.8+): Walk left 15 feet from the bolts and climb through the roof at the obvious notch (5.7; really fun). Continue straight as an arrow to the top, clipping pins and bolts as you go like some kind of sport climber. Another bolted anchor waits at the top.

Descent: One 60-meter rappel from this top anchor just barely reaches the GT Ledge, with rope stretch. Then one 60-meter rappel from the GT again barely reaches the top of the blocky ledge you started on. Although the rap stations have been placed well to the side, out of the way of climbers, please be courteous and look before you toss.

11. Cascading Crystal Kaleidoscope (CCK)   I, 5.8

The final pitch of CCK is surely one of the single best pitches of rock in the East. It has it all: a dramatic belay, a lot of variety, delicate moves, and sick positioning. If you ever wonder why people climb, I propose it is for rock like this!

According to Dick Williams's 1991 guidebook, the second pitch of CCK was rated 5.7, while the classic last pitch went at 5.8. Williams was the first ascentionist, so clearly it is his call. A general consensus, however, now regards the final pitch as being only 5.7. (Williams's 1996 guidebook reflects this.) Budding 5.7 leaders, though, should not get cocky. CCK's classic face may indeed be only 5.7 and fairly well protected, but it is the "dreaded" second pitch that should be regarded as the "business."

Last summer we had a stretch of 100-degree weather. I had three clients in the Überfall, and we were melting. Nearby, ranger Bill Cramer began hurriedly gathering equipment and consulting on his radio. Someone had pitched.

"If you need a hand, Bill, we have four able bodies ready to go," I offered before he sped off down the trail.

The accident turned out to be considerably more than the usual ankle-tweaker. From witnesses' accounts, the climber had traveled off route on CCK, thereby missing opportunities for gear. The second pitch may be serious, but it is not outrageous. The climber arrived at the notch in the roof 25 feet above the GT Ledge with no gear between himself and his belayer. In the heat, he slipped. As if his 25-foot fall directly on to the ledge below was not bad enough, he continued

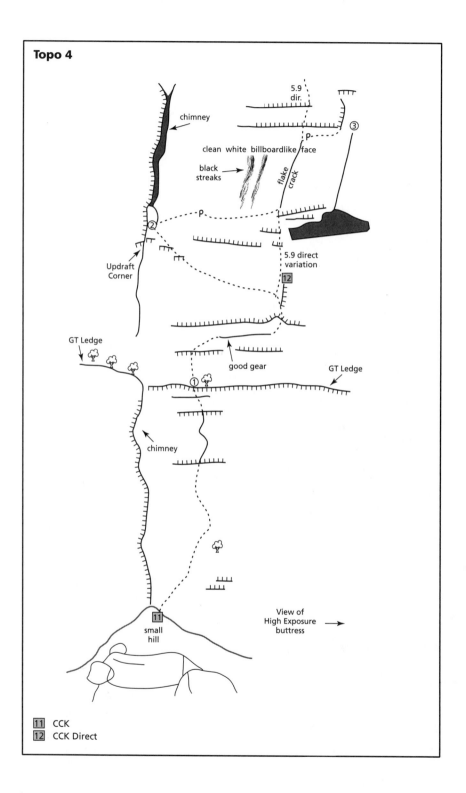

Topo 4

chimney

5.9 dir.

clean white billboardlike face

black streaks

flake crack

③

p

②

Updraft Corner

5.9 direct variation

12

good gear

GT Ledge

①

GT Ledge

chimney

View of High Exposure buttress

11

small hill

11 CCK
12 CCK Direct

to tumble. With no gear between them, the belayer was yanked violently around the other side of the tree, losing the rope. She tried to regain control, but was severely rope-burned. The climber hurtled down the first pitch.

Miraculously, a pair of climbers were preparing to rappel off that very tree at that very moment. Thinking quickly, they snatched the brake side of the rope, arresting the climber less than a dozen feet from the ground, saving his life.

With the Gunks emptied by the smoldering heat wave, we were probably the next closest climbers. Cramer was back collecting my party in short order, and my clients got an unexpected crash course in ferrying a litter down severe talus. We spent the remainder of the day in the shade discussing directionals and anchor building.

First ascent: Dick Williams and Richard DuMais, 1968.

Start: From the Überfall, walk the Undercliff carriage trail for about 12 minutes to the Andrew Boulder. This popular boulder is identified by a large, flat roof that hangs out over the carriage trail. Pass the boulder and follow the next yellow-blazed connector trail up the talus slope to exactly under the start of CCK. The large Updraft Corner is high up on the left. To your right is a clear view of the High Exposure buttress.

Route: Pitch 1 (120 feet, 5.5): A few feet right of the Updraft Corner, at the top of the small hill, diagonal up to the right across the face toward the small left-facing corner. Continue up and a bit left through the bulge above and then through

Bill Cramer at the top of CCK's perfect flake in the Gunks. Photo by Matt Calardo

the small overhang at a crack. Continue up to the GT Ledge and belay at the tree.

Pitch 2 (60 feet, 5.8): There are a few ways to climb this pitch. The original line (if you must, traverse 20 feet right, then up to a piton at a bulge; 5.7R) climbs dicey moves over a guaranteed ledge fall or worse. The pitch as described here uses part of the direct line (CCK Direct, climb 12). It is a touch stiffer, but not as awkward and much better protected.

Climb up directly behind the belay tree to a good stance at a ledge. Traverse right, under the roof, on good obvious holds to a notch in the roof. Climb up through the notch to a stance, then diagonal up left past old pitons to a belay nook in the Updraft Corner.

Pitch 3 (60 feet, 5.7+): Step down, then make the amazing traverse right to the base of the flake/crack out on the exposed face. Climb the flake/crack (yeeeeee-hah!) up to an old piton under the roof. Escape right and up to the top and belay.

Descent: Walk right (north) and descend from the bolted anchor just beyond High Exposure (climb 13). Three rappels from the newly bolted anchors get you down.

12. CCK Direct   I, 5.9

Climbing CCK via this direct linkup is fun, but it skips the classic "cocoon" belay in the Updraft Corner and the great traverse on the third pitch. But hey, if you are a rock climber, you should be used to making such decisions.

First ascent: Most likely in the 1970s.

Start: Same as for CCK (climb 11).

Route: Pitch 1 (120 feet, 5.5): Climb the first pitch of CCK (climb 11).

Pitch 2 (120 feet, 5.9): Climb up directly behind the belay tree to a good stance at a ledge. Traverse right, under the roof, on good obvious holds to a notch in the roof. Climb up through the notch to a stance. From this point, you leave the CCK route and climb straight up, following left-facing flakes past overhangs. This places you below the prominent flake/crack on CCK's third pitch. Climb the flake/crack (you can escape right as for the regular route from this point). Climb the roof above and out left to the top.

Descent: Walk right (north) and descend from the bolted anchor just beyond High Exposure (climb 13). Three rappels from the newly bolted anchors get you down.

13. High Exposure   I, 5.6+

Perhaps one of the most famous rock climbs in North America, High Exposure was first led in 1941 without preview and long before the arrival of technology that allows a leader fall. High E is still an aesthetic and intimidating line. Cowering beneath the crux pitch, you can truly appreciate the boldness of the late great Hans Kraus. Even today, turn the roof and have a look up the headwall you have just committed to . . . it is still a thrilling endeavor.

My first time on High Exposure was with my now good friend Phil Wolin. It was our first climb together; we had met only that morning. On the triangular belay ledge below the crux pitch, a party was chickening out.

"I lead 5.10 back home," one claimed, "but that," he said, gesturing to the roof above, "is sick."

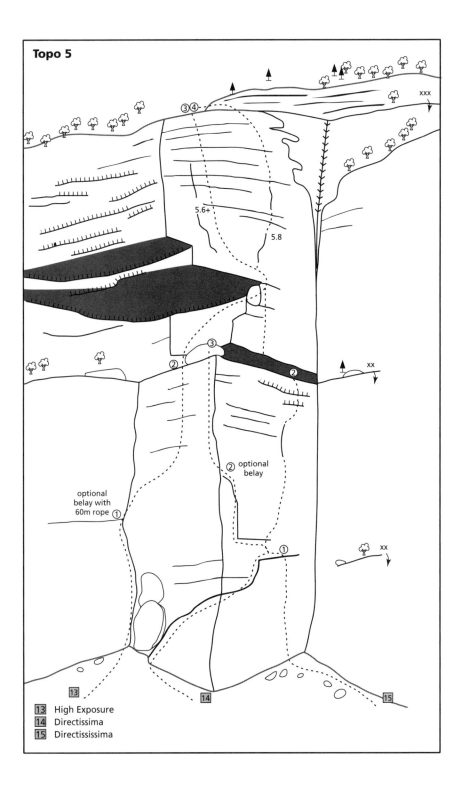

Topo 5

5.6+

5.8

③④

③

②

②

optional
belay

②

optional
belay with
60m rope ①

①

xxx

xx

xx

13 High Exposure
14 Directissima
15 Directissima

13

14

15

I wanted to at least have a look before we too made for the rappel. I led up to the lip and whimpered. I stemmed my toe way out, forced to stare down at the treetops so far below. I groped around above the roof and found a nicely in-cut hold. Instinctively, I yarded up on it. With no way to reverse from this position, I could almost hear the clock start ticking. I remembered being told that the upper section is really steep, but there are "good holds the whole way . . . so just keep moving." I stepped right and up the crack; I was alone on the breezy headwall and pumping out fast.

"Just stay with it; it's only 5.6, it's all there," I kept telling myself as I experienced the pump of all pumps. I was only a 5.7 leader at best in those days, and there I was on the 5.6 of all 5.6s. Eventually, I hauled myself over the top and whooped, "Off belay!" Phil followed the pitch and concluded that it was the hardest thing he had ever done.

You may notice, though, that I say I stepped right after the lip; of course, High Exposure steps left. I was so emboldened with beta, and at the same time intimidated by High E's reputation, that I had inadvertently led my first 5.8 (the last pitch of Directississima, climb 15).

That was many years ago now, and I have since guided this route many times. I take clients up the proper 5.6 version, though. Still, watching them fighting their way up the last 40 feet, eyes darting around desperately, always feels intensely voyeuristic, like watching them give birth or something. When they plop exhausted onto the ledge beside me, they usually all say the same thing Phil said to me years ago: "That was the hardest thing I have ever done."

First ascent: Hans Kraus and Fritz Wiessner, 1941.

Equipment: Big cams; 60-m rope avoids the first belay.

Start: From the Überfall, walk the Undercliff carriage trail for about 12 minutes to the Andrew Boulder. This popular boulder is recognized by a large, flat roof that hangs out over the carriage trail. Pass the boulder and take the second trail on the left (the first trail is to CCK, climb 11). You will catch a glimpse of the famous triangular buttress cutting high above the treetops like a massive ship's prow. If you come to the Boxcar boulder—about the size and shape of a boxcar—on the left side of the carriage trail, you have walked about 2 minutes too far. Follow the yellow-blazed connector trail up the talus to the left side of the base of the incredible arête. Get in line.

Route: Pitch 1 (80 feet, 5.5): Follow the large inside corner up past blocks and bulges, reaching ledges from which it is possible to start moving out right onto the impressive face. Belay from these ledges.

Pitch 2 (90 feet, 5.5+): Traverse and diagonal up to the right across the face. Then climb straight up the approximate center of the face past a few pitons to the famed High E ledge, the wonderful triangular ledge with the bazillion-dollar view. Pitches 1 and 2 can be joined only with a 60-meter rope and long slings.

Pitch 3 (60 feet, 5.6+): Climb the face behind the large Twinkie-shaped rock, starting on the left, then diagonal up and right to a ledge. A large cam and a long sling here save you from rope drag later. Climb through the notch in the roof just above the half moon–shaped scoop of rock. You are now in the arena. Once you turn the lip of the roof, climb a bit left and up to the top of the very steep headwall. Belay on the

Leif Johansson begins High Exposure's final headwall in New York's Shawangunks.
Photo by Dave Horowitz

ledge just below the true top of the cliff. If you keep going, you will not be able to communicate with your second, and you will find nothing but dead trees for anchors.

Descent: Easily climb the next 5 feet to the top of the cliff. Walk right (north) about 60 feet. Three rappels from the newly bolted anchors get you down.

14. Directissima   I, 5.9

If you can lead 5.9, this is the way to climb the High Exposure buttress. The 5.9 section is nice, but the 5.6 arête it leads to is one of the most well-situated lines on the cliff. And there is a lot of cliff.

First ascent: Hans Kraus and Stan Gross, 1956; first free ascent: Jim McCarthy, 1963.

Start: From the Überfall, walk the Undercliff carriage trail for about 12 minutes to the prominent Andrew Boulder. Pass the boulder and take the second trail on the left (the first trail is to CCK, climb 11). Follow the yellow-blazed connector trail up the talus to the left side of the base of the incredible arête. Start on a block just right of the start of High Exposure (climb 13).

Route: Pitch 1 (60 feet, 5.8): Climb up to the narrow ramp and follow it up and right around the corner. Keep going up easier rock to belay on a nice flat ledge.

Pitch 2 (40 feet, 5.9): Traverse an obvious hand crack out left for 15 feet until it is possible to follow a thin crack up on steep, reachy holds to a nook on the arête. If your second is not completely solid at 5.9, belay here. With a 60-meter rope, you can keep going to the High E belay ledge.

Pitch 3 (80 feet, 5.6): So very nice. Enjoy the stress-free arête, climbing up on great holds with good gear. Mantel classically onto the High E ledge and belay.

Pitch 4: Same as pitch 3 of High Exposure (climb 13).

Descent: Same as for High Exposure (climb 13).

15. Directississima (aka Double-issima)   I, 5.10b

One of the great things about the classic High E buttress, or Gunks climbing in general, for that matter, is the unlikely proximity of options at each level. On one side of the massive triangular prow, the fun, open gray ledges of High E are a delight. Just around the corner, though, the wall is as steep as it is orange.

If Directissima (climb 14) is a pump, Directississima, or "Double-issima," as it is more commonly known, requires at least twice the "issima." Welcome to the Gunks.

First ascent: Jim McCarthy, Hans Kraus, and John Rupley, 1957; first free ascent: John Stannard and Howie Davis, 1967.

Start: From the Überfall, walk the Undercliff carriage trail for about 12 minutes to the prominent Andrew Boulder. Pass the boulder and take the second trail on the left (the first trail is to CCK, climb 11). Follow the yellow-blazed connector trail up the talus to the left side of the base of the incredible arête. Start on the other (right) side of the High E buttress, at the flakes about 10 feet left of the inside corner/chimney on the right.

Route: Pitch 1 (50 feet, 5.8): Climb straight up to gain the first belay of Directissima (climb 14).

Pitch 2 (80 feet, 5.10b): From the left edge of the belay ledge, climb up and right to the steep face above. Continue up this to a short crack. Then move up and

Susan Sosin on the Trapps' Directissima in New York's Shawangunks. Photo by Matt Calardo

right and through a small overhang. Continue up to the Grand Traverse (GT) ledge. You are now below and to the right of the High E crux.

Pitch 3 (70 feet, 5.8): Climb the steep face and crack above to the top of the buttress. Step left to belay on the ledge at the top of High E.

Descent: Same as for High Exposure (climb 13).

16. Ants Line   I, 5.9

This single pitch is as perfect a climb as you will find. The dihedral itself is a dream. If you lieback, the jams are nice and secure. Lieback, though, and you will be toast by the time you realize there is no real rest before the crux.

So do not be timid. Stem way out there like you mean it, like you know you are supposed to. There, now you have the guns to hang in and figure out the crux. Good thing, too, because once you get past it, you learn there is no real rest *after* the crux, either.

Do not worry, though; the gear stays good the whole way, and if you are tenacious, the climbing becomes merciful again before you know it.

It should be noted that because Ants Line is a steep climb set deep under larger roofs and corners, it is the Gunks climb most likely to be dry when it has been raining.

First ascent: Ants Leemets, 1960s; first free ascent: Dave Erickson and Jim Erickson, 1968.

Start: From the Überfall, walk the Undercliff carriage trail for about 15 minutes.

Topo 6

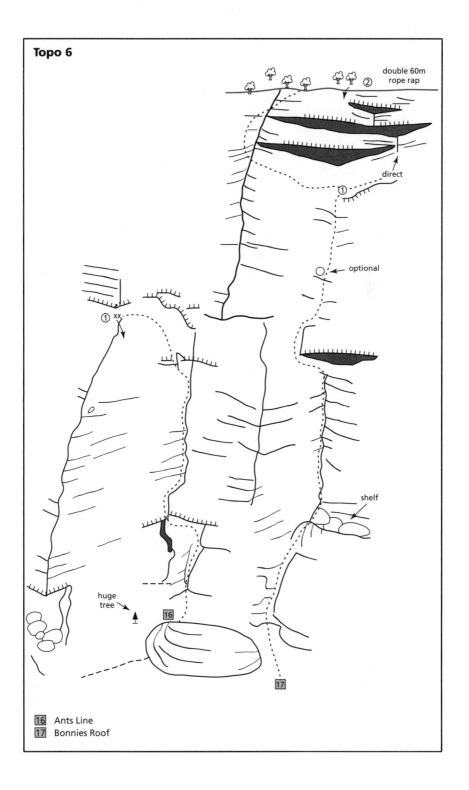

16 Ants Line
17 Bonnies Roof

Dave Horowitz on the crux of Ants Line in the Gunks. Photo by Phil Wolin

Stay on the carriage trail about 1,000 feet past High Exposure (climb 13). After a boulder with a thin roof that overhangs the trail 20 feet up, at an immense pine tree with a dead top, take the yellow-blazed connector trail up the talus. Climb the talus to the flat ground below the two impressive open books. Start below the beautiful open book 35 feet left of Bonnies Roof (climb 17).

Route: Pitch 1 (80 feet, 5.9): Climb onto the ledge below the roof on the right wall. Climb out left under the roof to gain the obvious line up the corner. Follow it until it moves left through a bulge. Then continue up, then left to the bolted rap anchor on the arête.

Descent: One rope gets you down from these bolts.

17. Bonnies Roof   I, 5.9

Welcome to the Dihedral District. If you enjoy great stemming, everything here must "go." This is one of the best sections of rock in the Gunks—really. Between Bonnies Roof, with its radiant orange rock, and the perfect inside corner of Ants Line a few steps to the left, you truly have two of the most perfect, inviting natural lines in the Gunks. This time I mean it.

Christopher Ross high on the regular finish of Bonnies Roof in the Shawangunks.
Photo by Dave Horowitz

First ascent: Bonnie Pruden and Hans Kraus, via a seldom done finish, 1952; standard second pitch by Hans Kraus, 1958; first free ascent: Dick Williams and Jim McCarthy, 1961; direct finish (highly recommended), Ivan Rezucha and Jeff Pofit, 1975.

Equipment: Big cams; two 60-m ropes for rappel.

Start: From the Überfall, walk the Undercliff carriage trail for about 15 minutes. Stay on the carriage trail about 1,000 feet past High Exposure (climb 13). After a boulder with a thin roof that overhangs the trail 20 feet up, at an immense pine tree with a dead top, take the yellow-blazed connector trail up the talus. Climb the talus to the flat ground below the two impressive open books. The taller one on the right capped by a three-tiered roof is Bonnies Roof.

Route: Pitch 1 (130 feet, 5.9): Climb the great inside corner and follow it up left through the roof. It is possible to belay at a stance right after the roof. Better to just keep going though to the ledge with stunning views under the huge roofs.

Pitch 2 (60 feet, 5.7): Traverse left out onto the spectacular wall to the arête. Turn the corner and continue to the top.

For the best thrill on this part of the Trapps, take Bonnies Roof Direct (5.9+): From the belay ledge, move a couple feet to the right, toward a pin, then crank up the alluring crack splitting the triple-tiered roof above. The first roof is the hardest. Good thing, too, because once you have committed, there is no turning back. But great gear and big jugs await, so go for it.

Descent: Two 60-meter ropes tied together off a tree to the right (atop the direct finish) place you on top of your packs. But be advised: this is the big air express; there are no local stops along this route. If you have only one rope, walk left and descend as for High Exposure (climb 13).

18. The Yellow Wall   I, 5.11b–c

The Gunks is the roof capital of the world. The Yellow Wall takes a line through some of the biggest and baddest roofs of 'em all. And who would have guessed it? The cruxes are height related. With huge moves through spectacular, colorful rock, the Yellow Wall is an enduring test piece.

First ascent: Dick Williams and Ants Leemets, 1966; first free ascent: Steve Wunsch (second pitch), 1973; John Bragg and Russ Raffa (entire route), 1977.

Equipment: Big cams, big guns, big huevos.

Start: From the Überfall, walk the Undercliff carriage trail for about 15 minutes. Stay on the carriage trail about 1,000 feet past High Exposure (climb 13). Pass a boulder with a thin roof that overhangs the trail 20 feet up, then an immense pine tree with a dead top, and continue on the carriage trail another 500 feet until you pass a few more obvious "bouldering" boulders. Take the next yellow-blazed connector trail up the talus. A pile of boulders makes a ledge about 30 feet high. The center of this pile has a wide crack choked with smaller boulders. Above you is the immense Yellow Wall (which appears orange).

Route: Pitch 1 (60 feet, 5.8): Scramble up the boulder pile. Climb up and left to the right-facing corner. Move left around the nose. Climb up the face to a horizontal crack and a pin; belay.

Topo 7

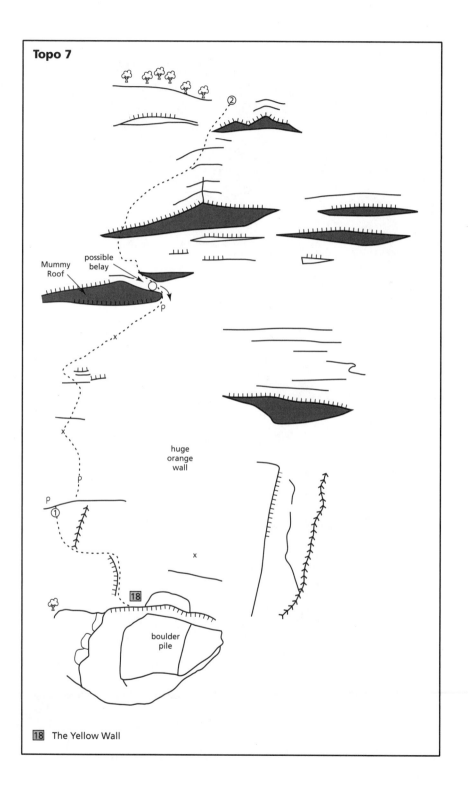

Mummy Roof

possible belay

②

①

p

x

x

p

p

huge orange wall

x

boulder pile

18

18 The Yellow Wall

Kirk Aengenheyster whipping off the Yellow Wall in the Gunks. Photo by Bill Cramer

Pitch 2 (130 feet, 5.11b–c): Continue up the face to the right, passing a pin, then up and left to a bolt. Diagonal up and right to another bolt. Climb up to the lip of the roof (called the "Mummy Roof" because it resembles a mummy's sarcophagus) with the big bong piton. Crank up to the alcove for a possible belay. Climb through the ceiling to an open book. Ease up to the small overhang. Step around the corner to the right and climb up to the roofs. Traverse off right to finish.

Descent: Walk left and descend as for High Exposure (climb 13).

The Near Trapps

The Near Trapps is the cliff visible from the overlook parking area on the left on US 44/55 just before the Trapps Bridge. "The Nears" consist mostly of huge roofs and soaring corners. Most of the climbing happens on the section of cliff nearest the road. This colorful rock is of the best quality . . . it is also the roofiest. This means that climbing in the Nears is either cranking big roofs or traversing this way and that to avoid them. Nevertheless, there are some remarkable routes here, unlike anything at the Trapps.

Approach

From the north end of the West Trapps parking lot, walk the path up to Trapps Bridge. Instead of climbing the steps to the carriage trail atop the bridge, carefully cross US 44/55. Walk downhill along the shoulder. Where the guardrail begins, a trail leads down into the woods in front of the Near Trapps. After a rocky start, the trail becomes flat earth under the cliff. See map 3.

19. Criss Cross Direct   I, 5.10a

The original line here, Criss Cross, traverses off right; the direct line is how it is more commonly climbed. Criss Cross Direct may be considered a "kiddie 5.10" by some, but with a powerful lieback start and crux moves close to the ground, it is still not a climb for the timid. It may be one of the easier 5.10s at the Gunks, but that is a bit of an oxymoron. It has been said that a 5.10 is a 5.10, except here at the Gunks, where it can be a 5.11. Nevertheless, if you have some technique and can think quickly under a pump, it is a fun challenge that has served as many climbers' first 5.10.

First ascent: Jim McCarthy (original line), 1968; Pete Ramis and John Stannard (direct line), 1971.

Equipment: Very small gear to back up the anchor.

Start: One hundred feet after the trail becomes flat, you come to a giant corner (the Disneyland arête) that hangs over the trail. Thirty feet right of the Disneyland arête, right of the smooth wall, is a piton in clean rock above a roof about 20 feet up.

Route: Pitch 1 (60 feet, 5.10a): Lieback the crack left of and below this first roof. Grab the jug and clip the piton. Think fast and climb up through the roof above. Continue straight up through overhangs and bulges to a cluster of old pins, which make a rap anchor. Small brass stoppers or tiny nuts are useful to back up these pins. Most people back up the anchor (one would hope), then lower from here and have the rest of the party top-rope.

(If you wish to continue, climb up left past a left-facing corner. Continue up,

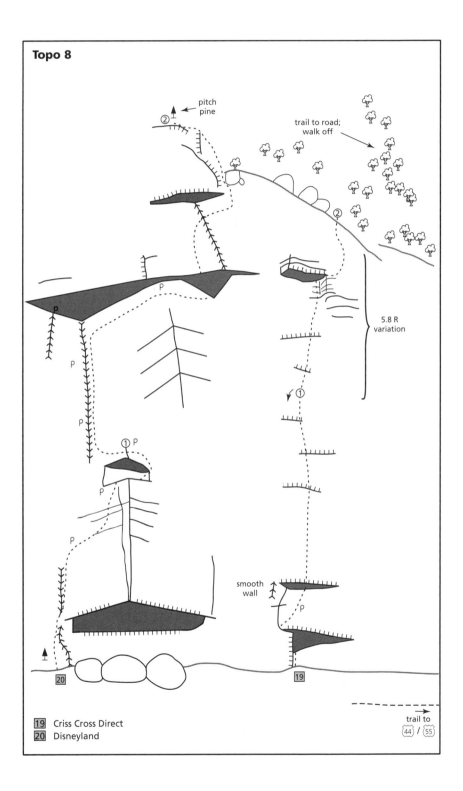

Topo 8

pitch pine

trail to road; walk off

5.8 R variation

smooth wall

19 Criss Cross Direct
20 Disneyland

trail to
44 / 55

passing an overhang, to a left-facing corner and a roof. Exit right and continue up to the top. Expect runout 5.8).

Descent: Walk back into the woods and follow the trail to the right (north) back toward the road. The trail forks and meanders. Stay right, following the ridge, not back into the woods. The height of the cliff decreases as you walk right, while the ground rises up from below, so a short scramble down to the base of the cliff comes up faster than you would assume. It is tough to locate if you are not familiar with the area. If you miss the scramble, you simply end up back at the road (US 44/55).

20. Disneyland   I, 5.6-

Fellow Gunks guide Rit Picone was walking out of the Near Trapps one day a few years back. As he approached Disneyland, he saw something unusual. "Hey, look. Pilot error . . . " he said, gesturing up in reference to a Black Diamond advertisement. An empty harness dangled lifelessly from a rope some 40 feet above the trail ahead. The B.D. ad, essentially the exact same image, was likely intended as a tongue-in-cheek reminder to check that your buckles are doubled back. This "pilot," though, needed to check a great deal more than that.

The climber had led the first pitch and was just above the belay nook, about to set an anchor, when he slipped. Fortunately, his fall was caught after only a few feet. Unfortunately, his rope had become wedged behind a flake. His belayer could not lower him, and he did not know how to ascend a fixed rope. What makes this guy's tale so unbearable is that where he was stuck, all he needed to do was ask (without even shouting) and a ranger could have gotten a ladder and had him down in a few minutes.

Instead, he devised a plan. He would unbuckle his harness. Then, he calculated, he could wiggle out of it, hang down, and jump to a boulder below. It was not a particularly good plan, but he went for it nonetheless. As soon as he undid the first pass of webbing, the remainder of the belt went whipping through the buckle uncontrollably. He was on the ground before he could say, "Agggggghhh!"

Winston Churchill once proclaimed, "A good plan now is better than a great plan later." But had Churchill been there that day to help Rit patch the guy up, he might have added, "A bad plan is, well, not very good at all, bro."

First ascent: Dave Craft and Eric Stern, 1959.

Equipment: Small cams for first pitch.

Start: One hundred feet after the trail becomes flat, a giant corner hangs over the trail. The pretty orange left side of this corner is the first pitch of Disneyland.

Route: Pitch 1 (45 feet, 5.6-): Starting in the inside corner, near the stout tree, climb up about 10 feet. Then traverse right and diagonal up across the face, passing fixed pitons. Move out to the upper-right corner and mantel up to inside the notch. Traditionally, climbers have set their belay in this little nook. The gear stinks, and it is awfully cramped. The savvy climber will continue through the notch, stepping out to the right, then up to a horizontal with a good piton above and left. Building your anchor here and setting a semihanging belay with your feet in the alcove is the way to do it.

Pitch 2 (110 feet, 5.5): Gain the previously mentioned horizontal with the piton above the notch. Climb out left past it and up into the big open book and climb it,

Jeanne Coleman on the first pitch of Disneyland in the Near Trapps at the Gunks.
Photo by Dave Horowitz

passing two pitons. At the top of the corner under the massive roof, there is yet another piton. From here, traverse right around the corner. The farther right you go, the easier the exit will be up to the final wall. Scamper up this lower-angle rock to the top.

Descent: Walk back into the woods and follow the trail to the right (north) back toward the road; descend as for Criss Cross Direct (climb 19).

21. Yellow Ridge   I, 5.7+

The thing about the Near Trapps is that with monstrous roofs lurking everywhere, you are either cranking through acres of overhanging rock or traversing radically to avoid it. Yellow Ridge is of the latter ilk, probably traversing as much as it rises. But given this climb's fantastic orange-yellow rock and quieting exposure, you certainly will not mind. Besides, the final face and stunning "yellow ridge" encourage some of the most pleasurable sequences this side of US 44/55.

First ascent: Fritz Wiessner, Ed Gross, and Ann Gross, 1944.

Start: One hundred feet after the trail becomes flat, a giant corner (Disneyland, climb 20) hangs over the trail. Continue past Disneyland a few hundred feet to a cluster of large boulders huddled against the cliff. Behind these boulders, an off-width splits the large left-facing corner about 30 feet up; a pin is at the base of the off-width.

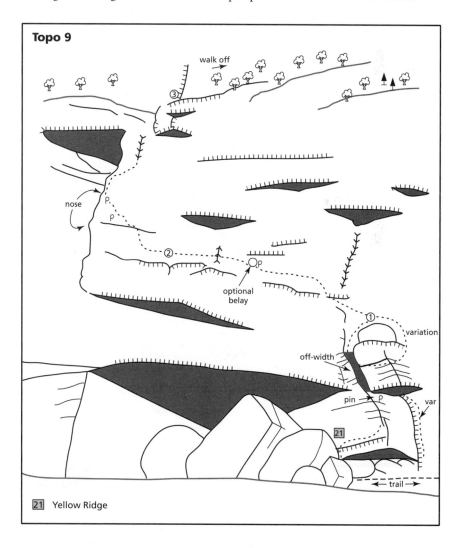

Topo 9

21 Yellow Ridge

Route: Pitch 1 (55 feet, 5.7+): From the foot of the inside corner, traverse carefully right to the nose. Climb straight up to the "thank-God" piton. Now move up toward the off-width and place some real pro. (You can also reach this point by starting around the corner to the right of the start described above and following the inside corner up, then left under the roof—better pro, but very out of the way.) Climb straight up the off-width to a ledge and belay. (Or escape the off-width at the first

"Smelly Aussie" David Weeks on the opening off-width of Yellow Ridge in the Near Trapps at the Gunks. Photo by Dave Horowitz

horizontal hand crack moving right across the steep wall, then up at the corner to the same ledge. This is a nice alternative, especially if you hate "awful-widths.")

Pitch 2 (50–70 feet, 5.5-): Climb the corner above and break out left. Keep following the ledge system out left. You can either belay on this ledge after another 20 feet, below some ancient pitons just before the corner with the small tree, or continue around this corner to the next open face and belay there.

Pitch 3 (80 feet, 5.7): Continue left. Climb up and left on the face, passing pitons, to the ridge. Now things get exciting. Make the fun, exposed moves up the nose, then up and right toward the roofs. Well, what did you think? A superclassic Gunks route wasn't gonna have a few ludicrously exposed roofs? Don't sweat it; they are only about 5.6, with very good gear. Belay on the big ledge just after the roofs.

Descent: Carefully follow the ledge right and back into the woods, where you join the climbers trail. Continue on it back toward US 44/55 and descend as for Criss Cross Direct (climb 19).

CHAPTER 2. THE CATSKILLS

Climbing type ▲ Ice
Rock type ▲ Shale
Elevation ▲ 1,000 feet
Number of routes ▲ 2 in this book

Millions of years ago, the Catskills were as tall as the Himalayas. But since they had a few million years' head start, they have eroded away to something quite a bit more manageable. The Catskills, never rising much taller than 3,500 feet, stand humbly beneath the bigger mountains to the north.

Some may mock the diminutive "CatsHills," but it is this nonthreatening scale, this miniature wilderness, that gives the woods of the lower Northeast its charm. The trees stand among you, they need not tower above. Rivers amble instead of rage. And although the mountains rarely break tree line, their lush flanks conceal many wonders.

Among these hidden delights are secluded cliffs laced with tumbling waterfalls. In the winter, these waterflows freeze into plenty of hard, steep, blue ice to bash your tools into.

Most of the climbing in the region is short and relatively easily accessed, making the Catskills a logical ice-climbing area for the multitudes of rock junkies waiting for the nearby Gunks to warm up. But it is not all "playgrounds" and top ropes. Deeper into the woods, there are a few longer, steeper challenges for those prepared to hike.

Although they are not necessarily a climber's "destination" area, the Catskills have become a favorite place for climbers to cut their teeth or dull their already sharpened picks. So if you are in the area and winter still maintains its icy grip, strap on your snowshoes and head for the "Hills."

Special Considerations

The Catskills are a mosaic of public, private, and state land; please respect usage and parking regulations. In all areas, parking is extremely limited, so please be

Marty Molitoris on Mephisto Waltz in New York's Catskill Mountains. Photo by Alpine Endeavors

considerate. The parking for trailheads to Devils Kitchen is within residential areas. Obey all posted signs.

Emergency Information
Call local police and fire departments (911); there is no mountain rescue team in the area, so competent rescue may be very long in coming.

Weather and Seasons
Late November to early March. The quality of climbing depends on the weather conditions for that season.

Standard Equipment

Six to ten ice screws. Two 60-meter ropes for descents (and for much easier sling-shot top-roping). Dress for typical winter hazards (hypothermia, frostbite, etc.)—and expect the temperature to be at least 10 degrees colder down in the Kitchen than above.

Getting There

From the New York State Thruway (Interstate 87), take exit 20 (Saugerties). After exiting I-87, make a left at the light toward Tannersville and Hunter. Exit right, following signs for Route 32 north and Hunter. After 5 miles, bear left at a yellow blinking light onto Route 23A toward Hunter. After another 2 miles, turn left at light, following Route 23A west, again toward Hunter. Continue through the impressive gorge, passing Kaaterskill Falls.

In another 6 miles or so reach Tannersville and continue through town. At the light just before the post office, turn left onto Hill Street. Go downhill and turn left over the bridge, then bear right past Byrne's Garage as the road becomes Railroad Avenue. In another mile or two, Railroad Avenue becomes Platte Clove Road. Pass the Eggery B&B on your right. At a "Y" in the road, stay left on Platte Clove Road.

After about 5 miles you reach Prediger Road. (It is possible to take a right on Prediger and hike in from the parking area on the right side of the road.) Continue past Prediger Road and past the Catskill Bruderhof. Cross over a small bridge at the bottom of the hill. Do not park in the small pullout on the right after this bridge. Instead, park 0.25 mile farther up the road on the left. Do not block driveways and obey parking signs; future access depends on this.

Devils Kitchen

As the more easily accessed roadside flows crowd with brightly festooned ice climbers emboldened by leaps in gear technology, this dark, icy cleft reserves a few tall cold ones for those willing to step a little into the Kitchen.

When I wrote this, the temperature was in the mid-90s and a sticky haze sat heavy on the Catskills. It was late July, and Devils Kitchen had long been devoid of ice curtains. I was attempting to write about days shivering on belay duty in this deep, frozen cleft. It was so hot, though, it was hard to remember what it means to be cold, how much it hurts when frozen hands thaw, how much time is spent pacing about incessantly and fantasizing about a hot beverage.

To describe the approach to this area, I hiked the route in summer with my faithful dog, Blackfoot. To make a long story short, we got lost.

Okay, not really lost, but we had a devil of a time finding the gully down to the Kitchen. What should have been an hour's round-trip stroll with the dog turned into a full-day project.

The official Catskill Forest Preserve map I had was not detailed enough to show where there is a cliff or a gully. Certain landmarks along the way were familiar, but everything was a dead end. We bushwhacked back and forth endlessly, stopped over and over by the continuation of the cliff band that makes up the Kitchen itself. Boy Scouts on the

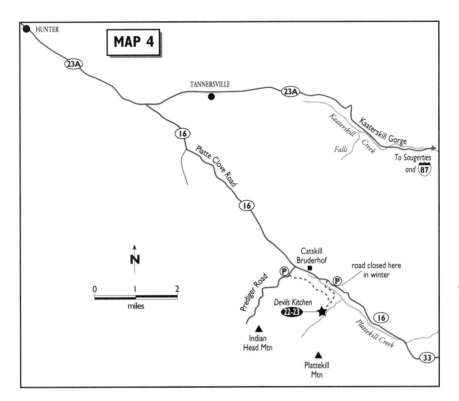

trails above marched loudly through the woods, making a mockery of our confusion.

We finally found the descent gully when the dog wandered off in a fortunate direction. The heat wave and drought had slowed the so-called Cold Kill Creek to but a warm, buggy, unrecognizable trickle.

This experience convinced me to make the directions in the Approach below painfully thorough, in hopes I can spare you the same aggravation. After all, we were just out for a hike. You will need your energy for the pump fest that awaits below in the cold, cold Kitchen. If it is ever actually going to be cold again.

Approach

From the parking area on the left 0.25 mile past the pullout near the bridge, walk back along the road to this pullout. Take Long Path South across the recently constructed "9/11 memorial" bridge over Plattekill Creek and follow the trail. After 0.9 mile, the trail from the Prediger Road trailhead merges in from the right. Just beyond this, a pair of signs indicate that Devils Kitchen Lean-to and Echo Lake are to the right and Prediger Road is back to the left. After 30 paces or so from these signs, a faint trail breaks off to the left. Walk this lesser trail for about 65 paces, then take a left into the woods, following the steep, wide gully straight downhill into Devils Kitchen. If other parties have gone before, you can follow their tracks through the snow and glissade down the gully. If not, take care in the forest because there are steep drops and cliffs on either side of this gully.

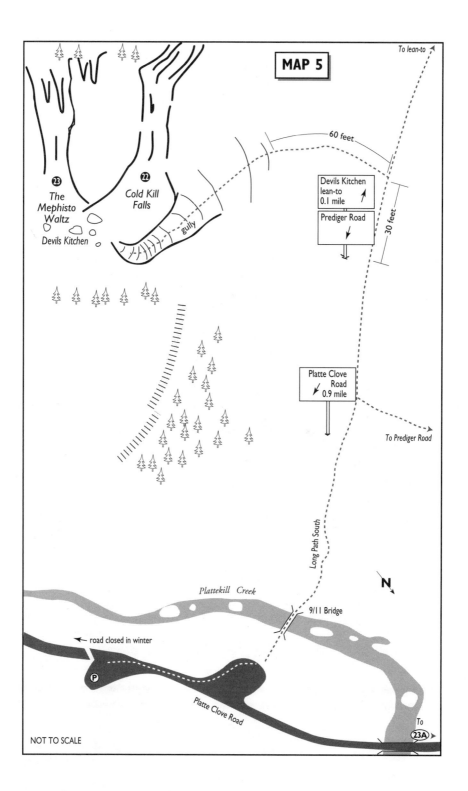

MAP 5

The Mephisto Waltz

23

Cold Kill Falls

22

Devils Kitchen

gully

60 feet

Devils Kitchen
lean-to
0.1 mile ↗

Prediger Road ↘

30 feet

To lean-to ↗

Platte Clove
Road
↙ 0.9 mile

To Prediger Road →

Long Path South

Plattekill Creek

N

9/11 Bridge

← road closed in winter

P

Platte Clove Road

To
23A ▶

NOT TO SCALE

22. Cold Kill Falls I, WI 3

This is a wide waterfall with demanding climbing in a remote, committing setting. As with most ice climbing, the history here is a bit fuzzy. It is safe to assume that these flows were first climbed in the mid-'70s or early '80s.

First ascent: Unknown.

Start: Begin at the far right end of this cirque of frozen curtains.

Route (175 feet, WI 3): In good years, this waterfall can accommodate multiple lines of ascent.

Descent: Climb to the top and walk to the right to descend to the approach gully, or rappel with two ropes.

Staying warm at the base of Cold Kill Falls in the Devils Kitchen in New York's Catskill Mountains. Photo by Alpine Endeavors

Chris Meyers on Mephisto Waltz in New York's Catskill Mountains. Photo by Alpine Endeavors

23. The Mephisto Waltz   I, WI 5

Mephisto Waltz is the tallest, steepest curtain in the cirque. Sometimes Mephisto will form with large windows, other times as one uninterrupted wall of vertical ice. No matter in which guise Mephisto appears, one thing is for sure: as climbers descend into the Kitchen, this dominant line never fails to drop a jaw or two. Now that you stand face to face with Mephisto, one question remains: "Shall we dance?"

First ascent: Unknown.

Start: Begin about 125 feet left of Cold Kill Falls (climb 22).

Route (190 feet, WI 5): Climb the vertical curtain past the rock roofs and belay. This is a long pitch.

Descent: Two ropes are needed to rappel. It is also possible, but not recommended, to bushwhack to the top and walk to the right, passing the top of Cold Kill Falls, to descend to the approach gully.

CHAPTER 3. THE ADIRONDACKS ——————————

Climbing type ▲ Traditional rock; ice

Rock type ▲ Anorthosite (most cliffs); granitic gneiss (Poke-O-Moonshine)

Elevation ▲ 2,000 feet

Number of routes ▲ 20 in this book

The Adirondacks, with an enduring remoteness, offer much for the climber with a pioneer's spirit. Six million acres of public and private land make up this, the largest tract of protected space in the contiguous United States. Unlike our national parks,

From high above New York's Adirondack Mountains, we see a wilderness overflowing with rock. Photo by Phil Wolin

the "'Dacks" are still, for the most part, as wild as they were in the days before tour buses and usage fees.

Adirondack State Park, located in upstate New York, or, as they say, in the "North Country," has been protected since 1885 by legislation and the 1894 New York State Constitution, which insures the land "shall be forever kept as wild forest lands."

Thanks to these measures and the fact that the Adirondacks are not near any major cities, the 'Dacks have remained a place where climbers can still hike a day into the woods and have a cliff all to themselves. If a climber cannot hear the belayer, it is more likely because of the roar of a river, not the drone of a highway.

While I was in the area researching this book, a local climber expressed concern. A book like this could lead to the horrific overcrowding that has infected other climbing areas (such as the Gunks). That climber need not worry. The nature of these mountains ensures that the 'Dacks will stay "forever wild." Weekend warriors and beginners, be advised: most of the climbs in the region have very involved approaches and descents, so even the "easier" routes are quite serious and committing. As the 'Dacks are less frequently traveled, there is rarely chalk to follow, and vegetation still grows from "clean" corners and cracks. Expert routefinding is a must, even when you are off the cliff.

Of course, these thick forests and rugged landscapes provide dramatic backdrops for any outings in the region. The mountains, some of the oldest on the planet, are ideal for just about every type of climbing. If you enjoy steep cracks or long blank slabs, isolated rock walls or vertical ice curtains, you will surely find what you are looking for in the Adirondacks. You may just need to do a bit of bushwhacking to get there.

Special Considerations
The Adirondacks are a rare treasure; please be kind to the land and leave no trace. Cliffs may be closed from May to August if peregrine falcons are nesting. Many climbers trailheads are marked with obvious signs asking climbers to respect nesting closures. Atop these signs, "CLIMBERS—GRIMPERS" (French for "climbers") is written in big yellow letters. Because many of the trails are hard to locate or are otherwise unmarked, these signs are good clues that you are in the right place.

Emergency Information
Call local police and fire departments (911); climbers here, especially, should be self-sufficient.

Weather and Seasons
Rock climbing: May to September. Blackflies can be very bad from spring to early summer. Ice climbing: early October until March. Expect mountain weather in the Adirondacks—expect the unexpected.

Standard Equipment
Rock climbs: a full set of nuts, including small brass or steel ones, cams to number 3 Camalot, and Tricams up to Blue. Since this is traditional climbing, bring a lot of 24-inch slings and only a few quickdraws. Two ropes for longer routes; if 60-meter ropes are needed, it is mentioned in the route description's Equipment paragraph.

Ice climbs: six to ten screws, a handful of nuts, and cams up to midsize.

For blackfly season, bring bug nets; for bushwhacks, long pants.

Getting There
The Adirondacks cover an enormous portion of New York State. Fortunately, most of the best climbing is concentrated in the northeastern portion of the park. This area, referred to as the High Peaks region, is fairly easy to negotiate from Interstate 87 (known north of Albany as the Northway).

For Rogers Rock: From I-87 take exit 25 and follow Route 8 east to Hague (see Map 1). Go north (left) on US 9N. In 3 miles, Rogers Rock State Campground is on the right. The approach to climb 24, Little Finger, starts from here—via canoe.

For the Chapel Pond area: From I-87 take exit 30 near Underwood. Take US 9 north for a few miles until it meets US 73 at a needlessly complicated intersection. Follow US 73 West toward Keene, Keene Valley, and Lake Placid. In less than 5 miles, you reach Chapel Pond (see Map 6).

For Pitchoff Chimney Cliff: Continue north on US 73 through Keene Valley and Keene, then the road heads west to Lower Cascade Lake and the Pitchoff Chimney Cliff (climbs 34–35; see Map 7).

For Mount Colden and Wallface: Both can be reached from the north by trails from Adirondack Loj. To reach the north trailhead, continue on US 73 West past Lower Cascade Lake. Just after the turnoff for Mount Van Hoevenberg cross-country ski area, take the next left and drive south to Adirondack Loj (see Map 7).

For Wallface south trailhead: Wallface can also be reached from the south from the Upper Iron Works trailhead. Take I-87 to exit 29 near Frontier Town, then take Route 2B west past Blue Ridge. After about 15 miles, go north on Route 25 (see Map 1); it becomes an unmaintained road for 5 of the last 10 miles to the Upper Iron Works trailhead (see Map 7).

For Moss Cliff: Continue northwest on US 73 West to Lake Placid, then take US 86 North/East out of Lake Placid toward Whiteface Ski Area and Wilmington (see Map 8). Five minutes or so from Lake Placid, you reach Wilmington Notch,

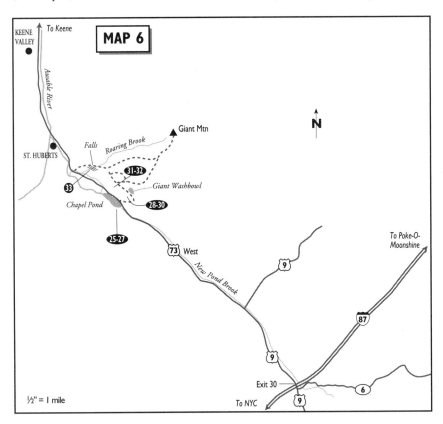

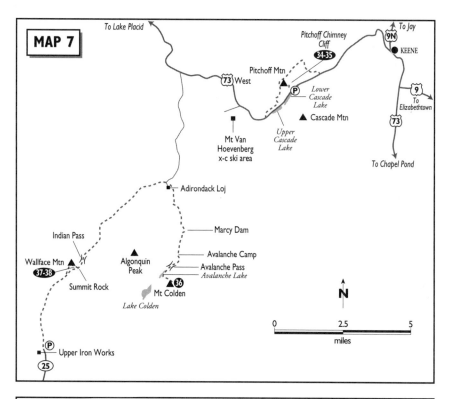

MAP 7

To Lake Placid

Pitchoff Chimney Cliff

34-35

To Jay

9N

KEENE

Pitchoff Mtn

73 West

P

Lower Cascade Lake

Cascade Mtn

9

To Elizabethtown

Mt Van Hoevenberg x-c ski area

Upper Cascade Lake

73

To Chapel Pond

Adirondack Loj

Marcy Dam

Indian Pass

Avalanche Camp

Wallface Mtn

37-38

Algonquin Peak

Avalanche Pass

Avalanche Lake

Summit Rock

36

Mt Colden

Lake Colden

N

0   2.5   5

miles

P

Upper Iron Works

25

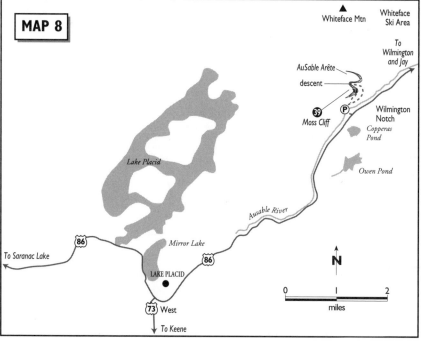

MAP 8

Whiteface Mtn

Whiteface Ski Area

To Wilmington and Jay

AuSable Arête

descent

39

Moss Cliff

P

Wilmington Notch

Copperas Pond

Lake Placid

Owen Pond

Ausable River

86

Mirror Lake

To Saranac Lake

86

LAKE PLACID

N

0   1   2

miles

73 West

To Keene

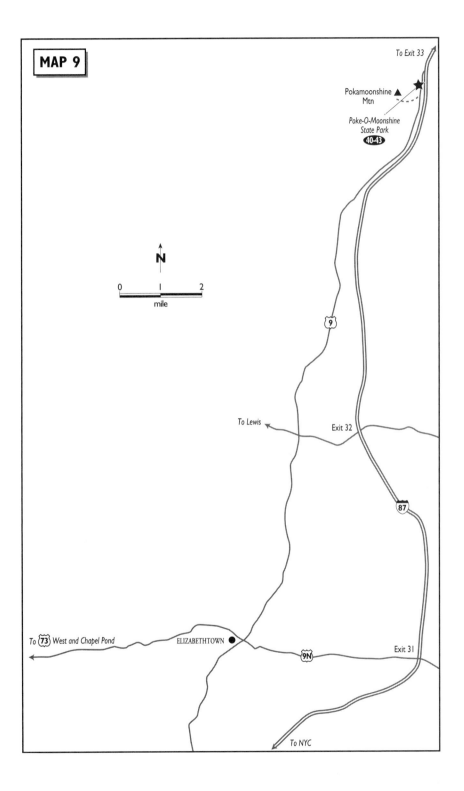

MAP 9

To Exit 33

Pokamoonshine ▲ ★
Mtn

*Poke-O-Moonshine
State Park*
40-43

N

0   1   2
mile

9

To Lewis ←   Exit 32

87

To 73 *West and Chapel Pond* ← ELIZABETHTOWN ●   Exit 31

9N

← To NYC

dominated by the commanding Moss Cliff (climb 39) on the left (north).

For Poke-O-Moonshine: From the south, take I-87 to exit 32 and then head west and follow signs toward Lewis to US 9. Take US 9 north to the state park campground under Pokamoonshine Mountain. From the north, take exit 33 from I-87, then US 9 south to the cliff. See map 9.

Rogers Rock

Rogers Rock, a 700-foot slab of rock, has but a few routes, and many of them are sickeningly runout. So why are you reading about it in this collection of selected climbs? Two words: canoe approach. With a cliff aspect that faces the water, you

Rogers Rock in New York's Adirondacks. Photo by Dave Horowitz

do not even see the climb until you get a look back from out in Lake George. Rogers Rock, reached by a short, pleasant paddle on the northern end of the lake, is without doubt one of the better places to be on a summer afternoon. Unless it starts hailing. . . .

Approach

When you enter Rogers Rock State Campground, go to the boat/canoe launch area at the northern end of the campground and put in. Paddle left, away from the swimming area, toward a break between Juniper Island and the shore. The paddling is easy and should take less than 20 minutes. Be prepared for choppy, deep water conditions, especially if motorboat traffic is heavy. Continue north along the shore until you see the slab.

24. Little Finger   II, 5.5

Named for Robert Rogers, leader of "Rogers' Rangers," a band of eighteenth-century English soldiers who battled the French, Rogers Rock stands tall above Lake George. Legend has it that Rogers, in an amazing act of derring-do, slid down the massive wall on a pair of snowshoes to escape a group of irate Native Americans. . . . Yeah, right.

The wall may be low angle, but it is not *that* low angle. For those of us who must obey the laws of physics, Little Finger is the easiest way up the slab. It is quite pleasant, too. A continuous crack provides good gear the whole way.

Many summers ago, I made my first of many paddles out to climb Little Finger. Phil Wolin and I had made it to the rock and almost 200 feet up the sunny wall when, way down on the lake below, we saw a tour boat circling back to give us another look. A tour guide's voice echoed over the boat's PA system and boomed off the lake. "If you look high up on Rogers Rock," the voice crackled, "you'll see a couple of rock climbers."

We could almost make out the collective gasp from the tourists below as they spotted us. It was very satisfying indeed. The sky was blue, the climbing was mellow, and we were, for the moment, rock stars. But how quickly things can turn in the mountains.

With no warning, the sky split in two. Hail and rain pelted down mercilessly. From behind the mountain, a swirling black cauldron of electricity descended on us with fury. The tour boat vanished, no longer interested in us stupid rock climbers. In a matter of seconds, we went from being the stars of the show to the fools in the rain. One could not really pick a worse place to be than ours in such a violent thunderstorm: high up on a rock in the middle of a lake, with tons of metal gear all over us, shackled to the crack that had become the mountain's main drainage flow—in other words, a waterfall.

Our two ropes tied together just barely saw us back to our canoe. We flipped it over and huddled beneath it to wait out the storm. Phil, always prepared, had

Opposite: *Phil Wolin on the Little Finger route (climb 24) on Rogers Rock in the Adirondacks.* Photo by Michelle Wolin

brought appropriate libations and our stay was a pleasant one. The next day, I made my second of many paddles out to climb Little Finger, or at least retrieve our anchor.

First ascent: Jim Kolocotronics and Bob Perlee, early 1970s.

Equipment: Two 60-m ropes; a canoe.

Start: In the center of the slab is the obvious finger crack that is Little Finger. Pull your boat out at the low point left of the finger crack. Drag it ashore and scramble right, to the base of the crack. Because Little Finger follows a low-angled crack system, you can belay just about anywhere you choose. This description is only one way to climb the route.

Route: Pitch 1 (200 feet, 5.4): Follow the crack and belay at a depression.

Pitch 2 (200 feet, 5.4+): Continue up the crack to another slight depression beneath the prominent bulge. Belay.

Pitch 3 (180 feet, 5.5): Follow the weakness out to the right around the bulge and up. (It is also possible to climb straight up through the bulge; 5.7.) Continue up as the angle eases and belay on the dirty ledges above. There is a rap station in the trees to the right.

Descent: Three 60-meter double-rope rappels bring you back to the ledge system at the base of the wall. The first rappel is from the trees to the right (north) of the final belay. (Set up this rappel carefully to avoid getting knots stuck in the roots when pulling the ropes.) Go over the large bulge below and the next rappel station is in the right-facing corner visible after passing the bulge. From the inside corner, rap down and right to another rappel anchor in the line of trees. One final rap from here gets you down.

Chapel Pond Area

One could almost call Chapel Pond the epicenter of Adirondacks climbing. However, the 'Dacks are far too vast and remote for such a thing to exist. Because it is the first obvious major climbing area off the Northway, it makes a heck of a landmark, admittedly. All around this peaceful pond, mountains race for the sky. There are gentle slabs, endless gullies, and steep, towering walls.

The Washbowl Cliff, opposite Chapel Pond on the east side of the road, is an impressive 350-foot wall standing high above the valley. With its intimidating positioning way up on the mountain, plenty of parties choose to back off while still in the parking lot. Those who go for it are rewarded with not only one of the larger cliffs in the region, but one with good, steep rock; reasonable protection; a sunny aspect; and a spectacular view.

The Spiders Web is also on the east side of the road, a bit north of Chapel Pond. To say the Spiders Web is steep is like saying El Capitan is big. The face, easily identified by a distinct weblike fracture on its upper right side, appears to be peeling out of the mountain above, top end first. The higher you go, the steeper the wall leans back. The climbing on the Web is relentless at best as you fight this graceful arc of nature. Most often it is not about a single move or even a sequence. It is usually about simply hanging in there.

Giant Mountain, slightly farther to the north, is home to Roaring Brook Falls.

If you need convincing that not all ice climbs are the same, have a look at Roaring Brook. Frozen midtumble in its picturesque cleft cutting down the side of Giant Mountain, this elegant route makes even the most winter-phobic rock rat want to come out in the freezing cold, if only to have a peek.

Approach (Map 10)

For Chapel Pond slabs: The slabs are obvious on US 73 West on the left just before Chapel Pond. The Emperor Slab is to the south (left) and Chapel Pond Slab is to the north (right). There is parking on the side of the road just before Chapel Pond, at a bridge over the creek.

For Chapel Pond and Washbowl Cliff: Chapel Pond is on US 73 West on the left just after the obvious, inviting slabs. Park in the pullout near the middle of the pond.

For the Spiders Web: Drive slightly north of Chapel Pond on US 73 West. The Spiders Web is visible high above the east side of the road. Park either at the pulloff on the left just north of the Spiders Web or at the camping area south of the cliff, at the top of the rise on US 73. On the east side of the highway, you will see a "CLIMBERS—GRIMPERS" sign, with a half ring of rocks behind the guardrail. This is the trailhead. (Directly across the highway from this trailhead, a dirt road leads into the camping area.)

For Roaring Brook Falls: Just northwest of Chapel Pond on US 73 at a low point of the hill, there is a parking area on the right; park here for the trail to the falls.

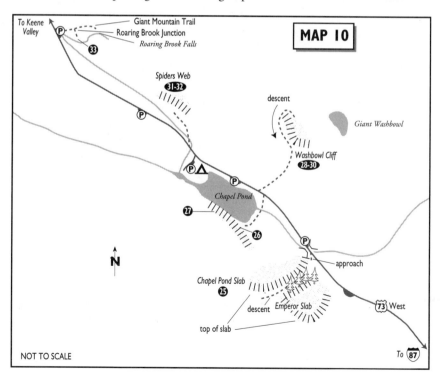

The Chapel Pond Slab in the Adirondacks. Photo by Dave Horowitz

Chouinards Gully

27

Crystal Ice Tower

26

Parking

Chapel Pond

73

Two ice climbs above Chapel Pond. Photo by Dave Horowitz

25. Chapel Pond Slab   II, WI 2–3

Chapel Pond Slab, with 700 feet of typically good ice, is the best route of its rating to be found in the region. Lower angled yet more technical and continuous than Mount Colden's Trap Dike (climb 36)—not to mention a lot easier to get to—it sees perhaps more traffic than any other ice climb in the area. As with all climbs in the Adirondacks, good routefinding skills are mandatory, especially for the descent.

Although this is a relatively easy and low-angled climb, Chapel Pond Slab is a long and committing route. Ice may be thin in spots and protection dicey. To add to the excitement, water may be surging just below the surface. Many climbers have learned this the hard way and gotten drenched.

First ascent: Jim Goodwin and Bob Notman (using no pitons or screws—merely belaying off stances chopped from the ice), 1936.

Equipment: Set of stoppers useful for belays in early season.

Start: From the parking area, walk US 73 east toward the slabs. After the highway crosses the stream, walk south into the woods on a short, flat trail a few hundred feet to the base of the slab. Look for the major left-facing corner.

Route (700 feet, WI 2–3): As with most ice climbs, the best route and belay stances depend on conditions and the time of the season. The first route to come in starts at the prominent left-facing corner. At about half-height on the slab, you reach the "Hummock" belay. This is the ledge system made up of three prominent hummocks or ridges. From the highest hummock, follow the best ice up the right side of the slab through the bulge. Continue up to the large roof. Pass the roof on the left and up lower-angled flows to the top. Again, depending on conditions, many variations may exist.

Descent: The most popular descent is to go left, down the gully that separates the Emperor and Chapel Pond Slabs. Follow the major chute down to a dropoff above a cave. The cave can be skirted to the north. Then regain the chute and follow it back to the base.

26. Crystal Ice Tower   I, WI 4

The typically well-formed tower can be seen from the parking area in front of Chapel Pond. This is a steep, short route that calls out to be climbed. Even in lean years, it is usually fat with ice and always guarantees a pump. As with many of the ice routes in the region, it is hard to know who climbed them first and in what manner. It is possible to continue up the snow and ice gully above it for two more pitches at about WI 2+. This continuation, known as White Line Fever, is worthwhile and highly recommended, given the fantastic setting.

First ascent: Unknown.

Start: When the pond is frozen, simply walk across and head for the rock walls to the left (south) of the pond and right of the slabs.

Route: Pitch 1 (60 feet, WI 4): Climb the tower. If you are interested only in the steep, hard stuff, this is the climb. Belay or rappel.

Pitches 2–3 (200 feet, WI 2–2+): Follow the gully that diagonals up and right above the tower.

Descent: If you have continued up the gully, it is best to rap the route.

27. Chouinards Gully   II, WI 3

When Chapel Pond is frozen and conditions are right, Chouinards Gully is one of the region's most aesthetic natural lines. Perfectly situated rising from the pond, the climb ascends 300 feet of moderate ice, with a relaxing section high up. But it is not all fun and games; early on, the steep waterfall is just about vertical, and in lean years the exit out of the gully can be an awkward squeeze.

Until the late 1960s, chopping steps and slogging up cold mountains was all the rage in ice climbing. But good old Yvon Chouinard changed all that. Just as his revolutionary idea, the chrome-moly piton, changed the way people climbed rock, his remarkable ingenuity also redirected the course of ice climbing.

One February weekend in 1969, together with one of the day's leading Shawangunks pioneers, Jim McCarthy, Chouinard led a group of New York and Connecticut climbers up to the icy mountains around Chapel Pond. The tools he carried were odd to climbers of that day. He had a short, wooden-shafted hammer with a curved, serrated pick, which allowed Chouinard to actually hang his weight from his arms while he repositioned his feet. This was big news for the day. But considering that

Mike Cross climbing the Crystal Ice Tower at Chapel Pond in the Adirondacks. Photo by Tad Welch

Chouinard and McCarthy were also introducing front-pointing, the group must have been dumbstruck. If they had only had Gore-Tex, they could have started a religion.

The prominent gully, near vertical in one spot, was among the many climbs exhibited by the pair; it would eventually bear Chouinard's name. The speed with which they ascended the lower-angled slab climbs in the vicinity of the pond was impressive. But it was Chouinards Gully that signaled a change in the way things would be done in the future. Its steep crux and continuous ice would have been impossible without these new tools and techniques. Unless, that is, you spent the whole weekend chopping steps.

First ascent: Yvon Chouinard, 1969.

Equipment: Two 60-m ropes for rappels.

Start: When the pond is frozen, simply walk across to the obvious scree cone with the ice-filled gully rising above it. If the pond is not yet safe to cross, it is possible, although not recommended, to go left around the pond. It is necessary to ascend a short section of 5.4 rock. You eventually rappel down to the aforementioned scree cone to begin the climb. Be sure to leave your rappel rope in place to get home, or you will be stuck there until Chapel Pond freezes over.

Route (300 feet, WI 3): The route is typically done in four pitches, and belay spots are determined by how the flow forms. The route is obvious, with a short, steep crux near the beginning, mellow climbing in the middle, and a funny escape out to the trees.

Descent: With two 60-meter ropes, two rappels get you back to the pond. One rope requires four rappels . . . oy!

Climbing Chouinards Gully above Chapel Pond in New York's Adirondacks. Photo by Mike Cross

The Upper Washbowl Cliff at Chapel Pond. Photo by Dave Horowitz

28. Hesitation   II, 5.7+

Starting at virtually the lowest point on the great Washbowl, Hesitation climbs one single crack system as it splits the cliff into two equal pieces. It does not stop until you have followed it up the final steep corner to the highest point on the great Upper Washbowl Cliff. Talk about a direct natural line. This climb is sustained and challenging, and may cause moments of, well . . . Hesitation.

Whether it is due to leaps in the technology of our safety equipment, the ceaseless growth of indoor gyms, or the effect of one too many Tom Cruise movies, rock climbing has become insanely popular. With the huge numbers of people joining our ranks each year, it is now almost considered a normal pastime.

Add to this the influence of sport climbing and hard bouldering, and we see why the level of performance has come such a long way. It is no longer news to see a sixteen-year-old cranking 5.12. The boulderer's "V" scale does not even begin to rate things until something roughly equal to 5.10a.

So if the everyman is "crankin' the rad" and little Tommy knows how to drop-knee before his training wheels are off, why do we consider a 5.7+ a must-do? How is it that a climb of this low a number can be considered by locals to still be some sort of a test piece?

Because real climbing is not about the numbers. A climb that is rated 5.7+, when you are out in the woods and on your own, is real climbing. I suppose they call it

Angelo Urrico ascends Hesitation on the Washbowl, in the Adirondacks high above Chapel Pond. Photo by Bill Cramer

"adventure climbing" these days. (I remember when the old-timers insisted that "traditional climbing" was a redundant phrase . . . ugh!)

It does not matter what you call it or how we rate it; this is climbing, pure and simple. Start at the base of a cliff and follow a single direct line to the top. You will encounter challenges along the way, and they will not be just of the gymnastic sort. Routefinding, protecting your second, and holding it together on spooky runouts . . . these are the things that make climbing different from other "sports." It is on a route like Hesitation where we are reminded that climbing is all about the "adventure." Without that, we may as well be playing golf.

First ascent: John Turner, Brian Rothery, and Irwin Hodgson, 1958.

Start: From the pullout near the middle of the pond, cross the road and walk slightly south (right) to take an unmarked trail that cuts down into the woods. It crosses a stream almost immediately. Follow this trail up and left as it passes a few short, steep cliffs and continue up a short section of talus (there are a few cairns along the way). The trail first hits the main cliff at the base of Hesitation. The approach takes about 20 minutes, assuming you do not get lost (not hard to do around here).

Route: Pitch 1 (70 feet, 5.7+): Climb the obvious open book above. Follow the crack until it is possible to exit right onto a small ledge. Climb the short, steep wall above to a sloping belay ledge.

Pitch 2 (75 feet, 5.7): Move again into the corner. Climb up to the roof and then go out right across the wall to the end of the roof (this is a common spot for rope drag; long slings are useful). Carefully climb the face back left to regain the main crack 20 feet or so above the roof. Belay.

Pitch 3 (100 feet, 5.4): Climb up the broken rock above. Belay beneath the beautiful open book.

Pitch 4 (75 feet, 5.6): Climb the dihedral to the top.

Descent: Walk the climbers trail down and left; the trail stays to the cliff side of the mountain. Cut back down the gully in front of the cliff and back around the base in about 20 minutes.

29. Wiessner Route   II, 5.5

This is one of the oldest routes in the region. And like just about every other Wiessner route in the country, it is a great deal of fun and follows a pleasing natural line. It is an impressive route, especially when considering how early it was first climbed, not to mention the commitment involved with heading so high up into the unknown. It may not be the most difficult line around, but set way up on the scenic Washbowl Cliff, it is a worthy adventure for even the more seasoned climber.

As climbers today, we reach fantastic heights by stepping quite literally in the footsteps of the giants who have gone before us. If you spend any time climbing in the Northeast, you have undoubtedly followed in the steps of the legendary Fritz Wiessner. Perhaps you have even clipped a few of his old pitons along the way.

Wiessner, who immigrated to the United States in 1929, was from Dresden, Germany (at the time, the home of the world's strongest free climbers). Although Fritz did not break onto the climbing scene here until 1931, he hit the ground running. Until Fritz's arrival, the mountains of the Northeast were quiet and had seen minimal technical climbing. Not to diminish the achievements of the likes of John Case, Robert Underhill, or Kenneth Henderson, but it would not be an exaggeration to describe Wiessner as climbing's original "hard man."

In Laura and Guy Waterman's *Yankee Rock and Ice,* they note, "It has been said that half the mountain ranges in the world have a 'Wiessner Crack.'" But if we focus on the cliffs and crags of the Northeast, that number is more likely to rise to about two-thirds. So prolific was he that this Wiessner Route, which ascends high above Chapel Pond on the imposing Washbowl Cliff, was, for Fritz, just a snack.

The Wiessner Route up Washbowl was climbed with M. Becket Howorth and

Bob Notman on the same weekend they put up a new line on the region's granddaddy of remote rock walls, Wallface (climbs 37–38), not to mention a first ascent on Indian Head as well. Granted, it was Memorial Day weekend, so they had an extra day.

First ascent: Fritz Wiessner, M. Becket Howorth, and Bob Notman, 1938.

Start: From the pullout near the middle of the pond, cross the road and walk slightly south (right) to the unmarked trail that cuts down into the woods and crosses a stream almost immediately. Follow the trail up and left past a few short, steep cliffs and up a short section of talus. The prominent arête 40 feet left and downhill of Hesitation (climb 28) is actually the major toe of the cliff.

From the trail, hike left below Hesitation around this corner. Slightly uphill you come to a large inside corner/weakness. This corner is directly under the rightmost edge of the large sloping terrace that can be seen from the road. If you look carefully, a dead tree lying across the trail has an ancient ring piton in it just past the base of the route.

Route: Pitch 1 (75 feet, 5.5): Climb the cracks inside the corner to a cubelike block that makes a roof about 45 feet up. There is a piton under the roof. Climb up to and over the block. Make certain to place gear to protect the second after the roof, because this whole corner leans out in an "odd" way. Continue up easier terrain to a spacious ledge and belay.

Pitch 2 (75 feet, 5.4): Continue up the corner, climbing the cracks and fractures past a dying white birch tree. Climb up then escape out left around the corner and up to a ledge. You can belay here at the gnarled fir tree with a rap station or continue up 20 feet to the start of the terrace.

Pitch 3 (120 feet, 4th class): Climb (walk) up the sloping terrace, passing the obvious inside corner crack of Partition (climb 30). Keep going until you reach the base of a short wall at the top of the terrace, where a large block leans into a corner with parallel cracks. Belay below these cracks.

Pitch 4 (40 feet, 5.5): Continue up either or both of the two large cracks to the large ledge (read: the top).

Descent: From the final belay ledge, which is still below a small, dirty rock band, walk left (north), passing a cairn. Continue down until under a clean, steep headwall. Below this, the trail heads steeply down, at first to the north. Carefully follow the ever-eroding trail back down to the base of the climb. Once you locate this trail, you will be back at your packs surprisingly fast.

30. Partition   II, 5.8+

This is the most obvious pitch on the entire Washbowl Cliff—a never-ending dihedral, an uninterrupted "partition." No surprises here; one look, and you know what is to come: a technical and sustained pitch, high up on an airy rock.

First ascent: John Turner, around 1960.

Start: Although there is a first pitch to this climb, it is vague and seldom climbed. This book describes the classic final pitch, reached by way of the Wiessner Route (climb 29). Climb the first two pitches of the Wiessner Route. Halfway across the sloping terrace, Wiessner's third pitch, you will see "the corner." Belay at its base.

Route: Pitch 1 (120 feet, 5.8+): Climb the corner to the top.

Descent: Follow the trail left (north) down toward the front of the cliff. Reach the ledge that is the top of the Wiessner Route. Descend as for the Wiessner Route (climb 29).

31. On the Loose   II, 5.9+

This route is a good introduction to getting your butt kicked on the Spiders Web. On the Loose is the easiest hard climb on the cliff. With good gear and positive jams, it is a popular intro to merciless crack climbing. The demands of this route are clear from low in the talus; the upper part of the wall overhangs 15 feet in 80.

First ascent: Henry Barber and Dave Cilley, 1977.

Start: From the trailhead (see Approach, above), cross the road to the "CLIMBERS—GIMPERS" sign and ring of rocks. Follow switchbacks down the steep bank. Take the trail left toward the Spiders Web. The trail briefly follows along the streambed, then into the birch trees, and then disappears altogether. Pick your way up and left through the talus field toward the cliff. Stay low on the talus, then head up where it gets more forested. The rightmost major crack system 30 feet from the south end of the wall is On the Loose. On the right side of the cliff, a pretty 5.11 hand crack (Romano's Route) shoots up the clean white wall. Just to the right of this, trampled earth leads to the top of some boulders and the base of On the Loose.

Route: Pitch 1 (80 feet, 5.9+): While being belayed from atop the boulders, climb to the base of the crack. Take a deep breath and go for it. Pump up the crack to the belay atop the loose blocks.

Pitch 2 (80 feet, 5.9): Climb out left under the roof and follow the wide crack up

The Spiders Web at Chapel Pond. Photo by Dave Horowitz

out of the wild cave. This is the original finish. Another possible finish goes right of the roof, up the hand cracks above the gash. This variation is easier but has some loose rock.

Descent: Walk off left (north) to return to the base of the cliff.

32. Drop Fly or Die   II, 5.11-

So you think you are a hard man? Well, consider that when Henry Barber first climbed this route, he did it as one long pitch, after having his partner add more rope, back-cleaning the traverse on the go. Most humans break the climb into two pitches. This steep, clean line is one of the most coveted lines on the Web, perhaps in the region. This is crack climbing. Period.

A funny thing happened while I was waiting to get a campsite at Yosemite's Camp 4 some years back. The "ADK" travel mug I was sipping from drew the attention of another climber in line. This guy had climbed just about everything in the Adirondacks, by just about every available variation. One could say he wrote the book on the place. Which, as he introduced himself, it turned out he did. . . .

He turned out to be Don Mellor, Adirondacks pioneer and author of *Climbing in the Adirondacks,* the area's thoroughly comprehensive guidebook. When Don noticed my partner leaving the next morning, he invited me to climb with him and his friend. They were heading for a 180-foot (5.10) hand crack on the toe of El Cap called Moby Dick. I confessed, before it became too obvious, that I was a Gunks climber and did not really know how to climb vertical cracks. Don's experience with stout Adirondacks cracks, and years as a teacher and guide, became evident.

"Just hang from the crack, stay under it, straight arms. Don't fight the fall line." He made a sidestroke swimming motion with his arms and remarked, "Just kind of swim up it." I was amazed. It was a "eureka" moment indeed, and when it was my turn, I climbed the thing as though I knew how to climb cracks all along.

If you are like I was, and you are presently racked up at the base of the Spiders Web, this info may come as too little too late for you. If it does, remember the other tip for steep Adirondacks cracks: move very quickly and do not let go.

First ascent: Henry Barber and Dave Cilley, 1977.

Start: From the trailhead (see Approach, above), cross the road to the "CLIMBERS—GRIMPERS" sign and ring of rocks. Follow the switchbacks down the steep bank. Take the trail left toward the Spiders Web. The trail briefly follows along the streambed, then into the birch trees, and then disappears altogether. Pick your way up and left through the talus field toward the cliff. Stay low on the talus, then head up where it gets more forested. You will see a large block roof in about the middle of the face, left of the "weblike" fracture. Slings are visible in the alcove under its left side; this is the top of the first pitch of Drop Fly or Die.

Route: Pitch 1 (80 feet, 5.11-): To begin, go down into the hole behind the major base rocks. Climb from the spike to a stance under the roof. Traverse left from here to gain the crack. You can either belay from a stance on a small ledge or at the anchor under the roof.

Pitch 2 (70 feet, 5.10+): Crank the roof and finish on easier rock above. Beware of loose stuff as the climbing gets easier.

Descent: Walk off left (north) to return to the base of the cliff.

33. Roaring Brook Falls   I, WI 3+

Roaring Brook Falls is actually a thunderous waterfall in the summer—not merely seepage that in winter freezes and accumulates against rock, as are many other ice climbs in the region. Consequently, the climb will not be fully in shape until after a long, deep freeze. Pay attention, because water may pound forcefully beneath the ice all winter long. Although Roaring Brook Falls was attempted in the 1930s by Jim

Mike Cross climbs Roaring Brook Falls on Giant Mountain in the Adirondacks. Photo by Tad Welch

Goodwin and Bob Notman, it was not successfully climbed until after a revolution in ice equipment and techniques.

Back twenty-plus years ago, when Peter Lewis was just a college kid, he went to climb Roaring Brook Falls one early April day—a day when the falls was living up to its name. Atop the first pitch, he put his partner on belay and took up the slack. Feeling resistance, he yelled "*On belay*" as loud as he could over the sound of the water pounding under the ice. He tightened up the rope, waiting to feel his partner begin moving. Nothing happened. He shouted again and then tugged on the rope. This little routine went on for a couple of frustrating minutes.

Finally he took a deep breath and yelled "*Alan!*" as loud as he could. "What?" came the sharp reply from just a step behind him, nearly causing a bladder accident. As it turns out, his partner had tied his pack onto the rope and then soloed up around the side as a joke. Ha ha.

First ascent: Unknown.

Start: From the pullout on the right, northwest of the Spiders Web, follow the Giant Mountain Trail. At the fork in the trail, Roaring Brook Junction, head right to reach the base of the falls. The walk takes about 5 minutes.

Route (350 feet, WI 3+): Typically this climb is done in three or four pitches; the climb is obvious and can be fully scoped out from the road.

Descent: At the top of the climb, head left (north) to find the hiking trail, which brings you back down to Roaring Brook Junction.

Pitchoff Chimney Cliff

"Pitchoff," situated stunningly above slender Lower Cascade Lake just off the highway, is the kind of cliff that makes you stop your car and gaze. In one of the best little nooks of an already mind-blowing mountain road, the parking pulloffs here are equally as popular with gapers as they are with climbers.

Pitchoff has a lot to offer climbers of all, including limited, abilities. This mostly clean cliff has something for beginning top-ropers (certainly unique in these parts) and moderately experienced multipitch climbers alike. Typically sound protection, a clean practice wall, and one of the easier approaches you will see in this chapter makes this little cliff a popular stop along the way to bigger things.

Approach

Between Keene and Lake Placid on US 73 West, on the pass along Lower Cascade Lake, there are three parking pullouts on the lake side of the road. Park in the middle one. See map 8.

34. Petes Farewell   I, 5.7

Among the many steep hand cracks on Pitchoff, this is one of the most popular. But do not be fooled by all that chalk; with a tricky crux and steep, exposed climbing, it is only by default that it is the easiest route on the main face.

Some twenty years ago, a climber—we will call him Peter Lewis—was young and, well, clumsy. He and a partner had just finished an ascent. So elated with success was Peter that, while walking off the cliff, he stumbled. He said he stepped out

Topo 10

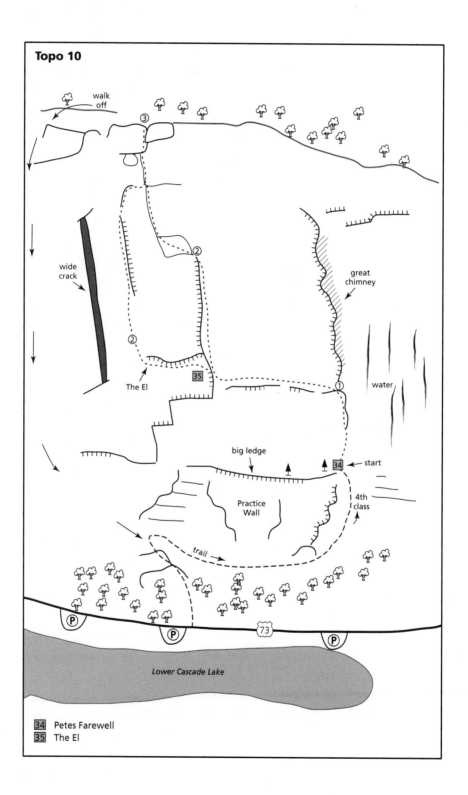

walk off

wide crack

great chimney

water

The El

35

big ledge

Practice Wall

4th class

start

34

trail

Lower Cascade Lake

73

P

P

P

34 Petes Farewell
35 The El

Peter Lewis at nineteen on Petes Farewell (climb 34) on Pitchoff Chimney Cliff in the Adirondacks. Photo by Mark Arsenault

onto the slab to avoid a bush. Anyway, he was falling off the cliff . . . totally airborne.

If it was not stretching the bounds of irony enough to "pitch" off of Pitchoff, the climb Peter fell from was Petes Farewell.

He saw the talus and road below as he plummeted. It seemed as if it was all over for our young climber. Magically, with arms pinwheeling him into balance, he landed on a small shelf some 20 feet into his fall. He broke both his ankles, but he was alive.

So impossible would it be for someone to survive the fall his partner had just witnessed, he simply started down the trail to his car to get the police to help clean up the mess. He later admitted to almost soiling himself when he heard Peter's voice calling out for help.

A few days later, legs in plaster, Peter would use this story to somehow impress the girl of his dreams. This girl would eventually become his wife (she still is).

A note of caution to new climbers: The above events, although true, are highly exceptional. It should not be expected that you can survive a fall off a 200-foot cliff any more than you should expect that admitting to such a blunder might actually get you a girl.

First ascent: Pete Gibb and Dave Gilyeat, 1968.

Start: Opposite the middle pullout (closest to the north side of Pitchoff Chimney Cliff), a trail leads up and right to the cliff. Follow the trail along the base past the alluring Practice Wall (great top-roping), then climb 4th-class rock up to the base of the great big chimney and the top of the Practice Wall.

Route: Pitch 1 (30 feet, 5.2): Climb up and out left to the outside corner and belay. The belay spot, which used to have a notable white birch tree, is roughly at the height of the top of the largest birch tree growing off the practice wall ledge.

Pitch 2 (75 feet, 5.6): Traverse left into the big right-facing corner. (It is possible to climb up higher before moving left, to skip the hardest part of the inside corner.) Climb up the crack to the exposed belay at a horizontal fracture.

Pitch 3 (50 feet, 5.7): Move left across the ledge to the perfect diagonal hand crack. Climb this and on to the top. Peter Lewis remembers when there were fixed chunks of wood in this crack with holes for protection slings; funny, he does not look that old.

Descent: Take the path that leads off the north (left) side of the cliff.

35. The El   I, 5.8

Like its namesake, the twelfth letter of the alphabet, this climb takes the shape of a capital *L*. Both the El and *L* start with a horizontal journey before taking a hard 90-degree turn to vertical. Good gear, unique challenges, and great positioning make this El one of the most classic "L"ines on Pitchoff.

First ascent: Grant Calder and John Wald, 1976.

Start: Opposite the middle pullout (closest to the north side of Pitchoff Chimney Cliff), a trail leads up and right to the cliff. Follow the trail along the base past the Practice Wall, then climb 4th-class rock up to the base of the great big chimney.

Route: Pitch 1 (30 feet, 5.2): Climb the first pitch of Petes Farewell (climb 34).

Pitch 2 (70 feet, 5.8): Move directly left until you reach a prominent right-facing corner (pitch 2 of Petes Farewell). Continue left around the exposed outside corner and out of sight. Be sure to protect your second along the way; this is the short stroke of the *L*. Keep heading hard left another 40 feet until it is possible to reach a stance 10 feet higher. This is one of the most exposed positions you can get just a half pitch off the ground.

Pitch 3 (60 feet, 5.7): Climb straight up the corner above. Good gear and great climbing.

Descent: Take the path that leads off the north (left) side of the cliff.

Mount Colden

With a vertical gain of roughly 2,000 feet, Mount Colden's Trap Dike is one of the longest and most unique features to be climbed in all of the Adirondacks. Climbing to the summit of Mount Colden, the state's eleventh-tallest mountain, the route follows a series of steep steps and waterfalls before breaking out onto the extremely exposed slides. Although the climbing here is not very difficult by today's standards, its isolation and duration make for one of the more enjoyable outings to be had in the whole Adirondack Park. In 1837 geologist Ebenezer Emmons made an early attempt of the Trap Dike; thirteen years later it was finally climbed.

Although the climbing is relatively easy, make no mistake: this is a long, secluded backcountry route. In winter, particularly after heavy snows, pay attention to avalanche possibilities. Once you are in the dike, the walls on either side become unexpectedly steep. The route may be easy to climb, but it would not be easy to escape. Teams should be self-sufficient and understand the commitment involved. Keep in mind the old adage, "there is no such thing as moderate mountaineering." Most parties take 2 days for this excursion, setting up camp at Marcy Dam or Avalanche Camp.

Mount Colden is deep within the Adirondacks. Photo by Dave Horowitz

Approach

Hike in from the Adirondack Loj trailhead—with a map and the skills to use it. Hike south about 2.5 miles to Marcy Dam (most parties set up camp here so they do not have to lug camping gear any farther). Continue another mile to Avalanche Camp, then another mile to Avalanche Lake via Avalanche Pass. Mount Colden is on the left (southwest) side of the lake. See map 8.

36. Trap Dike   III, WI 2 (winter) or 3rd–4th Class (summer)

We were past the Trap Dike's crux waterfall when the first snowflakes started falling. As the lake grew smaller beneath us, and since the technical climbing was done, we were sure we would make the summit—even if the snow was getting heavier. Deep ice moats and crevasses kept us moving rather slowly. The light began to flatten as we picked our way up the dike. By the time we finally gained the slides, it was apparent we probably should not have left camp so leisurely that morning. It was getting to be a long day. The snowfall had become a swirling whiteout and the snow on the slides was so loose and unconsolidated that each step forward, even with snowshoes, gained only a step and a half back.

Finally the snowfall dwindled, but then so did the light. Now under darkness and knee-deep in fresh snow, we did not think we would find the trail. We opted to descend the route. We down-climbed the route by headlamp, slogged back to camp (which had yet to be broken down), and then marched all the way back to the car and drove home in one push. Thirty-six hours of continuous motion.

I finally dragged my weary body up my steps, through the door, and into bed. When I finally closed my eyes, my next-door neighbor's alarm clock bleeped noisily through the thin apartment wall, confirming what I already knew: it had been a very long day.

First ascent: Robert Clarke and Alexander "Sandy" Ralph, 1850; first winter ascent: Jim Goodwin and Eddie Stanley, 1935.

Equipment: Summer, a rope, a few slings, possibly a light rack; winter, standard ice gear, snowshoes.

Start: Two-thirds of the way down Avalanche Lake, you can see a massive cleft in the mountain. This is the Trap Dike. In winter, simply hike across the frozen lake to the base of the dike. In the summer, take the trail around the far side of the lake to gain the base of the dike.

Route (2,000 feet, WI 2 or 3rd–4th class rock): Climb the steps up the gully passing a few short waterfalls along the way. Near the top of the dike, it is possible to escape out right onto the granite slides. If escaping the dike seems technical, you have not ascended high enough yet. Ascend the slides and continue through the scrub to the summit.

Descent: Take a trail down either left or right from the summit, or down-climb the route with a few short rappels.

Wallface

It does not get much more "Adirondack" than Wallface, tough to get to, deep within Indian Pass. Climbing here still feels as remote and isolated as in the days when trappers walked the dense trails below. In the 1830s it was this "sublime and terrifying sight" that

Dave Horowitz climbing the Trap Dike on Mount Colden in New York's Adirondacks.
Photo by Jim Ianora

The Adirondacks' Wallface can be reached from north or south. Photo by Mike Cross

lured the most notable adventurers, artists, scientists, and romantics of the day. Ebenezer Emmons, one such scientist/adventurer, remarked of Wallface that "probably in this country there is no object of the kind on a scale so vast and imposing as this." Roping up beneath this towering cliff, dwarfed by talus, you can appreciate his awe.

Approach
Wallface can be reached by trails from the north or south. Most parties hike in the day before and camp near the base of the cliff. Carry a good hiking map of the area; the trail deteriorates and the forest is thick. From the north trailhead at Adirondack Loj, it is about 6 miles in; from the south trailhead at the Upper Iron Works, about 4.5 miles. See map 8.

Hike in from your respective trailhead until south of Indian Pass. You can see the cliff if you look carefully through the dense woods as you approach. Summit Rock, a terrace on the trail south of the high point of Indian Pass, is the best place from which to get an actual view of the cliff. If you approach from the south via Upper Iron Works trailhead, Summit Rock is out of the way. Break into the talus when you recognize the major ramp.

37. The Diagonal   III, 5.8

The Diagonal is by far the most popular route on Wallface—the term "popular," of course, being completely relative. With the mountain's half-day approach, parties who climb the Diagonal often find they share the cliff with only the raptors that make the immense wall home.

Most of the climbing is fairly easy, yet this is no kiddy climb; routefinding on the approach and descent may present huge challenges, and the consequences of an accident in this isolated area would be grim. Teams should be self-sufficient and prepared for mountain weather.

Sometimes when I am out guiding, I feel as though everyone out there is sketchy. At the Gunks on a Sunday, you can almost smell the fear of panicked newbies as they threaten to shake themselves and all their shiny gear right off the cliff. I constantly puzzle as climbers amble off route on crack climbs.

When I come home from work griping about the hoards of "gumbies" who have discovered climbing, my girlfriend reminds me of stories I have told about what we "got away with" when I was learning to climb. Indeed, as I look back at my journals, I find that we were just as blissfully reckless as the masses who are now learning for themselves what not to do.

The Diagonal was an early objective for me and my friend Christopher Ross, full of our own brand of youthful bravado. I recall a sleepless night before the climb, afraid of the bears (or, more likely, raccoons) that sniffed about. And there was way too much unroped down-climbing up high when our rappels ran short.

Yet somehow, in our standard-issue "hypothermic death outfits" (jeans and cotton with no helmets), we did somehow succeed without incident. We had ourselves a great time sketching up and down this noble route. We took in some great views and indeed "got away" with something big . . . good thing it did not snow.

First ascent: Craig Patterson, Alvin Breisch, and Trudy Healy (finding pitons en route), 1965.

Equipment: Two 60-m ropes for rappels.

Start: The most prominent feature to look for is the huge ramp system that makes up the first few pitches of the Diagonal. There are no established approach

Near the top of the ramp on Wallface's Diagonal (climb 37). Photo by Christopher Ross

trails. Pick your way through the talus toward the base of the ramp. The terrain goes from boulders in the steep woods to full-on cliff with little warning.

Route: Pitch 1 (100–250 feet, 4th–5th class): Depending on where you exit the talus, it may take up to two pitches to get to the ramp. Belays and short pitches are needed before you reach the actual ramp. Gain the base of the prominent ramp and belay. (Parties climb this route in so many different ways that the accompanying route overlay does not show belay points.)

Pitches 2–3 (300–350 feet, 5.3): Climb the ramp up to the right to a tree beneath a bulge.

Pitch 4 (70 feet, 5.4): Make the slabby moves out right around the bulge and up. Belay on the long, grassy ledges above.

Pitch 5 (40 feet, 4th class): Scamper down and right on the ledge to a tree before some thin cracks.

Pitch 6 (50 feet, 5.8): Make a weird move up the cracks and continue up the steep corner above to a large ledge.

Pitch 7 (150 feet, 5.7+): Climb the obvious right-facing corner to the top. Catch your breath and belay.

Descent: There are several options for descent; they are all very involved. Take care and leave plenty of time for stuck ropes, miscalculations, and routefinding.

It is possible, but inadvisable, to walk off right. A machete, map, and compass are mandatory.

Some parties bushwhack left along the top to rappel a line of trees left of No Man's a Pilot (climb 38). The farther left you go, the easier the rappelling is, but there is more bushwhacking at the top and bottom.

Most parties find that rappelling the route is the least-confusing way to go. Tension rappelling is necessary to backtrack traverses.

38. No Man's a Pilot   III, 5.9

Partway up the Diagonal ramp, you cannot help but notice this intimidating route. Chimneys, big blocks, and thrilling exposure are all on the flight plan. The first-ascent party originally aided out the overhang as the finish; the free finish is described below.

First ascent: Pete Metcalf and Lincoln Stoller, 1974; first free finish: Alan Spero and Dane Waterman, 1975.

Start: There are no established approach trails. Pick your way through the talus toward the base of the huge ramp system that makes up the first few pitches of the Diagonal. The terrain goes from boulders in the steep woods to full-on cliff with little warning. Gain the ramp by climbing the first pitch of the Diagonal (climb 37). Climb up the first part of the ramp until you locate the prominent chimney system on the wall left of the ramp. Angle up and over toward the base of the chimney.

Route: Pitch 1 (80 feet, 5.9): Climb the chimney up over numerous stacked blocks and wedged flakes. Belay at a small plateau before a narrowing in the chimney system.

Pitch 2 (100 feet, 5.8): Continue up the chimney to a protected belay at a diving board of rock.

Chris Meyers on the crux of No Man's a Pilot (climb 38), on Wallface in the Adirondacks. Photo by Alpine Endeavors

Pitch 3 (60 feet, 5.3): Using the thin crack, move out left from the belay. Now that is a lot of exposure for 5.3, huh?

Descent: Descend as for the Diagonal (climb 37).

Moss Cliff

Perhaps no cliff in the Adirondacks is as imposing as Moss Cliff. Its flanks consist of, essentially, one sharp prow leaning deliberately out of the mountain. The left wall is fractured by a network of cracks. The right wall is steeper than seems possible. (Consequently, most routes are on the left wall.)

Moss Cliff towers like some impenetrable fortress guarding the mighty flanks of Wilmington Notch. And like any good fortress, Moss Cliff has a moat that climbers must cross first. The Ausable River, which at some times of the year can be a raging torrent, adds a unique obstacle for those intending to storm the castle.

Approach

On US 86 at the high point in Wilmington Notch, there is a dirt parking area on the left (north) under Moss Cliff. See map 8. A prominent right-facing dihedral in the center of the left face is visible from the road—Hard Times climbs this.

Moss Cliff and the Au Sable Arête in the Adirondacks. Photo by Dave Horowitz

39. Hard Times   III, 5.9

You may experience some Hard Times indeed on this remote climb: a hairball river crossing, steep talus, and unnerving solitude. But remember, no matter how bad things may get up there, it could always be worse. You could be going to work. Or, worse still, you could *be* at work.

So quit complaining. Like the tee shirt says, "Climbing may be hard, but it's easier than growing up."

First ascent: Al Long and Al Rubin, 1975; first free ascent: Henry Barber and Dave Cilley, 1977.

Start: From the parking area, follow the trail down the steep bank toward the Ausable River. If you find the river at a mellow summer pace, it may be possible to ford with the aid of a walking stick. A cable has been rigged for Tyrolean traverse crossings during higher water. At the time of this writing, the cable is in excellent condition. Do not assume that it still is.

Once you have crossed the river, follow a vague trail up the slope toward the cliff. Stay just left of center as you head up. Do not go so far right that you wind up in the talus. Uphill and left of a prominent outside corner, follow 4th-class terrain up and right to a bush-covered ledge atop a huge flake.

Route: Pitch 1 (140 feet, 5.8): Climb the hand crack and corners to reach lower-angled rock. Make your way left, to the left end of a tree cluster.

Pitch 2 (150 feet, 5.9): Chimney up to the top of the flake. (Some parties belay here.) Climb the tough roof above, then head up the face and an off-width to a flat ledge.

Pitch 3 (75 feet, 5.8): Follow the hand cracks to the top of the cliff.

Descent: Between the major steep right wall of Moss Cliff and the next cliff over to the north/right (the Au Sable Arête) is a huge depression. Head down this depression. A 75-foot rappel is necessary to get to the base of the wall.

Poke-O-Moonshine

Recently when I visited the Adirondacks, a Plattsburgh local remarked that the way he sees it, "There's all the climbing in the Keene Valley area . . . and then there's Poke-O."

By most measures, Poke-O-Moonshine is the single biggest climbing area in the region. A few cliffs in the Adirondacks may be taller or steeper, most are more remote, but none can match the sheer size and continuous quality of Poke-O. With rippling dike systems, bald faces, soaring corners, and unending hand cracks, Poke-O's main cliff contains many of the region's finest rock climbs . . . not to mention Positive Thinking, the single most-coveted frozen plum in the state.

Although that local may have exaggerated the point, he knew exactly what he was talking about. I only wish I had asked him what the heck a "Poke-O-Moonshine" was.

Approach

The climbing area is located in Poke-O-Moonshine State Park. See map 9. Please respect rules of the park regarding parking and fees. When the campground is closed, it is okay to park on the shoulder in front of the campground. Do not trespass on the private land under the cliff north of the campground.

The Adirondacks' Pokamoonshine Mountain. Photo by Dave Horowitz

At the back center of the campground is a large alluring boulder. The trail leading up to the cliff, marked by a "CLIMBERS—GRIMPERS" sign, begins here. Take the trail and at each fork you encounter, go right until you reach the base of the wall.

A few major features on the cliff will help you locate the climbs described. The Sky Nose, the large proboscis high on the main wall, is very apparent from both the road and approach trail. Continue along the trail under the Nose. Next you encounter a clearing where the trail dips down. The wall, expansive here, may be dripping; in the winter, expect thin ice.

40. Positive Thinking   III, WI 5

A lot of us share a similar trait, which probably attracted us to such a ridiculous thing as climbing in the first place: the knack for doing things the hard way. Anyone who has needlessly cranked a 5.8 move on a 5.4 climb, seeing that perfect jug only when it is at their feet, knows precisely what I am talking about. When you apply this tendency to the most talented climbers, amazing (terrifying) things get done.

Owner of the Gunks' Rock and Snow, Rich Gottlieb, is well known for pushing the possibilities of the region's climbing opportunities for decades. A few times while I have been ice climbing with a mutual friend, Marty Molitoris, Marty has pointed out some jumbled pile of frozen daggers lying busted up at the base of the most imposing feature in sight and told me that Gottlieb had led it, probably just the day before it detached. It came as no surprise, therefore, when I spoke with Rich about this book, that he agreed that Positive Thinking deserved all the accolades. Even if climbing it in the usual manner is not quite challenging enough for guys like him.

Twenty years ago, Rich was at Poke-O with Austin Hearst and Rusty Reno one cold day to climb Positive Thinking for the umpteenth time. This time, though, Rich was armed with new inventions from Europe called "mixed picks" (this was long before M ratings, before mixed climbs were even a concept). Thinking they would be great for hooking rock nubs on the thin first pitch, he was psyched.

You have probably never heard of mixed picks. That is because, as Rich learned in about 5 feet of scratching around, they do not work particularly well for mixed climbing. They were actually designed for low-angle alpine ice, but they never caught on for that either.

Despite the ferocious heckling that ensued, Rich came back down and took one tool from each of his friends and started back up the pitch. Now armed only slightly better with hopelessly wobbly picks that had no grippy rubber, he climbed on undaunted. That is, until he noticed that the constant hum of belayer banter had at some point ceased.

He looked down the thin ice smear to see what was wrong. He had been working so hard at keeping those sketchy tools planted that he had not noticed the 90-foot ground fall he was flirting with. A white flash of reality made him shudder. Despite a deafening silence, he successfully eked his way to the belay. The banter and all its comfort resumed.

40 Positive Thinking

Positive Thinking in winter at Poke-O-Moonshine. Photo by Rich Gottlieb

If Gottlieb had just brought proper tools in the first place, the climb would still have been rated WI 5; but, like the rest of us, even the best sometimes find themselves doing things the hard way.

First ascent: John Bragg and John Bouchard (via the hand crack), 1975.

Equipment: A few medium to large nuts; rock rack for the hand crack start; thin ice pro for the smear.

Start: Continue along the base of the cliff to the first prominent clearing. The wall sweeps out in front of you. This is Positive Thinking. The first pitch, usually just a thin smear of ice in winter, creeps up the wall toward the corners and chimneys above.

Route: Pitch 1 (150 feet, WI 5): Climb the smear to gain a good-size belay ledge in the dike. The 5.9 hand crack is just right of the smear. It is also possible to follow the rising dike traverse in from the left.

Pitch 2 (150 feet, WI 5): Climb the bulges and steep central column to the roofs at the top of the chimney.

Pitch 3 (150 feet, WI 3-): One final, less demanding pitch of ice ascends to the trees.

Descent: From the top of the cliff, walk left (south) then scramble down the huge eroded dike above the campground.

41. Gamesmanship   II, 5.8

This continuous line is among Poke-O's best. The endless hand-crack pitch that opens the climb is unmatched in these parts. First climbed during one of John Turner's blitzes in the late 1950s, Gamesmanship was one of the first 5.8s on the cliff—one of the first in the region, for that matter. Before you get lulled by the vintage of this climb, be advised: "There are 5.8s, and there are Turner 5.8s."

Many qualities made the enigmatic Turner a remarkable figure, but it was his willingness to climb with unflappable self-assurance that made his mark on Poke-O so everlasting. He climbed in a bold style that was very rare for the day. In a time when a crack wider than an inch was unprotectable, he took his climbing way beyond the "leader must not fall" conservatism. This willingness to push the limits earned him a reputation. "Tumbledown Turner," as he became known, would not be stopped by some silly little runout.

Or, in the case of his 1959 ascent of Gamesmanship, before nuts and cams, he would not be stopped by some giant, knee-knocking runout either. (Do not despair; for modern climbers, the crux pitch is very well protected.)

First ascent: John Turner, Brian Rothery, and Wilfried Twelker, 1959.

Start: Continue on the trail a minute or so past Positive Thinking to a very obvious hand crack that starts a few feet off the ground and continues straight up the wall as far as can be seen. A scooped "belay-seat" tree from days gone by lies rotting at the base of the route.

Route: Pitch 1 (145 feet, 5.8): Gain the block/flake under the crack. Realize it is getting ready to pop, and use something else. Let the games begin . . . jam up the crack to a belay stance at some old pitons.

Opposite: *Rich Gottlieb does some Positive Thinking on the Adirondacks' Poke-O-Moonshine.* Photo from the Gottlieb collection

Pitch 2 (120 feet, 5.7): Climb to the left-facing corner system above. Climb to ledges at the large traversing dike system and belay. Handle the broken rock in the dike cautiously.

Pitch 3 (100 feet, 5.4): Diagonal up and right to some trees under the left-facing corner.

Pitch 4 (150 feet, 5.7): Step around the block to the right. Climb the hand crack up and continue until a belay at the bushy ledge.

Pitch 5 (150 feet, 5.1 R): Climb the easy slab to the trees.

Descent: From the top of the cliff, walk left (south) then scramble down the huge eroded dike above the campground.

42. Bloody Mary   II, 5.9+

At the time of its first ascent, Bloody Mary was considered the boldest lead in the region. It remained the single hardest climb in the Adirondacks for more than fifteen years. Put up during one of John Turner's infamous seiges of the North Country, its steep, committing climbing was, like Turner himself, years ahead of the conservative style of the day.

Half a century later, the climb is still an inviting challenge at the upper end of its rating; it just protects a lot better.

First ascent: John Turner, Dick Strachan, and Dick Wilmott, 1959.

Start: Continue to the right along the base of the cliff about 100 feet past Gamesmanship. Around the corner, you come to a large clearing with a lot of eroded broken rock. At the left side of this clearing is a large inside corner. Up in the flaring dihedral, a prominent flakelike crack splits the open book, then arches right.

Route: Pitch 1 (50 feet, 5.6): Climb up the broken rock to gain the major part of the corner.

Pitch 2 (100 feet, 5.9+): Climb up the corner and the left wall to a small belay stance under the next corner.

Pitch 3 (75 feet, 5.8): Squeeze up the dihedral to easier climbing and belay.

Pitches 4–6: Finish either by scrambling left across broken rock to join Gamesmanship (climb 41; only 5.7 from this point) or move up and right to reach Fastest Gun (climb 43; 5.10).

Descent: From the top of the cliff, walk left (south) then scramble down the huge eroded dike above the campground.

43. Fastest Gun   III, 5.10-

Fastest Gun, which takes a stunning line up one of the more impressive cliffs in the region, is 500 feet of continuously outstanding climbing. From the enjoyable lieback crack/flake start to the wild roof near the end, each pitch of this climb could be considered a regional showpiece.

In most other climbing areas, at least a handful of routes are touted to be the route to do. 'Round these parts, no one challenges the Fastest Gun.

First ascent: Geoff Smith and Dick Bushey (first two pitches), 1977; Jim Dunn (final two pitches), 1978.

Start: Continue to the right along the base of the cliff about another 100 feet

Photo by Dave Horowitz

past Gamesmanship. Around the corner you come to a large clearing with a lot of eroded broken rock. At the top of this clearing, and about 60 feet right and uphill of Bloody Mary, a deep flake/crack inside a small dihedral shoots up the cliff. Just left of this flake/crack is a large dead tree that is broken off at the top.

Route: Pitch 1 (100 feet, 5.9): Climb the flake/crack to the rap slings. Belay here, or continue left then up to belay atop the blocks.

Pitch 2 (140 feet, 5.9): From the left of the blocks, follow the twin cracks up

Route detail of Poke-O's Fastest Gun. Photo by Dave Horowitz

Bill Cramer on the Fastest Gun in the Adirondacks' Poke-O-Moonshine area. Photo by Ralph Schimenti

past a slot at the roof to the dike. It is possible to belay either here or on the ledgelike flake above and left.

Pitch 3 (150 feet, 5.9+): Move right and follow a thin crack past an old bolt. Continue up to the base of the big left-facing corner with a roof.

Pitch 4 (150 feet, 5.10-): Crank the roof to gain the corner. Escape left, passing sketchy flakes, then up to the top.

Descent: From the top of the cliff, walk left (south) then scramble down the huge eroded dike above the campground.

PART II
CONNECTICUT _____

Opposite: *Looking up at the Wiessner Slab on Connecticut's Ragged Mountain.* Photo by S. Peter Lewis

onnecticut is a climbing enigma. Though only Delaware and Rhode Island are smaller and Connecticut has no mountains to speak of, there is a wealth of rock climbing here far out of proportion to the state's tiny dimensions. Tucked among the suburbs and small towns that dot the central part of the state are dozens of diminutive cliffs that sport thousands (yes, thousands) of rock climbs. Though none are taller than a pitch, if linked top to bottom, they would form a climb many miles high.

The rock here is traprock, an igneous mix of basalt and dolerite. Traprock outcroppings are found throughout Connecticut (although climbable traprock is found almost nowhere else in New England); the rock is typically steep (just about vertical on average), dense and fine-grained, fractured vertically at regular intervals, and littered with little holds. For the climber, this means a lot of strenuous cracks that protect well and face climbs that often do not protect well with conventional gear but have a lot of holds. If you like jamming steep cracks and crimping on vertical walls, you will love Connecticut climbing.

Climbing began here in the early part of the twentieth century with the first routes following the obvious jam cracks. The faces in between, peppered with edges of various shapes and sizes, have been explored since the 1960s—and these faces have been so scoured that probably nowhere in the state is there more than 10 feet between climbs.

Connecticut is trad country—if you are looking for sport routes, look elsewhere. Leading on removable gear (including hooks on some of the neckier face climbs) and top-roping are the accepted methods here. There are almost no bolts and fixed pitons, and local sentiment is that it should stay that way.

With more than 2,000 recorded routes in the state, it was a daunting task to pick a handful of favorites for this book. Since no routes are longer than a pitch and this book has trended toward the longer routes in the region, we decided to pick Connecticut's premier crag, Ragged Mountain, and describe a selection of some of its best routes from 5.4 to 5.11a. This smorgasbord of pitches, when strung end to end, provide more than 750 feet of some of the finest climbing in all New England and would make a very satisfying hit list for a weekend trip. Most of the routes chosen will protect very well, though all can also be easily top-roped.

CHAPTER 4. RAGGED MOUNTAIN ————

Climbing type ▲ Traditional
Rock type ▲ Traprock
Elevation ▲ 600 feet
Number of routes ▲ 9 in this book

Ragged Mountain is in the town of Southington in central Connecticut 30 minutes north of New Haven and 30 minutes south of Hartford. The 56-acre parcel of land including the cliff is owned by the Ragged Mountain Foundation (RMF), a nonprofit membership organization that is a "conservation group dedicated to preserving natural resources and maintaining public access to Connecticut's high and wild places." Through long negotiations, the RMF has secured long-term access to Ragged and preserved a vital Northeast climbing treasure.

The view from the summit of Ragged looks out on classic southern New England countryside with hills, forests, reservoirs, and small towns. It may not be very high or very wild compared to other areas in this book, but it is charming and the climbing is wonderful.

Ah, Ragged—this is where I was bitten by the climbing bug way back in 1976. I had just gotten my driver's license and one day I drove up to Southington and hiked into Ragged. I felt the handholds at the bottom of the routes as I walked along the base, saw my first rock climber, and that was it. I was bitten.

I got some rudimentary gear, including 16 feet of 2-inch webbing for a swami belt, and started making trips to the mountain nearly every weekend. Even through the haze of years, I have many recollections of working through the ratings. It took me four years to work up to top-roping 5.8 with any kind of style, and I vividly remember thinking that 5.9 was it, that if I could ever top-rope just one 5.9, I would have "arrived." Alas, college intervened and the hard climbs of Ragged had to wait a few years. But my climbing world expanded and over the next two decades I climbed all over the country, got better, climbed 5.9 and a bit beyond, and came to realize that Ragged, diminutive as it was, had been a wonderful place to fall in love with climbing.

Recently I drove back to Southington and hiked through the oak woods to Ragged. I met a friend and his girlfriend there on a hot summer morning as the cicadas were buzzing the air from the treetops. We spent a pleasant morning, with them climbing and me taking pictures, until it got too hot and sticky. I walked around the north end of the cliff to retrieve my hat from the summit and while walking past Vector, I knocked what I thought was a rock off the path and into the woods. It turned out to be a small painted turtle. It was hot and dry and very far from water, so I carried it back with me in my back pocket to put in in the pond below the cliff when we walked out. I showed it to Dave and Jennifer when I came down. Jennifer seemed somewhat alarmed. We had just met that morning and she did not know that this kind of behavior was par for the course for me. Dave just said, "You really are from Maine, aren't you?" I put the turtle back in my pocket.

A little while later, while Dave and I were bouldering the opening moves on Subline, I made a high step with my left leg that must have disturbed the turtle because it stretched out its pointed little snout and clamped onto my backside. I whooped and jumped down, did a little dance, and fished the turtle out of my pocket. It stretched its neck way out and hissed at me. A quarter century after I first tied in to a rope, I was back at Ragged, fingering the holds and bitten again.

Special Considerations

Because of its location in the middle of southern New England suburbia, access to Ragged has become increasingly problematic. Parking is an especially difficult issue (the RMF has no parking lot as of this writing) and trail access is also limited. Because of the changing access situation at Ragged, only general guidelines are provided here—go to the RMF website (*raggedmtn.org*) to find out the latest parking and trail access information. Please heed any "NO PARKING" signs, do not block mailboxes or driveways, pick up after yourself, and be polite and courteous to the people who live in the neighborhood.

Emergency Information
Call local police and fire departments (911).

Weather and Seasons
Year-round, with April through November the main season and spring and late fall best. Summers can be uncomfortably hot and humid.

Standard Equipment
A selection of standard nuts and cams to 3 inches for the cracks; smaller nuts and cams on face climbs. There are no bolts on any of the routes described. It is often difficult to rig gear anchors at the top of the cliff (the rock is typically shattered), so bring an extra rope to reach to the trees (at least 50 feet back) for top-rope anchors.

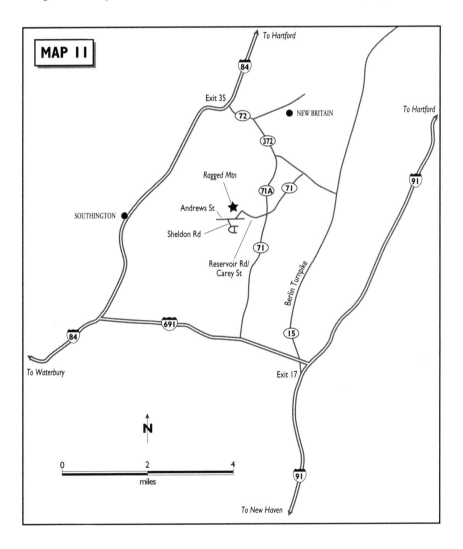

(If leading a pitch, you should be able to reach the trees, tie off your lead rope, and then belay by clipping in to a loop back from the edge.)

Getting There
From the north: Heading east or west on I-84, take exit 35 in New Britain to Route 72 (Black Rock Avenue), head east to make a right onto Route 372, then another

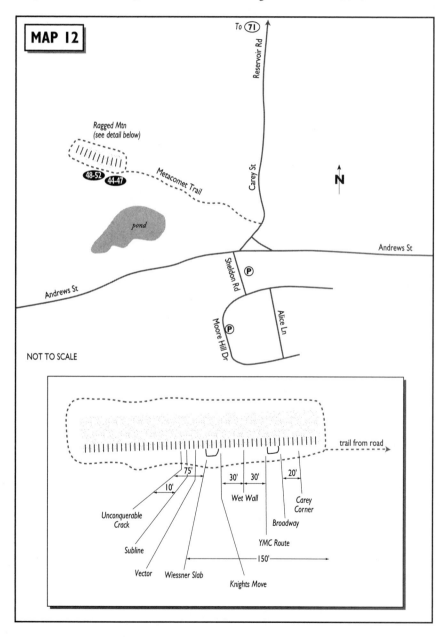

right onto Route 71A, and follow 71A south for several miles to Reservoir Road, where you turn right. After several miles (passing the reservoirs), this road becomes Carey Street (which ends at Andrews Street). Bear right and then take an immediate left onto Sheldon Road.

From the south: Take I-91 to exit 17, go north on Route 15 (Berlin Turnpike) to Route 691, take 691 west to Route 71, then follow 71 north to a left onto Route 71A and almost immediately a left onto Reservoir Road; then follow the directions above.

At the time of this writing the closest parking is on two side streets, Sheldon Road and Moore Hill Drive, both south of the cliff off Andrews Street. Consider parking at Ferndale Plaza on Route 71A a few miles north of Ragged and carpooling to limit the number of cars parked on either Sheldon Road or Moore Hill Drive. You may park either on the east side of Sheldon or continue a few hundred feet south to Moore Hill Drive, where additional street parking may be available.

Approach

From the intersection of Sheldon Road and Andrews Street, walk east on Andrews a few yards; at the fork take a left onto Carey Street, and follow that northeast for several hundred yards to the Metacomet Trail on the left; it starts up a dirt driveway through an orchard—look for blue blazes. The trail follows the driveway, then turns sharply left and divides—stay left for Ragged and in just about 5 minutes you will pass the Ragged Mountain Foundation kiosk (check for updated climbing bulletins) and then intersect the bottom of the cliff at its southeast end. The trail runs west along the base of the 600-foot-long cliff, and steep gullies provide easy access to the top at both its east and west ends.

Descent

For all routes, walk to the north to reach the trail that encircles the mountain, and then walk either west or east to return to the approach trail at the cliff's southeast end.

44. Carey Corner   I, 5.7

As you look up from its base, the bottomless dihedral of Carey Corner hangs down brooding and almost ugly. Steep, shaded, and looming, the lower section is fortunately blessed with great hand jams and footholds. Halfway up, a spacious ledge allows you to pause and contemplate the left-facing corner. At first glance you may see only one crack shooting up the wall, and it looks like one long, grunting lieback is in order. But closer inspection shows a second crack, perpendicular to the first, and all of a sudden the grunt turns to pure fun—albeit with few rests.

First ascent: Fritz Wiessner, Bill Burling, and Henry Beers, 1935.

Equipment: Larger pieces for the upper corner.

Start: From the southeast end of the cliff, walk west along the base for about 70 feet. The obvious hand crack connects to a hanging left-facing corner.

Route: Pitch 1 (90 feet, 5.7): Jam the crack strenuously to a ledge at two-thirds height, rest, then continue up the corner above—cracks facing both ways give you a lot of jamming and gear options, but few rests.

Ragged Mountain in Connecticut. Photo by S. Peter Lewis

45. Broadway   I, 5.8-

This is one of Connecticut's all-time classic moderate routes. I remember the loose chockstone halfway up the block on Broadway that provided a welcome rest twenty-five years ago. The liebacking and stemming up the right side of the block is considerably harder than it was when that chockstone was still in place. Just thinking about reaching up for that chockstone makes me feel older than my years. If you like face climbing, jamming, liebacking, and stemming, all with great protection, then this route is for you.

First ascent: John Reppy, Gil Young, and Frank Carey, 1958.

Start: About 20 feet west of Carey Corner (climb 44) are two parallel cracks about 15 feet apart on either side of a huge square block (the Skull and Bones block) that sticks out of the wall about 50 feet up. Broadway follows the right-hand crack.

Route: Pitch 1 (90 feet, 5.8-): Climb the crack to a strenuous lieback up the right side of the Skull and Bones block. From the block's flat summit, the crack continues (easier) to the top.

Dave Horowitz on Ragged Mountain's Broadway route; the striking crack in the background is Carey Corner (climb 44). Photo by S. Peter Lewis

46. YMC Route   I, 5.8–5.9-

When I first top-roped this climb in 1976, I was so scared to make the moves left at the block that I hung there and whimpered for about a half hour. It took me three attempts to make the scary moves (on a top rope) around the crux of YMC.

First ascent: John Reppy and Will McMahon (with a couple of aid moves), 1963; first free ascent: Dick Williams and John Reppy, 1964.

Start: About 20 feet west of Carey Corner (climb 44) are two parallel cracks about 15 feet apart on either side of the Skull and Bones block, which sticks out of the wall about 50 feet up. Follow the crack on the left side of the Skull and Bones block.

Route: Pitch 1 (90 feet, 5.8--5.9-): Tricky moves and hard-to-get gear lead to the base of the Skull and Bones block. To keep the route at 5.8, step several feet left on small holds, then climb up and back right to a flake and the top of the block (exciting). If you are up for the challenge, continue straight up the corner above to the top of the block (5.9-). Easier climbing leads to the top of the cliff.

47. Wet Wall   I, 5.6

If the quality of a route depended on its name, then Wet Wall would be junk. And while it is true that the opening overhang does seep a bit after a rain, more often than not it is bone dry. If the name keeps folks away, then you are in luck because the route sports excellent moderate climbing from bottom to top. The steep start around the little roof can be disconcerting but, fortunately, there is good protection for these, the crux moves. Above, a welcome rest ledge is found (a vintage photo shows a climber from the 1930s giving a shoulder belay from here), and then a long corner leads to another ledge just below the delightful final crack on Knights Move (climb 48).

First ascent: Fritz Wiessner and Donald Brown, 1934 or 1935.

Start: About 30 feet west of Broadway (climb 45) and YMC Route (climb 46) is a right-facing corner that hangs down and turns left, forming a small overhang about 8 feet off the ground.

Route: Pitch 1 (90 feet, 5.6): Climb the overhang strenuously, then lieback the

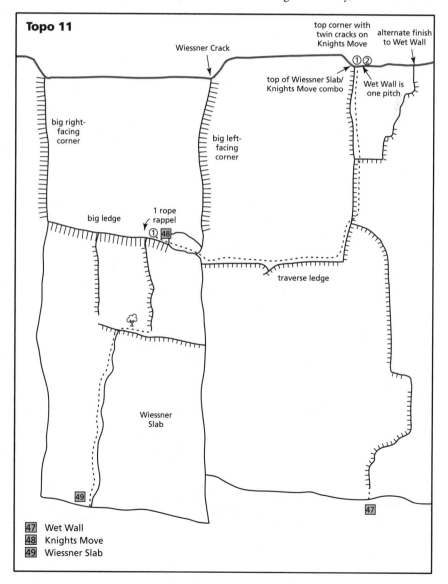

Topo 11

top corner with twin cracks on Knights Move

alternate finish to Wet Wall

Wiessner Crack

① ②

top of Wiessner Slab/ Knights Move combo

Wet Wall is one pitch

big right-facing corner

big left-facing corner

big ledge

1 rope rappel

① 48

traverse ledge

Wiessner Slab

49

47

47 Wet Wall
48 Knights Move
49 Wiessner Slab

corner until you intersect the traverse ledge of Knights Move. Either continue up that route's final corner or climb a series of steps immediately to the right.

48. Knights Move   I, 5.4

After climbing straight up the Wiessner Slab (climb 49), the way ahead appears to be forever barred by ominous cracks, arêtes, and faces that clearly are harder. But, like the knight on a chessboard with an opponent directly ahead, a deft sideways move takes you toward victory: A quick cut right puts you on a foot ledge all but invisible from below and allows an easy line across a stunningly steep wall. Then turn straight ahead again and gallop up easy ground to a perfect corner that leads to the top. This is Ragged's only multipitch climb and one of its greatest easy pleasures.

First ascent: Unknown.

Start: Climb Wiessner Slab (climb 49).

Route: Pitch 1 (50 feet, 5.4): From the fixed anchor atop the slab's right end, climb down under the boulder to the right to an obvious foot ledge that leads to the right. The transition from the gently angled Wiessner Slab to the vertical face to the right, even though the moves are easy, is a little like stepping out onto a window ledge. Follow the ledge to a short left-facing corner and then continue up a beautiful, narrow dihedral with double cracks.

49. Wiessner Slab   I, 5.3

Sometime in the distant past, a huge chunk of Ragged simply slumped down into the woods. Perhaps a torrential rainstorm loosened things up enough, or maybe a bitter winter's frost finally had its way, but whatever happened, in a moment the

Dave Horowitz and Jennifer East on Ragged Mountain's Wiessner Slab. Photo by S. Peter Lewis

Wiessner slab was born. For the Ragged climber, this fallen slab provides a welcome rest from the surrounding vertical walls. This route was a regular event for me when I was first learning to climb in the mid-1970s. It is a wonderful little wall where you can climb anywhere you want and every move is a delight. Too bad it is over so soon.

First ascent: Fritz Wiessner and Bill Burling, 1933.

Start: From the southeast end of the cliff, walk west along the base for about 150 feet to the bottom of the obvious slab that has slid down the cliff and settled lower into the woods.

Route: Pitch 1 (80 feet, 5.3): Start from some stone stairs on the left side of the slab and climb a finger crack to a ledge at midheight. Traverse right past a clump of bushes to a small right-facing corner and follow it to the wide ledge atop the slab and a fixed anchor around a boulder on the right side. At this point, you are blocked by harder routes above, including the awesome right-hand dihedral of Wiessner Crack (5.8).

Descent: Either rappel, climb Wiessner Crack, or continue on Knights Move (climb 48).

50. Vector   I, 5.8

This is another classic, moderate crack with a deceptively easy start and a stinging finish. The upper crack on Vector is described in an early guidebook as terrifying, and when I tried it in my third season, I was indeed terrified. If you get gripped with a cam at your waist on the upper crack, it may help to envision Fritz Wiessner making the impressive first ascent with a hemp rope around his waist, tennis shoes, and probably little protection.

First ascent: Fritz Wiessner and Roger Whitney, 1935.

Start: About 40 feet west of the Wiessner Slab, the trail goes uphill and passes a free-standing pillar about 15 feet high that leans against the cliff.

Route: Pitch 1 (80 feet, 5.8): Climb behind the pillar on the left to a left-facing corner that leads to a small roof. It has been easy so far, but get ready. Pull the little roof and then jam the strenuous and technical hand crack above to the top.

51. Subline   I, 5.11-

If you climb our list of Ragged classics from easiest to hardest, you will find Subline staring you down at the finish line. If you have any guns left (or have wisely taken a rest day), then what awaits you is 100 feet of Connecticut's finest. A stout little roof, hard jams, tweaky face moves, and intricate climbing with

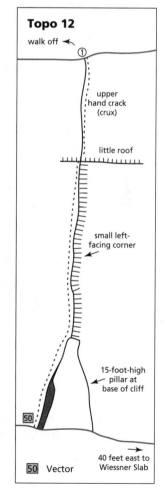

Topo 12

walk off

① upper hand crack (crux)

little roof

small left-facing corner

15-foot-high pillar at base of cliff

50

40 feet east to Wiessner Slab

50 Vector

Looking up the Vector route on Ragged Mountain. Photo by S. Peter Lewis

no rests until the very top make this one of the cliff's hardest routes to tick without winging off (or weighting a top rope). And if you find yourself shaking your head and wondering what to do, remember that Gunks legend Kevin Bein managed the first free top-rope ascent way back in 1969.

First ascent: Sam Streibert and John Reppy (with aid), 1963; first free ascent: Henry Barber and Bob Anderson, 1972.

Start: Start 10 feet east of Unconquerable Crack (climb 52).

Route: Pitch 1 (100 feet, 5.11-): Step off a boulder into the jaws of the toothy overhang (well protected) and swing out on good holds, then follow the thin, snaky crack line up the dead-plumb wall above. You have to be a master of many climbing techniques, be able to fiddle gear in while hanging from tweakers, and have great staying power to get up this sublime route.

52. Unconquerable Crack   I, 5.10-

This is perhaps Ragged's most stunning line—a dead-vertical crack running the full height of the cliff. Starting the lead, you look up at a fissure that just goes and goes. Opening jugs lead to jams of every description, and if you think that the wide spot

Photo by S. Peter Lewis

halfway up looks like the crux, you are right. The climbing is pumpy and sustained, and a successful ascent is a great achievement. Writing about the climb in his 1997 guide *Hooked on Ragged,* Ken Nichols, Connecticut's most prolific climber, issued one of the shortest challenges in the book: "Climb it."

First ascent: Sam Streibert and John Reppy (with a smattering of aid moves), 1963; first free ascent: Sam Streibert and John Reppy (Reppy leading), 1964.

Ragged Mountain's Unconquerable Crack, Connecticut. Photo by S. Peter Lewis

Equipment: Gear to 3½ inches.

Start: From the Wiessner Slab, walk west along the base of the cliff for about 75 feet to a shallow amphitheater with a fallen slab forming its left wall and an obvious toothy overhang on the main wall about 10 feet off the ground. Unconquerable Crack tackles the obvious hand crack that shoots up the wall to the left of the overhang.

Route: Pitch 1 (100 feet, 5.10-): The start is very steep but the holds and gear are good. Above, the crack widens and the crux beckons; farther above that, the crack just keeps on its unrelenting course.

PART III
VERMONT ─────────────

Opposite: Ryan Stefiuk on the crux pillar of Ragnarock at Smugglers Notch in Vermont. Photo by Alden Pellett

Rolling hills, tiny towns tucked into hollows, maple syrup, autumn leaves, and cows with short legs on their uphill side pretty much describes Vermont. And while the Green Mountain State does have a few outcrops of nice gneiss and granite and some nearly secret rock climbing, if it were not for two amazing places, Vermont would just be a hilly spot that climbers drive through between the Adirondacks and the White Mountains. But oh, those two places! Smugglers Notch and Mount Pisgah/Lake Willoughby are more than enough reason to pull to the side of the road, grab your ice gear, and head up the hillsides.

Smugglers Notch, just 25 miles or so northeast of Burlington, the state's largest city, is much like New Hampshire's roadside attraction, Frankenstein Cliff, but its alpine flavor, stout ski or snowshoe approach, and dramatic routes give it an aura of seriousness that is decidedly not roadside. Several dozen routes, from moderate slabs and gullies to steep pillars and mixed climbs, provide enough variety for everyone.

Many consider the Lake Willoughby area to have the best ice-climbing cliff in North America. Along a 1-mile stretch of a small road in the remote Northeast Kingdom of Vermont stretches the west face of Mount Pisgah. Upward of 600 feet high in places, Mount Pisgah is home to more than thirty ice climbs of such unrelenting verticality that WI 4 pillars are rare—this is WI 5 country. If you want to climb pitch after pitch after pitch of vertical ice, this is the place.

CHAPTER 5. SMUGGLERS NOTCH ⎯⎯⎯⎯⎯⎯⎯

Climbing type ▲ Ice
Rock type ▲ Schist
Elevation ▲ 1,800 feet
Number of routes ▲ 4 in this book

Smugglers Notch is a wild place with buttresses, slabs, gullies, and perhaps more mixed climbing potential than anywhere else in the Northeast. It has been a favorite haunt of ice climbers since the 1970s. Low-key and decidedly off the beaten path, Smugglers has been somewhat overshadowed by its New Hampshire counterpart, Frankenstein Cliff. Both places offer scads of superb ice climbing up to several pitches long clustered in a small area, but their characters are really quite different.

Frankenstein is a true roadside crag with a flat railroad right-of-way running conveniently along its base; it is mostly a pure ice playground, and you are never out of earshot of logging trucks. By contrast, Smugglers feels like it is in the mountains. The approach up a narrow road puts civilization way behind you, and the often thrashing approaches and descents make the climbs feel decidedly more "out there." You do not hear any traffic.

Special Considerations
Smugglers Notch is located in Smugglers Notch State Park. No fees or restrictions in winter. Because of its relatively high elevation, the road through the notch is closed

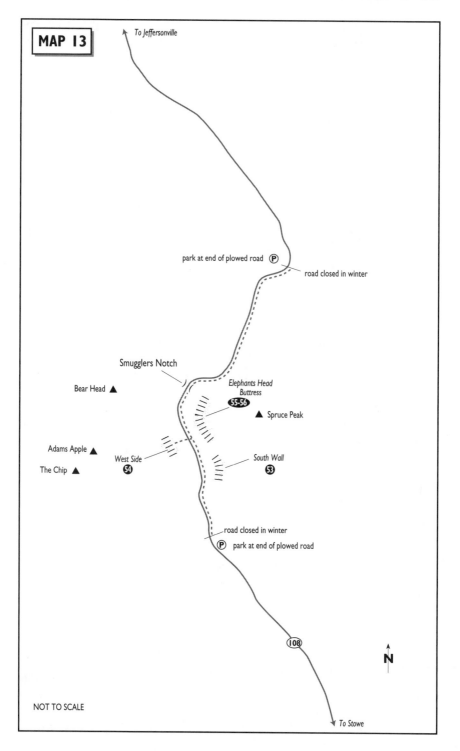

in the winter, leaving climbers with about a 1-mile approach from either end—allow extra time. Avalanche danger can be high on many of the approach gullies, especially after a big storm.

Emergency Information
Call local police and fire departments (911) or Stowe Hazardous Terrain Evacuation Team (802-888-3502 dispatch or 802-253-9060 regular phone). Do not count on help arriving quickly.

Weather and Seasons
Late November (especially for mixed climbing) until early April. Smugglers can be a very cold and windy place.

Standard Equipment
Six to ten ice screws; a small rock rack to 2½ inches for the area's scratchier routes. Two ropes for rappelling—often the best way down.

Getting There
Smugglers Notch is located on Route 108 between Stowe at the south end and Jeffersonville to the north, about a half hour northeast of Burlington.

For the south end: From I-89 in Waterbury, take exit 10 and follow Route 100 north to Stowe, then take Route 108 north to the notch.

For the north end: From the Burlington area, take Route 15 east through the town of Cambridge to a right turn onto Route 108 in Jeffersonville; follow 108 south to the notch.

From either direction, park where the plowed road ends. The unplowed stretch of road through the notch is approximately 2 miles, with the high point about in the middle and most of the climbing just south of there. See the Approach for each area for details on hiking, skiing, or snowshoeing up the notch.

South Wall
The South Wall's centerpiece is Daves Snotcicle, which drips spectacularly off one of the biggest roofs in the notch. Down and left of Daves Snotcicle is Blue Room, another classic notch moderate, and to the right of Daves is Prenuptial Agreement (WI 5+), which climbs one of the steepest pieces of ice in the area.

Approach
Hike up from the south (Stowe) end of the notch for 1.1 miles to the Big Spring parking area. A trail leaves from the back of the parking area.

53. Daves Snotcicle   II, WI 3–4+
Daves Snotcicle is right out in the open, infused with blue ice and sparkling in the sun. The route looks really hard. Fortunately, because of the way it forms each season, the variations on each pitch allow you to dial in the rating anywhere from WI 3 to verging on WI 5. This route, one of the most reliable in the notch, can be crowded,

Standard
ramp finish

Much
harder
finish

Harder
first pitch

Easier
variation

Daves Snotcicle
53

The South Wall at Smugglers Notch, Vermont. Photo by Brian Post

but "when the sun is shining, it's a fantastic place to be," says notch regular Alden Pellet. First ascent information on this route is sketchy, although you could assume that it was some guy named Dave.

First ascent: Unknown.

Start: Follow the trail most of the way to the obvious cliff band, then head up and right to the base of the route.

Route: Pitch 1 (120 feet, WI 4): Climb up the center of the flow to a belay in a huge cave below the roof. (An easier variation starts around to the right and wiggles up to the cave on lower-angled ice.)

Pitch 2 (60 feet, WI 3–4+): Climb out and left on a ramp, bypassing the final steep column (or tackle it directly; WI 4+).

Descent: Make one long rappel to a tree on the left, then rappel again or walk off (with caution).

West Side

This is the prominent amphitheater on the west side of the notch just south of Elephants Head.

Approach

Hike up from the south (Stowe) end of the notch past the Big Spring parking area at 1.1 miles and continue about 0.1 mile until below the obvious amphitheater on the left (west). See map 13.

54. Blind Fate   III, WI 4

In 1974 ice climbing in Smugglers Notch was an exciting, risky business. The gear was bad, there were few climbers, and if you got hurt you might not be found until spring. But there were a lot of new routes to be done.

John Bouchard was a student at the University of Vermont then, and one day a young Rick Wilcox drove over from New Hampshire, picked John up, and headed into the notch in search of new things (John had an aversion to second ascents). Picking a steep line in an amphitheater on the west side of the notch, the pair swung leads to the final, crux pillar. Bouchard led the pillar and soon had Wilcox on belay. "These were the real old days," Wilcox told me in 2002. "We had long axes with wooden shafts and leather triple boots."

Up on the vertical pillar, Wilcox started getting tired, really tired. Struggling with the low-tech screws, eventually he had to make a choice: Finish the pitch or clean the screws—he could not do both. He climbed, unclipping and leaving each screw where he found it. He assumed the pair would hike down from their new route; "I figured that when I reached the top, I could switch screws with John and he'd never know the difference," Wilcox said.

Arriving exhausted at the top, Wilcox realized his ruse would not work when he heard Bouchard say, "Well, there's no way down, we'll have to rappel." Wilcox tried to talk John into a long bushwhack down. But no way. Bouchard quickly rigged and disappeared over the edge. Wilcox did not have long to wait for what he knew was coming. "*You &%$(*@& jerk!*" Their friendship remained strong (it was just a couple of screws, after all), but to this day Wilcox still prefers to walk off from a climb rather than rappel.

First ascent: John Bouchard and Rick Wilcox, winter of 1974–75.

Special considerations: Avalanches have occurred on the approach snow gullies; take extra caution after a storm.

Start: Follow one of several long snow gullies below the amphitheater (the best-packed trail should be obvious) to the base of the route, which climbs an undeniably bold line up the very center of the amphitheater.

Route: Pitch 1 (140 feet, WI 3+): Climb over steep bulges to a belay at the base of the final steep column.

Pitch 2 (100 feet, WI 4): Climb straight up the final vertical drip—very spectacular. It is sometimes possible to avoid the final difficulties by heading right up a ramp to an easier bulge and the trees.

Descent: Hike right (north) through the woods and then trend down the tree-covered buttress on the right side of the amphitheater until a short rappel is needed to reach easy ground. Or rappel the route with long ropes and V-threads.

Smugglers Notch's West Side. Photo courtesy Rick Wilcox

Elephants Head Buttress

The gigantic Elephants Head Buttress is on the east side of the road just south of the top of the notch.

Approach

From the north (Jeffersonville) end of the road, it is 1.4 miles; from the south (Stowe) end, 1.6 miles. Look for a large boulder with a brass plaque on it (the King Rock). See map 13.

55. Ragnarock   III, WI 4+

Saying John Bouchard is fiercely competitive is like saying that the northern New England winters are really long. Spend any time up north or with John, and the character traits of both become obvious. In the winter of 1974–75, Bouchard and his frequent partner Steve Zajchowski continued reaping their crop of new routes in Smugglers Notch by climbing a major new route, along with several variations, on the right side of the Elephants Head Buttress.

Ragnarock proved to be one of the longest, hardest, and most spectacular routes in the notch, and they were justifiably proud of this all-time Smugglers classic. However, in an early version of the guidebook to the area, the description of Ragnarock was vague enough that a variation was climbed by another pair of climbers who assumed it

Elephants Head Buttress at Smugglers Notch. Photo by Brian Post

Climber on Ragnarock at Vermont's Smugglers Notch. Photo by Alden Pellett

to be a new route. According to guidebook author Rick Wilcox, Bouchard was livid and wanted Wilcox to recall the guidebooks, fix the error to give him the credit he was due, and reprint the book. But the books were already out and a recall would have been prohibitively expensive, so the description of the "Creighton-Korman Route" stayed. The error persisted through the second edition of the guidebook, and Bouchard was not vindicated until the third edition—in 2003!

First ascent: John Bouchard and Steve Zajchowski, winter of 1974–75.

Equipment: Add rock gear.

Start: A trail leaves the road about 75 feet downhill from the King Rock and goes to Elephants Head Buttress; head to the right side of the buttress.

Left-Hand Route: Pitch 1 (120 feet, WI 3+): Climb what is usually a fat smear on the left to a fixed belay (back up with rock gear) at the base of the big right-facing corner.

Pitch 2 (70 feet, M5): Climb up and right, following the approximate line of the corner, on thin ice and some rock (rock gear in corner) to another fixed belay.

Pitch 3 (80 feet, WI 4+): Climb up and slightly right, then back left, following the best ice. When the column on the far right is in shape, it offers an alternate steep finish.

Right-Hand Direct Route: Pitch 1 (150 feet, WI 4): Climb straight up thin ice on the right, following a crack (rock gear) to a screw belay below the final column.

Pitch 2 (75 feet, WI 4+): Finish straight up the steep column above. This does not always form completely, but the terrain is such that you can wiggle left or right and climb mixed ground to the top.

Descent: Hike north to the top of Elephants Head Gully (climb 56) and rappel that route with two ropes.

56. Elephants Head Gully   I, WI 3-

You would be hard pressed to find a more spectacular moderate ice climb than Elephants Head Gully. High above Smugglers Notch, the route weaves its way up the big corner formed by the looming Elephants Head Buttress and the wall to its left. Decidedly alpine, this modest climb can often look and feel as if it were high on some peak in the Canadian Rockies.

"For people just starting to climb, the surroundings can be very intimidating; dark, and cold," said Alden Pellet, longtime Vermont climber and photographer. While the nearby routes to the south are bathed in bright sunshine, the cleft of E-Head Gully is brooding and breathing. "It's always colder in there," Pellet told me. "The wind roars down, then the updraft brings it back up. Sometimes it comes down from the top and up from the bottom at the same time—but where does it go?" Fortunately, such mysteries are only meteorological; the route itself is a straightforward romp up what is mostly WI 2 ice.

First ascent: Chet Callahan, Bob Olsen, and Chuck Bond, winter of 1969–70.

Start: A trail leaves the road about 75 feet downhill from the King Rock. Elephants Head Gully climbs the dark groove that forms the left side of the buttress.

Route: Pitch 1 (130 feet, WI 2): Start at the lower-left corner of the buttress and follow low-angled ice to a fixed belay on the right at two bolts.

Photo courtesy Rick Wilcox

Pitch 2 (50 feet, WI 3-): Climb up and left over one short, steeper section to the top.

Descent: Rappel the route with two ropes: the first from a fixed anchor on a tree, the second from the bolts at the top of pitch 2. Be cautious rappelling when other climbers are below.

CHAPTER 6. MOUNT PISGAH/LAKE WILLOUGHBY AREA

Climbing type ▲ Ice
Rock type ▲ Granite
Elevation ▲ 1,500 feet
Number of routes ▲ 4 in this book

Willoughby is the most spectacular ice-climbing cliff in the United States. There, I said it. With our apologies to Vail and Ouray in Colorado, several canyons in Montana, and the entire community of climbers in Valdez, Alaska, we stand on our claim that no area in the country combines ease of access and dependable conditions with as vast a quantity of steep ice. The west face of Mount Pisgah, in the remote Northeast Kingdom of Vermont, is home to dozens of ice routes from 150 feet to well over 500 feet

high and is famous for its unrelenting WI 5 pillars. If you want to climb pitch after pitch of arm-pumping ice in a spectacular setting, then "the Lake" is the place to go.

Special Considerations

The land around Lake Willoughby is managed by the Vermont State Department of Natural Resources (DNR). Local climbers have been working with the DNR for several years to ensure that ice-climbing access remains open. Please climb (and park) responsibly.

Emergency Information

Call local police and fire departments (911) or St. Johnsbury State Police (802-748-3111).

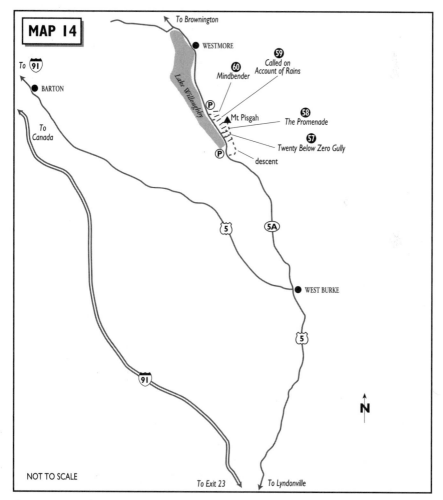

Opposite: *Mark Moran leading the first pitch of Mount Pisgah's Mindbender route in Vermont.* Photo by Peter Cole

Weather and Seasons
Mid-December until sometime in March. The cliff faces southwest and the ice gets baked later in the season, creating potentially unstable conditions.

Standard Equipment
A large rack of ten to twelve ice screws; two ropes for rappels (the best alternative for at least two of the routes listed here).

Getting There
Lake Willoughby is located in northeastern Vermont about an hour and a half east of Burlington and 25 miles north of St. Johnsbury. From I-91, which travels along the west side of the Connecticut River as it divides Vermont from New Hampshire, drive north of St. Johnsbury and take exit 23. Follow US 5 north through Lyndonville, and several miles outside of town, take a right onto Route 5A in West Burke. In about another 7 miles, you reach Lake Willoughby. Park at the south end of the lake in an unplowed area across from a campground or on pulloffs below your route (avoid these during storms, as you may get plowed in).

Approach
Walk down the road to under the intended route and hike up the snow slope to reach the base, typically 15–30 minutes from the road.

57. Twenty Below Zero Gully   II, WI 4+
In January 1974, Henry Barber, Michael Hartrich, and Al Rubin turned the last corner on Route 5A in northern Vermont and beheld the west face of Mount Pisgah for the first time. "Someone had told us 'there's something over there,' so I had to check it out," Barber told me recently. "Our first response was "Holy &$%#!," he said. "We thought we'd tapped into the mother lode." With the face plastered end to end in more vertical ice than any of the three had ever seen, the first challenge was to pick a line.

The future big routes in the Last Gentleman amphitheater looked harder than the benchmark of the times, the Black Dike (climb 62) on Cannon Cliff's Whitney-Gilman Ridge in New Hampshire, so the trio looked farther right, where the cliff mellowed somewhat. They soon spotted a rock buttress with an obvious flow down its right side. "It looked like a line; it looked do-able," Barber said. "And we hoped there might be some stemming" to keep the pump factor down. Hartrich led the first pitch and Barber took the second. He led the crux pillar wielding a 70-centimeter ax and a short hammer—neither with wrist loops. This route was the first climbed at Lake Willoughby.

I asked Henry if after their successful ascent of Twenty Below Zero Gully, they had tried to keep the place quiet so they could bag some of the other plums. "You don't keep much hush, hush with Rubin," he said with a laugh. Sure enough (though certainly not just because of Al telling a few friends), word soon got out and the major lines began to get ticked. Today, almost thirty years after three guys stared slack-jawed at Mount Pisgah for the first time, Twenty Below is still considered one of the Lake's best routes—even if it is only moderately difficult by today's standards.

Earl Anderson leading Twenty Below Zero Gully on Mount Pisgah above Lake Willoughby. Photo by Peter Cole

Of course, if you do it without wrist loops. . . .

First ascent: Henry Barber, Michael Hartrich, and Al Rubin, January 1974.

Start: Although in a good year the right end of the cliff is almost completely draped with ice, in most years there are distinctive clumps of ice. Twenty Below is typically the fifth obvious ice flow from the right end of the cliff. Walk the road until below the route and then head straight up—there is usually a well-beaten path.

Route: Pitches 1–2 (150 feet, WI 3+): Take the line of least resistance up and

Vermont's Mount Pisgah yields a trove of ice climbs. Photo by Bernie Mailhot

around bulges for either two short or one long pitch to a belay below the final pillar.

Pitch 3 (80 feet, WI 4+): Climb the big, steep pillar to the top. Believe it or not, this is one of the easiest routes here.

Descent: Hike straight back into the woods and turn right on a (usually packed) trail that leads back to the road at the south end of the cliff.

58. The Promenade   IV, WI 5+

The Promenade is the centerpiece flow in the obvious amphitheater just north of Twenty Below Zero Gully (climb 57). It is perhaps the longest, steepest, most aesthetic ice climb in the Northeast. If Lake Willoughby has some of the steepest ice in the Northeast, the Promenade has some of the steepest ice at Lake Willoughby. Its middle and top pillars just go up and up and up. The historic first ascent was made over 2 days.

Alden Pellet, a Willoughby regular, was on a nearby route one day and watched a drama unfold on the Promenade. A climber tackling the plumb middle pitch paused to put in a screw and then decided to go on without it. Not a big deal yet. Fifteen feet higher, he repeated himself. Now he had Alden's attention. "Put something in," Alden shouted over to him. The climber went up. He started to look a little shagged.

Way up now, he struggled again with another screw, then again clipped it back on his harness and continued up. *"Put something in,"* came the universal admonishment from the audience, much louder now. The climber reached the very top of the pillar, completely runout and obviously fried. He got a tool in over the top, crooked his arm over the top of it, and sagged down to rest. Pellett, confident now that the guy was going to make it, turned his attention to his own climbing for a moment. "The next thing I heard was Gore-Tex flapping," Pellet told me.

The guy fell down and down and down, 40 feet, 60 feet, 80 feet, 100 feet, and never let out a peep. The guy was in the air so long that Pellett had enough time to reach for his camera, put it up to his eye, and take a photo while the climber was still falling. Amazingly, a screw near the base of the pillar held, and the climber dangled below his belayer completely unscathed. According to Pellet, the guy looked up at his belayer and with perfect composure said, "You want to lead this pitch."

Because of its unrelenting verticality, only at Lake Willoughby can you fall more than 100 feet and still pull off a great one-liner.

First ascent: Tim Rouner, Rainsford Rouner, and Peter Cole, January 1977.

Start: Hike straight up the slope to the base.

Above Vermont's Lake Willoughby. Photo by Peter Cole

Route: Pitch 1 (140 feet, WI 5): Climb the center of the flow (can be thin at the start) to a ledge (possible belay) and continue with greater difficulty to a belay in a cave.

Pitch 2 (120 feet, WI 5+): Climb out of the cave into the land of verticality and pump your way up a long column.

Pitch 3 (100 feet, WI 5+): Blast your way up the final dead-vertical column (some stemming may ease the strain) to the trees.

Descent: Hike straight back into the woods to the descent trail, turn right, and follow it to the road at the south end of the cliff.

59. Called on Account of Rains IV, WI 5+

In late December 1977, Clint Cummins and John Imbrie were sorting their gear below the west face of Mount Pisgah. Dozens of unclimbed plums dripped above them, and they had their eyes on one particular route in an obvious amphitheater. Soon two school friends, Rainsford Rouner and Gustavo Brillembourg, showed up. "They were better organized and started up the gully to the amphitheater ten minutes ahead of us," Cummins recounted in *Lake Willoughby Ice Climbs: A Few Climbing Yarns* (1979). "Silent competition arises even among friends."

Assuming that Rouner and Brillembourg had a different objective in mind, Cummins and Imbrie thought they were "getting a free ride by letting Gus and Rainsford break trail for us." It soon became apparent, however, that Cummins and Imbrie were being beaten to the punch as their friends headed straight for their intended route. "John quickly stifled my impulse to muscle in, and we glissaded back down the gully, embarrassed," Cummins said.

Cummins' and Imbrie's second choice for the day was a long, skinny drip in the center of the wall that did not quite touch down. They planned to aid up to reach the ice, but the rock proved too rotten and the attempt failed.

The next weekend the pair came back, traversed a long ledge in from the left, and reached the upper ice pillars on their consolation route. Having worked out a system for steep ice that involved hanging from their tools while placing screws, the pair climbed "two nice ice pitches . . . in a giant corner," said Cummins, somewhat understatedly, considering the WI 5+ rating of the first pitch.

The following winter, Cummins and Imbrie returned and found the lower part of their route touching down—although just barely. Finding the ice a mere half inch thick at the bottom, they decided to go for it anyway. "Having made the approach, I was willing to ignore the dangerous nature of the pitch. I rationalized that the ice would probably never reach the ground again," Cummins wrote. Tricky climbing on bad ice with weird and suspect protection got Cummins to thicker ice, and they were soon repeating the familiar pitches above. "The last 'first' we cared to do was finished, and we groped down the descent trail to a feast of chocolate chip cookies," Cummins said.

And this is how one of the most spectacular and enduring test pieces at Lake Willoughby came to have its first ascent. All because Cummins' and Imbrie's first choice had been "Called on Account of Rains"—Rainsford Rouner, that is.

Opposite: *Perhaps the Lake Willoughby area's most dramatic route, Called on Account of Rains takes the right-hand line.* Photo by Peter Cole

Earl Anderson on the skinny first pitch of Called on Account of Rains, Mount Pisgah, Vermont. Photo by Peter Cole

First ascent: Clint Cummins and John Imbrie, December 28, 1977.

Equipment: Some rock gear (including pitons), especially on the thin opening pitch; extra gear, including headlamp, recommended.

Start: Park in a pullout almost directly below Mindbender (climb 60) and walk south on the road for about 800–1,000 feet until below the climb and then head right up the hill.

Note: If the route does not touch down, the upper pitches can be reached by climbing the Ledge Approach Variation (the way Cummins and Imbrie reached the ice the first time). Climb up the big snow slope down and left from the start of the route, then head up and left to a big amphitheater (the ice climb here is Stormy Monday, the route that Rouner and Brillembourg grabbed from Cummins and Imbrie). Gain a ledge system and climb several scrambly mixed pitches to the right to reach the ice.

Route: The route is described as it is typically done, in three long pitches. This is a long and serious route that ascends the uncompromising white stripe down the steep wall in about the center of the cliff. If the route is not touching down, be prepared for desperate (if not impossible) mixed climbing on the first pitch. **Pitch 1** (200 feet, WI 4+, M4 R): This pitch is often terrifyingly thin. Climb the sheet of ice (anticipate a lot of mixed moves and potentially sparse protection) to thicker ice and belay on the big ledge above. This pitch can be split.

Pitch 2 (125 feet, WI 5+): Climb the sustained pillar off the ledge to its top.

Pitch 3 (125 feet, WI 4): Climb the final long, easier pitch to the top.

Descent: The route is typically descended via three double-rope rappels. From trees at the top, rappel to an obvious cedar tree on the ledge, then down to a V-thread anchor (often there is a fixed thread anchor here) and again to the ground.

60. Mindbender   II, WI 5+

This is the central line on the trio of flows that are in an amphitheater at the far north end of the cliff. I once spent several hours dangling off Mindbender while my friend John put on a show on this arm-blowing route for my camera. The hike around to the top was miserable, extremely steep, and scary, but soon enough I was at the top and draping my ropes over a curved cedar tree that hung its trunk out over the void in a perfect crook.

I had trouble shooting John. I just could not get a good perspective. He was a great climber, awesome to watch and stylish, but as he climbed toward me, nothing looked dramatic; he just kept getting bigger. Later we rappelled off my perfect tree and part of the photo mystery was solved—our feet never touched the ice until we were on the ground.

When I got the film back, the whole thing became clear. I had been looking down a sheer, blue-white tower that sat on a steep, blue-white snow slope. I had spent all day trying to shoot one of the most dramatic ice climbs in the Northeast, and I had forgotten one of the first principles of photography—to show scale and perspective, you have to have a reference point. When everything is on the same plane and is the same color, things get pretty dull.

Now John would argue that there was nothing dull about his trip up Mindbender, but his perspective was a bit different from mine.

First ascent: Clint Cummins and John Imbrie, February 13, 1977.

Start: Park in a pullout almost directly below the route and hike straight up to the base.

Route: Pitch 1 (90 feet, WI 5): Climb straight up on very steep ground to a belay in or near the cave that usually forms on the right side of the flow.

Pitch 2 (75 feet, WI 5+): Climb out of the cave and head up one of the unrelenting pillars above. In a fat year, the whole top fills in as one uninterrupted wall of vertical ice. Expect pumped arms.

Descent: Rappel with two 60-meter ropes from nearby trees.

Photo by S. Peter Lewis

Gary Kuehn on the second pitch of Mindbender, Mount Pisgah, Vermont. Photo by Peter Cole

PART IV

NEW HAMPSHIRE ————

Opposite: *Bruce Luetters on Cannon Cliff's Whitney-Gilman Ridge, New Hampshire.* Photo by S. Peter Lewis

New Hampshire's well-deserved nickname, the Granite State, shows how fitting a place it is for climbing. More than any other Northeast state, New Hampshire is blessed with huge quantities of this hard igneous rock. Sheer faces, smooth slabs, a huge exfoliating dome, and a spine of rugged little mountains all are built of the state's foundation stone.

No other areas this book covers have so many excellent routes of so many different types and ratings. There are sport crags of wide renown, short trad crags, cliffs with great winter mixed climbing, and even great bouldering areas. Choosing just a handful of routes from this diverse area posed a unique challenge.

We chose to focus on the longer traditional rock routes and great multipitch winter routes that have made the region famous for decades. We cover two distinct regions in New Hampshire: the expansive cliff of Cannon Mountain on the west side of the White Mountains near Lincoln, and the crags and mountains of the Mount Washington Valley on the east side of the range. The first recorded roped ascent in the region was on a rock climb on Mount Washington back in 1910, and since then the area has become well known for its long, naturally protected rock climbs and superlative winter routes.

You could spend a lifetime here on the crags of northern New Hampshire (as many of us have) without running out of new challenges. It is no wonder that so many Northeastern climbers who have trained here on such varied terrain have gone on to raise eyebrows on routes around the world.

From 5.5 to 5.11+, from slabs to cracks to face, from short afternoon romps to mixed free and aid routes that will take a very long day, from 1,000-foot snow climbs to long WI 5 ice pillars, from roadside crags to windy ridges above timberline, there is something in New Hampshire for everyone that will get your blood pumping and make your heart glad.

CHAPTER 7. CANNON CLIFF/ FRANCONIA NOTCH

Climbing type ▲ Rock, ice
Rock type ▲ Granite
Elevation ▲ 2,500 feet
Number of routes ▲ 6 in this book

Cannon Cliff is a huge face about 0.75 mile wide and almost 1,000 feet high, gracing the west side of Franconia Notch. One of the largest cliffs in the East, it is home to many classic rock climbs, including some of the longest, hardest free and aid routes in the region as well as a host of classic ice climbs. While smaller crags dot the hillsides of the notch, the focus here is on the long, historical rock and ice routes of this alpine face.

Special Considerations

Cannon is located in Franconia Notch State Park. There are no climbing regulations, but use the voluntary sign-in/sign-out box at the parking area at Profile Lake. The box is checked every day by park officials, and the system has proven invaluable in emergencies. Cannon is a big alpine face with the characteristic challenges of routefinding on long climbs, some suspect fixed protection and belays, and loose rock. In the last few years, Cannon has had several large rockfalls that have sloughed hundreds of tons of granite into the talus. In May 2003, the famous profile of the Old Man of the Mountain—the state symbol of New Hampshire for as long as anyone can remember—slid off the north end of the cliff, wiping out Lakeview, an intended classic route for this book. Please take extra caution to protect yourself and other climbers when climbing on Cannon: wear helmets, do not knock off loose rock, test holds, do not trust fixed gear, start early, move fast, and do not get in over your head—Cannon is not a place to practice leading or to test your limits.

Emergency Information
Call local police and fire departments (911) or Mountain Rescue Service (603-356-7013 or 356-5433 extension 14).

Weather and Seasons
Rock climbing: mid-April through mid-November; May, September, and October are best. Ice climbing: mid-November through early April; December through February is best. Be prepared for very nasty weather—Cannon's winter environment is decidedly alpine.

Standard Equipment
Because most Cannon routes are long and many wander, a larger rack is often needed. Rock climbs: a generous selection of nuts and cams up to 4 inches and a lot of slings. Any special gear requirements, including an ice rack, are noted in the route descriptions. Helmets are essential due to the cliff's alpine (i.e., deteriorating) nature. Two ropes (smart on all Cannon routes even if you plan to walk off), foul-weather gear, headlamps, food, and water are all a good idea.

Getting There
Cannon is located about halfway up the center of New Hampshire on the west side of Franconia Notch, about 10 miles north of Lincoln on Interstate 93. The parking area is just north of the cliff at Profile Lake and is only accessible southbound on I-93 just south of exit 35B.

Northbound on I-93, pass the huge bulk of Cannon Cliff on your left and then take exit 35B at the top of the notch and reverse direction, driving south on I-93 a short distance to the parking area on the right.

Approach
For Whitney-Gilman Ridge: From the south end of the parking lot, follow the bike trail south for about 0.25 mile to a marked climbers trail on the right. Hike through a short section of woods until you emerge onto the talus near a huge boulder (the Little Matterhorn, a useful landmark for relocating the trail from above). Follow cairns up to the base of the Whitney-Gilman Ridge.

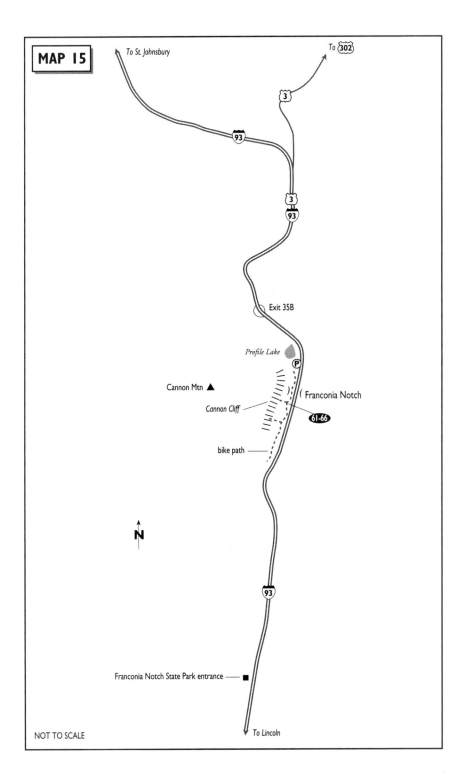

MAP 15

To St. Johnsbury

To 302

3

93

3
93

Exit 35B

Profile Lake

P

Cannon Mtn ▲

Franconia Notch

Cannon Cliff

61-66

bike path

N

93

Franconia Notch State Park entrance ■

NOT TO SCALE

To Lincoln

For the "big-wall" section of the cliff: From the south end of the parking lot, follow the bike trail south a short distance to the top of a rise and look for a marked climbers trail on the right near a huge boulder. Follow the trail through a short section of woods to a knoll and then follow cairns to the base of the cliff in the vicinity of Vertigo (climb 66).

On either approach, take care in the talus field—in summer the blocks can shift and poison ivy is abundant; in winter, avalanches are not unheard of.

61. Whitney-Gilman Ridge   III, 5.7–5.8

"What do you think I should put in here?" The question came from my dear friend Polly as she started up the first 5.4 pitch of the all-time classic New Hampshire climb, the Whitney-Gilman Ridge. I hissed condescendingly and said, "It's 5.4, for crying out loud. I wouldn't put anything in." Polly down-climbed, tossed the wad of gear on the ground, and then the silence of outer space filled all of Franconia Notch for several very long minutes. Finally, staring as I had the whole time at the stones between my feet, I whispered, "I'm sorry. I'm a jerk. I'll lead."

The "Whitney-G," as it is often called, is perhaps the coolest climb in the East. Climbing a perfect fin of granite for hundreds of feet, it has some of the wildest positions anywhere. With its stunning geometric line, it is somehow fitting that it was first climbed by famed Harvard mathematician Hassler Whitney. In 1929, Whitney and his cousin Bradley Gilman made the climb in more than a dozen short pitches (climbers of the day typically stopped to belay on every decent ledge). The route that was to bear their names was considered the hardest rock climb in the country at the time, and is likely New Hampshire's most famous rock climb.

About a third of the way up the 600-foot route, the pair found their way up the left side of the fin blocked by an overhanging wall. Historians Laura and Guy Waterman wrote about the crux pitch in *Yankee Rock and Ice.* "With cool nerve, they swung around the corner of the knife edge for one particularly exposed and delicate pitch, poised airily over the evil void of the Black Dike." On a subsequent ascent, in 1931 legendary climber Kenneth Henderson (with Robert Underhill) drove a piece of pipe into a crack to protect the moves over the void—creating the "Pipe Pitch," perhaps the most famous 20-foot section of granite anywhere in the Northeast.

By the time Polly and I arrived at the belay below the pipe pitch, we were talking again and having the time of our lives. Soon I was peering around the corner straight down into the Black Dike—surely the oddest place for a climber to want to find a piece of water pipe. But there it was, and a sling around it gave me the courage to begin stemming up the corner above. Clipping into every '30s vintage piton I could find and trying to fiddle in nuts between them, I wormed my way up and out left, shaking like a leaf, and finally pulled over left and up to the ledge. It had been a very short and rather reasonable pitch; I was just scared.

After Polly had followed the pitch effortlessly and handed me back the big wad of slings, 'biners, and nuts, far out of proportion to the length and difficulty of the pitch, she did not say a word.

First ascent: Hassler Whitney and Bradley Gilman, August 3, 1929.

Start: Follow the Approach to the Whitney-Gilman Ridge.

walk off

6

5

4

5.7 crux on
north wall
of buttress;
pipe pitch

3   3a

5.8 variation

2

1

alternate start
on right side
of buttress

1a

A

61 Whitney-Gilman Ridge

Whitney-Gilman Ridge in New Hampshire. Photo by S. Peter Lewis

Approach pitch (50 feet, 4th class): From the very base of the ridge, traverse a ledge system left onto the front of the buttress and belay below an obvious crack.

Route: Pitch 1 (100 feet, 5.5): Climb the crack in a right-facing corner up the front of the buttress to a low-angled slab on the right and belay at the base of the next steep section.

Alternate start (replaces approach pitch and pitch 1) **Pitch 1a** (140 feet, 5.4): Start up the gully on the right side of the ridge about 50 feet and climb up and right to reach the ledge at the top of the regular pitch 2.

Marc Chauvin on the crux of the Whitney-Gilman Ridge of New Hampshire's Cannon Cliff. Photo by S. Peter Lewis

Pitch 2 (80 feet, 5.5): Lieback a crack on the right (the left crack is 5.7) to a spike, step left, and climb straight up to a spacious ledge.

Pitch 3 (125 feet, 5.6): Climb up, then left on a slab to a short groove/chimney; move right above this, passing blocks, to a belay on a ledge at the base of a 4-inch crack.

Pitch 3a (75 feet, 5.8): Climb straight up the crest of the ridge to an obvious hand crack and climb it strenuously to a small belay ledge.

Pitch 4 (100 feet, 5.7): The infamous Pipe Pitch. Climb the wide crack off the ledge (do not stick your knee in it—trust me), then traverse right around the arête and onto the extremely exposed north wall of the ridge (look low for the pipe). Climb up cracks and the shallow corner above to a hard move left at the top, then climb up a short slab to the right and then back left to a belay around a corner.

Pitch 4a (40 feet, 5.7): Climb up a small corner and then the face above to join the regular fourth pitch right at the pipe.

Pitch 5 (100 feet, 5.5): Climb up a slab past a block and traverse left to a short corner leading to a ledge. Continue up another corner on the crest of the ridge to a small belay stance.

Pitch 6 (100 feet, 5.7): Continue up left of the ridge via the most reasonable line, with one hard move getting out of an alcove, and finish up a corner.

Descent: From the very top of the ridge, hike straight into the woods for a couple hundred feet, then turn sharply left and follow the obvious climbers path down around the left (south) side of the cliff. (**Note:** It is a long way across the top, so do not cut down early; stay on the most obvious path.)

62. The Black Dike   III, WI 4–5 M3

In 1971 the leader of the revolution in ice-climbing technology, Yvon Chouinard, described the Black Dike in the Sierra Club journal *Ascent* as "a black, filthy, horrendous icicle 600 feet high. Unclimbed." Though it may seem odd to nonclimbers, this is just the kind of language that can keep ice climbers up all night scheming away.

Though many of the most skilled climbers of the day had their eyes on this route, most peered at it through prerevolution eyes, and their visions of swinging straight picks and chopping endless steps up the near-vertical ice of the "horrendous icicle" kept them at bay. "Hugo Stadtmuller had gone up to look at it and backed off. Little lion-hearted Jorge Urioste had weighed it and pronounced it suicidal," said historians Laura and Guy Waterman in their history of Northeast climbing, *Yankee Rock and Ice.* Even with all the hype and a seeming taunt from Chouinard, the country's most visionary climber, no one did better than scratch around the base. In the end, the coveted first ascent would fall to a nineteen-year-old kid named John Bouchard "who had never cut a step and knew only the revolution," wrote the Watermans.

On December 18, 1971, Bouchard—alone, because his would-be partner, John Porter, had had to work that day—climbed the talus below the Black Dike carrying a rope and a few pitons with an eye on a reconnaissance. A short way above the first hard moves, his rope jammed. He dropped it and continued. A little higher, he broke the pick off his hammer. Still he continued. Then he dropped a mitten and the afternoon light began to fade. But there was no going down. The Watermans describe the next few minutes as Bouchard confronted a 10-foot pillar near the top of the route: "Employing a variety of aid techniques in utter desperation, fighting down panic, he somehow clawed over it" and crawled into the woods, "having soloed by far the hardest route yet done in the Northeast. John Bouchard had seen the future and it worked."

At Franconia Notch's Cannon Cliff. Photo by S. Peter Lewis

Achieving almost mythic proportions, an ascent of the Black Dike in the mid-'70s was worthy of real hero worship. But like many milestones, as the years have passed and with the continuing revolution in ice-climbing equipment, the route has lost much of its sting. It is no longer a myth to be tested only by the elite. Today, on many a fine winter's day, a line is queued up at the base of the route. Invariably the line includes some with decidedly modest climbing résumés, and there may even be those who have never heard of the revolution.

And yet, regardless of your age or experience, when you are high on the route staring at that final pillar, try to think of what it must have been like more than three decades ago. Imagine mushy leather boots instead of plastic ones, flexing crampons instead of sturdy monopoints, an ice dagger in one hand and a primitive curved-pick tool in the other. Imagine you have no partner, no rope, and one bare hand. And imagine that you have no idea that the route above is even possible. Now squint your eyes so that the day dims to twilight, and feel the shiver run up your spine.

First ascent: John Bouchard, December 18, 1971; first winter ascent (for those who are sticklers, winter begins December 21): Bouchard, John Bragg, Rick Wilcox, and Henry Barber, 1973.

Special considerations: This early season route is typically in its best shape early December through January; its difficulty ranges from WI 5 in typical (thin) conditions to WI 4 (when fatter). Due to popularity, a very early start is advised (even midweek). Climbing beneath other parties on this route is extremely dangerous because stuff falls all the time.

Equipment: 6–10 ice screws, including some short ones; rock gear often useful.

Start: Follow the Approach to the Whitney-Gilman Ridge. The start of the route is obvious up in the huge, dark corner right of the Whitney-G.

Route: Pitch 1 (200 feet, easy snow then WI 3): After trudging up what is typically 100 feet of steep snow, climb a shallow groove straight up to a belay ledge that is about 30 feet right of the very back of the right-facing corner that forms the climb.

Pitch 2 (150 feet, WI 5 M3 in typical conditions, WI 4 if fat): The crux pitch climbs straight up for a few feet and then concocts a leftward traverse on blocky holds (may be 5.8) to reach the steep yellow runnel in the back of the corner. Follow the runnel steeply up over bulges to a good ledge with a fixed anchor.

Pitch 3 (150 feet, WI 3+): The final pitch climbs up and right to a short, steep wall then trends up and left following the main corner to the top.

Descent: Head straight into the woods for 100–200 feet and then turn sharply left (south) and follow a usually well-packed climbers trail as it contours down and around the left end of the cliff. Turn left (north) on the bike path and return to the parking lot. Allow about an hour.

63. VMC Direct Direct   IV, 5.10d

In 1996 I called Steve Arsenault and Sam Streibert to ask if they would return to VMC Direct Direct so I could shoot some photos for a magazine article. They were

Opposite: *Ray Omerza climbs the Black Dike '80s style on Cannon Cliff.* Photo by S. Peter Lewis

2 pitches
5.5/5.6

7

Cows Mouth

5.10d

6

5.9

5

5.10d

4

5.9

3

5.10d   5.10

5.10+

2

5.10+

1

5.7

VMC Direct Direct   63

New Hampshire's Cannon Cliff. Photo by S. Peter Lewis

Steve Arsenault on the second pitch of VMC Direct Direct in 1996. Photo by
S. Peter Lewis

both keen to head back and eliminate the few points of aid from their route of
twenty-seven years past.

We had a bit of a reunion in the parking lot and then I was soon huffing to keep
up with these two guys in the talus—neither had gone soft in a quarter century. The
first pitch was a walk, and soon Steve and I were watching Sam negotiate the thin
undercling crux out the ceiling above. As aggressive as he had always been, Sam tried
valiantly several times, but it was just too thin, and with a final expletive he pulled on

the draw and rode the trolley over to the corner, which he dispatched with ease (5.9).

I ascended a fixed rope and photographed next to Steve as he repeated the undercling performance, with the same complaints of fat fingers and the same pull on the draw. Both men were frustrated with the single aid point, but determined that that would be it. On the third pitch, a burning stem fest up a hanging dihedral, we watched as Steve hung in there and cranked every move. At the roof, he paused and fiddled in some small nuts. I knew the spot well and that the next moves were really hard, but Steve just yarded over the roof and was soon whooping at us from the belay. Sam followed as if on a hike. We rapped off, having had a great day together, but both men paused as they passed the roof, looked at that teeny undercling, and shook their heads.

A couple of years later, I was on Cathedral Ledge when a really fit Steve Arsenault came cruising by without a rope. We chatted for a couple of moments and then started climbing again. After a couple of moves, he turned back and looked at me. "Hey, I went back to VMC Direct Direct," he said. "How'd you do on the undercling? I asked. "Cruised it," he said with a big grin, and then he disappeared above.

First ascent: Dick Williams, Art Gran, and Yvon Chouinard (pitches 5–9), two days in September 1965; Steve Arsenault and Sam Streibert (entire route), June 7–8, 1969; first free ascent: Jeff Burns with Hans Larsen, June 1975.

Special considerations: This is a long route; be prepared for a fairly long day (unless you bail after pitch 3, as many folks do).

Equipment: Additional small pro; extra clothes, headlamp, etc.

Start: Follow the Approach to the "big-wall" section of the cliff, then hike south along the base of the cliff for 700–800 feet until below the highest part of the cliff. VMC Direct Direct starts on the right side of a small buttress in the center of the cliff—look for the razor-cut right-facing corner that starts about 150 feet up with a small roof at its base arching to the right.

Route: Pitch 1 (120 feet, 5.7): Follow the right side of the buttress up corners and cracks to a good ledge.

Pitch 2 (140 feet, 5.10+): Climb up the tiny right-leaning corner above, then a left-trending ramp, then undercling the obvious ceiling to the right (many consider this the crux) to enter the dihedral proper. Follow the stunning dihedral to another good ledge.

Pitch 3 (130 feet, 5.10+): Continue stemming and liebacking the corner above and pull a small roof (another crux) at its top to a very small ledge and bolts. Instead of pulling the roof, you can also undercling right (5.10) and then climb a short corner to the belay. Many people rappel from here, because the climbing above gets a bit scrappy.

Pitch 4 (100 feet, 5.9): Climb up a gully (5.5) to a big hanging block, step across the block to its left side, and face climb to a ledge and the junction with the VMC Direct (a classic 5.11 route that follows arching corners to the left).

Pitch 5 (125 feet, 5.10d): A difficult move off the belay gains a flake and a long ledge, which is followed left for 30 feet to a shallow, right-facing corner that leads to moderate slabs, a small overlap, and short headwall.

Pitch 6 (100 feet, 5.8–5.9): Climb over the headwall then right to a shallow, left-facing groove and more moderate climbing to a belay in the obvious alcove above—the Cows Mouth. This is the last place where rappelling is an option.

Pitch 7 (40 feet, 5.10d): Struggle out an overhanging crack on the right side of the Cows Mouth, then up to moderate slabs.

Pitches 8–9 (200 feet, 5.5–5.6): Two more scruffy, low-angled slabs lead to the trees at the top of the cliff.

Descent: Many people do just the first three pitches and then rappel. If you go to the top of the cliff, either rappel from the top of pitch 6 (much easier) or finish the last couple of pitches, bushwhack up and right on slabs and through malevolent, pervasive, ubiquitous, impenetrable brush, and follow vague trails north until at the top of the former Old Man of the Mountain, where an established trail leads back to the parking lot.

64. Labyrinth Wall   V, 5.8 A3 or 5.11

The Lab Wall is one of the only real big-wall routes in the Northeast. Unless you are some kind of super hotshot, you actually will end up spending the night on it. When I did it way back in 1984 with my friend John, it still had an aura of seriousness about it, and we were somber and kept our brows furrowed as we lugged our big haul bag up the talus. We chose to do the route in late June so that we would have as much light as possible. Unfortunately, this was also the height of the notorious black-fly season. But what the heck, Cannon is a big cliff and it is not squeezed into the forest like so many other Northeast crags, so how bad could they be? And besides, John had brought the bug dope. What? He thought I had brought it? Oh well; no worries. We would be 500 feet up in the breeze in no time.

All day long we picked our way up the first half of the route, John leading anything harder than A2, and arrived at the bivy ledge with 3 hours of light left. From here, things went downhill. First, John brought out dinner: tins of sardines and crackers, which had been powdered by the ride up the wall in the haul bag. Then we discovered that one of our jugs of water had leaked inside the haul bag, and my sleeping bag had been below it. These were just minor setbacks, however, and we settled in to enjoy the summer evening and tremendous views of the Franconia Range across the valley.

Did I mention that it was a windless evening? In the calm, the blackflies flew all the way up to our ledge. We snuggled in, cinched our bags over our heads, and tried to sleep. Did I mention that the bivy ledge is not flat? Well, we spent most of the night slowly sliding closer and closer to 500 feet of air.

We got up (note I did not say "woke up") at dawn and John started off. The hardest aid pitches of the route lay above us and since John was the trinket master, he would be leading from here on in. It was hot. It was dead calm. At the top of the ninth pitch, I hung on a hanging belay. John was going slowly (it was A3). The blackflies were everywhere. I had a mound of welts encircling my bare neck that made it look as though I was wearing a thick, red bandana. I was sitting astride the haul bag, numb from the waist down, feeding out occasional slack through an ascender as John slowly inched up the wall above. I lay my head on the top of the bag, 650 feet up, shrouded in flying bloodsuckers, and fell sound asleep.

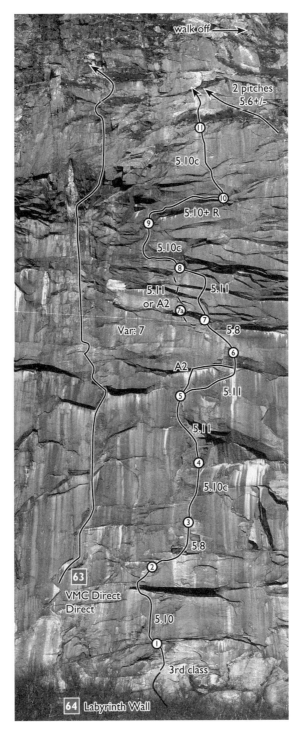

The Labyrinth Wall at Cannon Cliff. Photo by S. Peter Lewis

First ascent: Paul Ross and Michael Peloquin (to top of pitch 7 and then exited right), August 12–13, 1971; Peter Cole, Rainsford Rouner, and Mark Hudon (complete route, after several tries), November 1974; first free ascents: Chris Kulcyzcki (first few pitches), 1980; Mark Richey (couple pitches higher up, finishing to right), May 24, 1981; Neil Cannon and Alison Osius (complete route), October 1984.

Special considerations: This is a big, complex route. If attempting it in a day, get an early start and move fast. If you bivy, at night make sure your headlamp does

John Tremblay on pitch two of the Labyrinth Wall in 1984. Photo by S. Peter Lewis

not shine out toward the highway—passing motorists may think it is a distress signal. This route is all free and can be climbed very clean; please keep your pounding and bashing to a minimum.

Equipment: A generous rack, including a lot of small pro, some hooks, bashies, pitons to 1 inch (if aiding upper pitches); a belay seat for the many hanging belays; three-season sleeping bag, foam pad, some extra clothes for a bivy.

Start: Follow the Approach to the "big-wall" section of the cliff, then hike south until under the center of the cliff. The route starts about 100 feet right of the VMC Direct Direct (climb 63). Look for an obvious triangular recess about 200 feet up the wall, and start below and to the left of this.

Route: Pitch 1 (50 feet, 3rd class): Climb up easy rock to a belay below the left end of a large horizontal overlap.

Pitch 2 (100 feet, 5.5 A2 or 5.10): A bolt leads to a small corner (pins); then go left around a roof and up to a two-bolt belay.

Pitch 3 (80 feet, 5.8): Go right and then up a left-facing corner, then move right to a belay.

Pitch 4 (80 feet, A2 or 5.10c): Three bolts lead to a slab; trend left and climb into the base of the huge triangular recess above, then belay at its base on the higher of two ledges.

Pitch 5 (75 feet, A2+ or 5.11): Climb steeply past bolts out the recess's left side to a hanging belay above.

Pitch 6 (100 feet, A2 or 5.11): Climb a short dowel ladder, then aid along the bottom of an arch until you can break through its right end. If free climbing, traverse low (bolts), then straight up to the break.

Pitch 7 (70 feet, 5.8 R A1 or 5.10+ R): Climb left on friction to bolts, step left under an overlap, then step over it to the right of a thin, vertical crack (5.8 R) and then up to a small stance.

Pitch 7a (90 feet, A2 or 5.11): As an alternative, instead of belaying continue left after the bolts and climb the original "A4 seam" on the left, the route's original line. This variation leads directly to the bivy ledge (top of pitch 8).

Pitch 8 (35 feet, 5.11): Climb a left-trending arch with difficulty to the right end of the bivy ledge.

Pitch 9 (80 feet, 5.8 A3 or 5.10c): Traverse left along a flake for 30 feet, then climb over a break and follow difficult aid until you can free climb to a stance with three pitons. This is a strenuous free pitch.

Pitch 10 (60 feet, 5.10+ R): Climb a slab to the right below the big arch above to a belay with a lot of bolts.

Pitch 11 (100 feet, 5.10c R): Angle left, staying generally below and left of the aid route's fixed gear, to a thin flake that is climbed to a corner to the right of a slab. Climb the corner to a brushy ledge.

Pitches 12–14 (250 feet, 5.3–5.6): Climb a short corner above two slabs, then continue up easy, brushy slabs until the trees get big enough to be called the top. This is particularly nasty if you have done the route in 2 days and are dragging a haul bag.

Descent: Thrash through the woods to the right for several hundred yards until you can hike down and to the right to reach the top of the former Old Man of the Mountain and then down the trail.

65. Moby Grape   III, 5.8

From high on the soaring corners and cracks of Moby Grape, it is pretty easy to imagine that you are on a high alpine peak in the far West—Pingora in the Wind Rivers, perhaps, or maybe Cathedral Peak in the High Sierra. Clean, white, heavily fractured, clearly exfoliating (granite slabs stacked like the rings of a peeling onion), and perched atop a huge talus slope, the route certainly looks western. That it is in tiny New Hampshire, perched at under 4,000 feet, and less than an hour's walk from the road seems somehow incongruous.

If you choose the Reppys Crack start (highly recommended), you get that western feel right off the deck. Cleaving the front of a clean buttress, this crack soars and soars—and if you do not keep moving, you will be sore too. The angle is laid back and the crack is smooth and friendly and readily accepts gear, but oh, it is unrelenting. Most of the time your feet are torqued at odd angles in the crack, and if you dawdle you pay for it with painful ankles. The climbing is secure (except for the awkward pod at three-quarter height) and not particularly strenuous, so just climb.

Above, the climb weaves its way up the wall, over a pretty big overhang on pitch 3, jamming nice cracks and stemming short corners above, and finally lands you below perhaps the most notorious feature on all of Cannon—the Fickle Finger of Fate. Jutting crazily out of the cliff like a big cleaver, the Finger gives pause on an otherwise low-key granite stroll. You cannot avoid this thing. You are going to have to climb it. Our advice is not to get too worked up about it; the gear is okay, the holds are fine, it is really quite short, it is not as strenuous as it looks, and when you get on top the typical reaction is, "Oh, that was not too bad."

As you stand on the big ledge above, surrounded by white granite and with peaks soaring above timberline to the east, it is not hard to imagine you are in Wyoming—and hey, think of the airfare you saved.

First ascent: Jan Conn and Herb Conn (pitch 5), 1945; Phil Nelson and Alan Wedgewood (final three pitches), May 6, 1965; Joe Cote and Ben Read (added fourth and sixth pitches), 1971; Joe Cote and Roger Martin (the whole route), July 1972; Kurt Winkler and John Colebaugh (alternate finish), October 1986.

Equipment: Several large cams to 4 inches for Reppys Crack.

Start: Follow the Approach to the "big-wall" section of the cliff, then hike south about 300 feet to an obvious buttress with a striking hand crack in its center.

Route: Pitch 1 (145 feet, 5.8): Lieback the outer overlap on the left side of the buttress and then climb a finger crack to a step right. Lieback up the corner to a move right and then head up and right across the front of the buttress. Belay at a piton (back it up.)

Pitch 1a (200 feet, 5.8), Reppys Crack: Jam the wonderful crack (it gets big) on the front of the buttress to either a semihanging belay at the top of the crack (120 feet) or continue up a corner on the right to the top of the buttress and belay from bolts.

Pitch 2 (150 feet, 5.7): Climb a short crack, then scramble on easy ground to the top of the buttress and belay on a ledge directly below a triangular roof above.

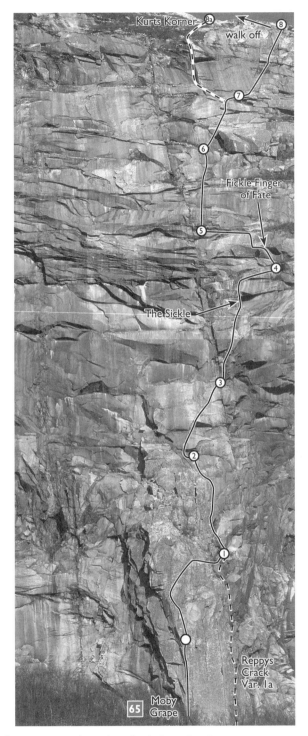

Cannon Cliff in New Hampshire. Photo by S. Peter Lewis

Pitch 3 (110 feet, 5.8): Climb a finger crack to the triangular roof, pull it on the left, and then climb more easily to a belay on a good ledge above.

Pitch 4 (150 feet, 5.7): Climb a right-trending corner on the right, then left to flakes and cracks, then straight up to another ledge on the right, then up a right-trending arch to the Sickle and over it to a belay at the right edge of the Fickle Finger of Fate.

Pitch 5 (90 feet, 5.7): Climb the right side of the Fickle Finger, step onto a slab, then climb to a large ledge (possible belay and escape to the right) and belay on the left end at a dike.

Pitch 6 (150 feet, 5.7): Make a boulder move, then follow an easy dike straight up 50 feet, then trend right to a scabby wall with thin flakes; friction up and right to the base of a left-facing chimney.

Pitch 7 (150 feet, 5.7): Climb the chimney, pull the roof, then climb up and right following obvious weaknesses for a full rope length.

Pitch 8 (150 feet, 5.6): Climb straight up over a small overlap to easier ground and the top.

Pitch 8a (140 feet, 5.7+): This nice finish (Kurts Corner) climbs out left after the chimney of pitch 7 into a long left-facing corner.

Pitch 9a (200 feet, 4th class): Climb very easy slabs to the top.

Descent: Bushwhack north to the top of the former Old Man of the Mountain and follow the obvious trail back down to Profile Lake.

Betsy Harrison at the top of the fifth pitch on Cannon Cliff's Moby Grape route. Photo by Peter Cole

66. Vertigo   III, 5.9 A0

Cannon is one of those places where stuff just plain happens. The cliff is big, the rock is funky, routefinding can be a nightmare because of all the cracks and slabs, and you just never know what is coming over the top from the west. The rest of New Hampshire can have a cloudless day, and seventeen lightning bolts can still skip and skitter Cannon.

If you like cracks, you will love Vertigo . . . or at least most of it. If you love all cracks, including off-widths, you will love all of Vertigo.

After a nebulous first pitch, the climbing gets really interesting. Skirting the right side of an overhang, you soon are jamming a nice finger crack. But then it ends at a bolt (it used to end at a manky pin; the bolt is much nicer). Clip the bolt and then ask your belayer to lower you down at least 30 feet. Now start running—and I mean running. Your goal is the base of a left-facing corner about 25 feet to your right. With sticky shoes, good balance, and great momentum you should just be able to skid your way over to the corner and toss in a finger jam. Unless you are leading on two ropes, avoid the strong urge to put in gear right away (your second will be really mad when it is his or her turn to repeat the pendulum). Instead, just start jamming the corner. It is not too hard and soon you are high enough to put in a piece.

The third pitch is an arching finger crack on the left wall and then an incredibly awkward pull around to the right. **Hint:** Do not belay in the first cramped little niche, but continue around to the better ledge. Pitch 4 climbs a nicely widening hand crack to a good ledge.

Now, if you have been clever, you have worked it (lame excuse about the wrong shoes, flip of a two-headed coin, etc.) so that your partner leads pitch 5, the infamous off-width Half Moon pitch. Forget lacing the pitch with big stuff; after just a few feet, it does not matter anyway. What does matter is which way to face: left or right? Funny, but I cannot quite remember just now. But not to worry; it is nasty either way.

One fine summer day a bunch of us headed over to Vertigo for a fun romp. I was there to take pictures so it was not hard to weasel my way out of leading any pitches ("Gee, fellas, with all this camera gear, I should probably just follow"). The day was grand and the wall dry as we headed up.

I was hanging down from the third pitch belay shooting my friend Bruce as he stretched out to reach for the crack at the end of the pendulum when the black cloud of death drifted over from the west and let fly at us. The wind picked up to about 25 miles per hour in just seconds and hail the size of marbles started banging off the walls. In 2 minutes we went from completely comfortable to completely miserable. Hail was piling up everywhere and we were forced to ram our foreheads against the wall and just grimace.

Like I said, at Cannon stuff just happens. At least we had a good excuse to bail on the Half Moon pitch.

First ascent: John Bragg, Michael Peloquin, and Paul Ross, July 1971; first free ascents: John Bragg and Ajax Greene (upper parts), August 10, 1973; Doug White and Tad Pheffer (pitch 2 was except for pendulum), 1975.

Equipment: Some big cams (the biggest you can find) for Half Moon Crack on pitch 5—although there is too much crack even for them near the top.

Crescent Moon variation

Half Moon Crack

pendulum right

66 Vertigo

Cannon Cliff. Photo by S. Peter Lewis

Bruce Luetters stretching the pendulum on pitch two of Vertigo on Cannon Cliff, New Hampshire. Photo by S. Peter Lewis

Start: Follow the Approach to the "big-wall" section of the cliff, then hike south about 100 feet. Vertigo is about 200 feet right of the start of Moby Grape (climb 65). Look for a left-arching corner about 100 feet up (pitch 2 of neighboring Union Jack).

Route: Pitch 1 (75 feet, 5.5): Climb up a hand crack to a right-trending crack to a belay (same as pitch 1 of Union Jack).

Pitch 2 (100 feet, 5.8 A0): Climb cracks to the right side of an overhang, then a thin flake to a bolt; clip the bolt, then lower down 30 feet or so and pendulum to the right over a corner and into the base of another corner with a crack in a left-facing corner, then climb the corner to a stance. (**Note:** Take extra care here to make sure your system allows for the best protection of your second. Double ropes make it easy and safer.)

Pitch 3 (80 feet, 5.9): Climb the curving crack on the wall left of the corner to a difficult pull-around to the left at the top, then continue around to the right to a good ledge.

Pitch 4 (50 feet, 5.9): Step with exposure to the right and another crack, which widens steadily to a big ledge below the obvious off-width. (Pitches 3 and 4 can be combined.)

Pitch 5 (80 feet, 5.9 R): Grunt up the curving Half Moon Crack (it is traditional to whine near the top) to a good ledge. Even a #5 Camalot will not fit in this nasty crack. Many people choose to rappel the route from here.

Pitch 5a (80 feet, 5.9): The Crescent Moon pitch bypasses the Half Moon Crack to its left. Climb to the piton at the start of the Half Moon, then traverse left into a left-facing corner. Climb the corner to an overlap and then up a finger and hand crack to the ledge above the Half Moon Crack.

Pitch 6 (80 feet, 5.6): Climb over an overhang on the right, then continue up a corner.

Pitches 7–8 (250 feet, 5.2–4th class): Continue up and left to ever easier ground and the top.

Descent: Bushwhack north to the top of the former Old Man of the Mountain and follow the obvious trail back down to Profile Lake.

CHAPTER 8. MOUNT WASHINGTON VALLEY ___

Climbing type ▲ Traditional, aid, alpine, ice, mixed

Rock type ▲ Granite

Elevations ▲ Cathedral and Whitehorse Ledges, 500 feet; Frankenstein Cliff, 1,500 feet; Mount Willard, 2,000 feet; Mount Washington, base 2,000 feet, summit 6,288 feet

Number of routes ▲ 23 in this book

The Mount Washington Valley, an hour east of Cannon Cliff/Franconia Notch, is loosely centered around the village of North Conway and offers an incredibly wide variety of summer and winter climbs. Within a 30-minute drive, you will find sport crags; trad cliffs up to 600 feet high; multipitch aid climbs; alpine rock, snow, and ice routes above timberline; and frozen waterfalls by the score.

We give a grand tour of this beautiful area, starting with Whitehorse Ledge just west of North Conway Village in the south and working north. The biggest cliff in the region, 500- to 700-foot Whitehorse Ledge has a split personality—it cannot decide whether it is a slab, a steep face, or a crack climbing area. Right next door is Cathedral Ledge with its soaring corners, cracks, and faces.

We then move 20 miles northwest to Crawford Notch to sample some of the finest waterfall climbing in the Northeast, as well as one really neat rock climb. Frankenstein Cliff is located in Crawford Notch State Park; Mount Willard is just a few miles north.

Charlie Townsend at the top of Mount Washington's Lion Head; Tuckerman Ravine is in the background. Photo by S. Peter Lewis

Then we head northeast for our last stop in New Hampshire, the crown of the state, Mount Washington. Located at Pinkham Notch in the White Mountains, Washington has been the training ground for alpinists for almost 100 years.

Special Considerations
Because climbing areas in this chapter are so diverse, see each area for this information.

Emergency Information
Call local police and fire departments (911) or Mountain Rescue Service (603-356-7013 or 356-5433 extension 14).

Weather and Seasons
Rock climbing: mid-April through mid-November (June through September on Mount Washington); May, September, and October are best. Winter and ice climbing: mid-November through early April; February and March are best.

Standard Equipment
Because climbing areas in this chapter are so diverse, see each area for this information.

Getting There
For Whitehorse and Cathedral Ledges: To get to North Conway Village (see Map 1): From the south via the Boston area, take I-95 north to Portsmouth, New Hampshire, and the junction with Route 16 (the Spaulding Turnpike); follow Route 16 north for 2 hours to North Conway Village. From the south via I-93, get off at exit 23 (New Hampton) and take Route 104 east for 10 miles; turn south on US 3 for 1 mile to the center of Meredith and then take Route 25 east for about 30 minutes to Route 16; turn north onto Route 16 and drive about 20 minutes to North Conway Village. From the west at Cannon Cliff, take I-93 south to exit 32 (Lincoln) and hook up with Route 112, the Kancamagus Highway, which leads east to Route 16 just 5 miles south of North Conway Village. From the east via the Portland, Maine, area, US 302 leads directly to North Conway Village.

  For Frankenstein Cliff: Continue north out of North Conway Village to Glen, where you stay left on US 302 for 20 miles west. (US 302 continues northwest to I-93 about 12 miles north of Franconia Notch, chapter 7.) See Map 1.

  For Mount Willard: Continue north on US 302 to the very top of Crawford Notch, 5 miles north of Frankenstein Cliff.

  For Mount Washington: From North Conway Village, head north to Glen, where you stay right on Route 16 to Pinkham Notch, 18 miles north of North Conway Village (see Map 1).

Whitehorse Ledge
Whitehorse Ledge is one of the most impressive hunks of granite in New Hampshire. The slabs of Whitehorse jut out of the forest floor and rise in sheets of white granite for hundreds of feet. There is not a speck of lichen, no loose rock—and often a dearth of protection. Bill Crowther, a brilliant leader of his time, says in *Rock*

Climbs in the White Mountains of New Hampshire, about the first ascent of Sliding Board (climb 67), "I liked the slabs, and it didn't bother me too much being 100 feet out from my protection." If you are armed with sticky rubber and a calm approach, these immaculate slabs offer little to fear and much to desire—nowhere will you find stone as pure and fine.

The right side of Whitehorse is an immense monolithic slab with few features and long stretches of blank, perfectly clean granite. Around the corner to the left, the South Buttress rears up to nearly vertical and sprouts cracks and small face holds. The South Buttress of Whitehorse Ledge is one of the most breathtaking walls in New Hampshire. Free of ledges and cracks for most of its 500-foot height, the face was considered to have little potential when nearby Cathedral (with all its cracks) was being devoured in the 1970s.

Upon closer inspection, however, the face was found to be covered with face holds, and a few climbers began making forays. Today a cliff like this might be bolted from the top down and have a full complement of routes in just a few seasons. But in New Hampshire in the 1970s and 1980s, the traditional ethic was strong (and still is, for the most part), and the forays were made from the ground up with hand drills. Routes went up slowly and with great care, put up by climbers with the nerve to

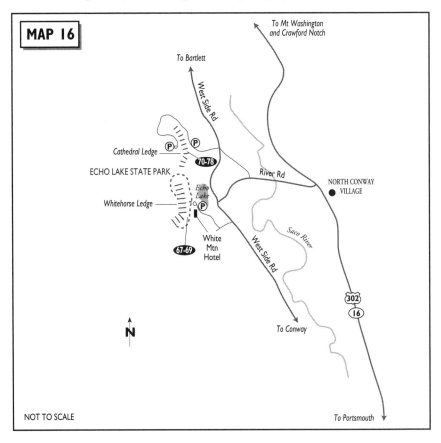

climb—at times quite far—into the unknown, resulting in long runouts on easier ground and well-protected cruxes. If you venture onto this wall, known as the Wonder Wall, you should be the sort who does not mind being 25 feet out on 5.8.

We describe just three routes here, but the combination gives you more than 1,200 feet of the finest climbing found anywhere, requiring your best friction, face, and crack climbing efforts—as well as willingness to run things out a bit.

Special Considerations
Whitehorse Ledge is in Echo Lake State Park. There are no climbing restrictions except for spring raptor closures (they rarely affect the routes listed here); please check the kiosk at the base of Cathedral Ledge before you climb.

Standard Equipment
A range of nuts, Tricams, and cams from ¼ inch to 3 inches (with emphasis on the ¾-inch to 2-inch sizes). Do not skimp on slings. Sixty-meter ropes are useful but not necessary.

Approach
On the west side of Route 16 in the north end of North Conway Village is a town park. At the second traffic light north of the park, turn left onto River Road. Follow it over the Saco River and then take the first left, onto the West Side Road. Go a mile and then turn right into the driveway for the White Mountain Hotel. In just 0.25 mile, turn right and park at the small lot below the hotel near the maintenance sheds. Parking for Whitehorse is restricted: *Do not* park at the hotel's upper lot unless you are a paying guest. See map 16.

67. Sliding Board   II, 5.7
I have climbed Sliding Board perhaps a hundred times, almost always with clients on their first big multipitch climb. With its sweeping granite and friendly nature, no place is better to get folks off the ground and help them learn to love rock climbing. But not all ascents are routine.

There used to be a little flat hold—the "Nickel"—right in the middle of the crux groove on the second pitch. I would always get a little thrill when I dipped in my chalk bag, reached up, and hit the Nickel dead on—without looking. When I was awash in acres of stone, it gave me a sense of connection to the ground to pull up and stand on that little hold.

But one day I reached up and the Nickel was gone. It just was not there. I looked and looked. Nothing. My legs began to shake and I struggled up to the belay, very saddened that my friend was gone. Higher, on the fourth pitch, I got off route onto steeper ground and found my feet skidding. I was bewildered and shaky. Soon the sixth pitch loomed overhead. The tricky liebacking and edging on this vertical dike had always given me a bit of the creeps. I stepped up, placed the No. 4 Rock just like always, chalked up, and swallowed.

Then I saw it. Under a fold in the dike, there was a tiny edge that I had never seen before. I leaned left, peered low under the little fold to make sure, high-stepped

Whitehorse Ledge in New Hampshire's Mount Washington Valley. Photo by S. Peter Lewis

onto the new hold, and liebacked through the crux with such grace as had never been seen before. There I was, awash in acres of stone, standing on a little hold—connected once again.

First ascent: Bill Crowther and Bob Gilmore, 1959 or 1960.

Equipment: A small rack to 2 inches (one 3-inch cam for belay atop pitch 4)— most leaders place just a couple of pieces per pitch, so do not bring a big rack (there are few cracks); 60-m rope for direct start.

Start: Walk to the upper hotel parking lot and from its right-hand corner follow a climbers path straight toward the cliff, crossing a well-maintained hiking trail at 50 feet and continuing straight toward the cliff on the climbers trail for about 200 feet to the base of the cliff. Turn left and walk about 100 feet to a flat area beneath the center of the slabs. You will know you are in the right spot if you see a really big, partly dead tree right next to the cliff and a series of ledges 100 feet up and to the right. Scramble up to these ledges, referred to as the "Launch Pad."

Route: Pitch 1, the direct start (200 feet, 5.2 R): From a belay at the left end of the Launch Pad, climb up and slightly left to a two-bolt anchor 20 feet left of the ledge at the base of the obvious arch in the center of the slabs. If you do not have a 60-meter rope, arrange a belay with Tricams from two solution pockets 10 feet apart about halfway up the pitch (you will need several long slings).

Pitches 1a–2a (250 feet, 5.3): This two-pitch option allows you to reach the

Dennis Goode padding up classic friction on Whitehorse Ledge's Sliding Board. Photo by S. Peter Lewis

regular pitch 2 start with a 50-meter rope (and may help you avoid traffic). From the right end of the Launch Pad, climb up and slightly right past flakes to a two-bolt belay in the obvious "Toilet Bowl."

The next pitch climbs up and then left, passing flakes, to the ledge at the base of the obvious arch that sweeps up the center of the cliff. You can either belay at the fixed anchor at the base of the arch and approach the regular pitch 2 from the right or continue traversing left to the two-bolt anchor described at the top of the direct start.

Pitch 2 (50 feet, 5.7): Move 10 feet right and up, clip a bolt, step left into a shallow groove, and smear delicately past another bolt to a semihanging belay in a finger crack with an old piton. Alternatively, you can continue past the crack and up and left to another two-bolt belay (more comfortable stance, harder to see your second).

Pitch 3 (130 feet, 5.5 R): Climb up and left from the crack belay (straight up from the bolted belay on the left) and then straight up a white streak, passing one lonely bolt halfway, to a two-bolt belay at the Park Bench—a wonderful small ledge. On this pitch, beware of getting suckered off into no-man's-land to the right.

Pitch 4 (110 feet, 5.6): Angle up and right to the obvious hanging, left-facing corner, lieback up it, then follow the weakness above past pockets to a small sloping ledge and belay off small nuts, Tricams, and a big cam (making a good anchor here takes some imagination).

Pitch 5 (125 feet, 5.5 R): Climb straight up the brown rock above with little protection, following a faint dike. When the dike steepens and becomes more obvious, climb 10 feet above a small tree then traverse straight right to an even more obvious dike and two-bolt anchor at a tiny stance below a vertical wall.

Pitch 6 (75 feet, 5.6): A great finale. Climb straight up the vertical dike above, very well protected, to the lower-angled slabs above and a belay in a diagonal crack. (You will not be able to see your second easily and it may be hard to hear, so do not run the rope out.)

Pitch 7 (125 feet, 5.0): Continue up the same dike in the low-angled slab above, aiming for the left end of the large overlap above. Belay (awkwardly) at a short, stout evergreen at the overlap.

Pitch 8 (250 feet, 4th class): Angle up and left on a really easy dike, passing one bolt; continue up and left and then angle back up and right to the top of the cliff and a belay off trees.

Descent: Head north (toward Cathedral) and follow the cliff's edge on a climbers path that enters the woods after 100 feet or so. Follow the trail down to the saddle between Whitehorse and Cathedral, turn right at the first trail junction, and continue downhill (steeply in one spot) to an intersection with an old road. Turn right, pass a dilapidated old shack in a field, and in 5 minutes you reach the base of the cliff at its northeast edge.

68. The Last Unicorn   III, 5.10b

Of all the routes on the Wonder Wall, the Last Unicorn is perhaps the most representative of the character of the wall. Over 2 days in August 1978, longtime local climbers and visionaries Ed Webster and Jeff Pheasant wove their web up the face. Picking their way carefully along, they pieced together tiny features, placing bolts from tenuous aid

Whitehorse Ledge. Photo by S. Peter Lewis

placements (Pheasant wearing sneakers on pitch 3!) or from tiny free stances, then pulling their ropes and leading each section completely free. When they were done, they had finished linking the finest sections of granite the cliff had to offer into 275 feet of the most stunning face climbing in the state. For their efforts, the crowds began to flock up the new route, and they have continued ever since.

I once hiked to the top of Whitehorse with my good friends Marc Chauvin and Bill Pelkey to shoot some photos of them on the route. After a most miserable thrash, we finally found ourselves at the top, contemplating a horizon shift from brushy slopes to 500 feet straight down. We checked and rechecked everything before stepping off for the ride down the sheer wall.

As Marc and Bill organized themselves at the belay, I looked around. I was perched high in the air over one of the most beautiful valleys in all of New England with nothing below me but shimmering golden granite. It was a simply gorgeous summer day. It had rained recently and the wall was clean and bright. I looked down at my friends and marveled at the lack of features between us. Surely from above I should see holds, but I saw little evidence that they would be able to climb past me.

As Marc began, carefully piecing together the moves, his little dabs of chalk revealed the magic line—an edge here, a side pull there, a hidden jam off to the

Marc Chauvin on perhaps the best face climb in New Hampshire, Whitehorse's Last Unicorn; Bill Pelkey belays. Photo by S. Peter Lewis

side. Yes, from above, with the sun over my shoulder, if I looked really hard, I could see the holds. But then I thought of Ed and Jeff so many years before and how from below, no matter how hard the two looked, the holds were veiled, the edges blurring into wall as they squinted into the sun. I was amazed. Thank you, Ed and Jeff, for seeing what was not there and making it possible for the rest of us to enjoy this golden wall.

First ascent: Ed Webster and Jeff Pheasant, August 10–11, 1978.

Equipment: Nothing bigger than 2 inches; there is much fixed protection.

Start: From the right-hand corner of the upper hotel parking lot, follow a path straight toward the cliff for 50 feet, then turn left on a well-maintained trail. The trail parallels the cliff for 1,000 feet, then turns right and steepens, reaching the base of the South Buttress after another 500 feet.

Approach pitches (300 feet, 4th class–5.4): From the base of the cliff at the start of Hotter than Hell (climb 69), walk about 50 feet to the right and scramble up a blocky section for another 50 feet. Then trend right and slightly up, following the most obvious weaknesses (mostly 4th class), aiming for an obvious ledge system with a white pine tree on its left end. Traverse the broken ledge system to its right end, then down-climb to the obvious foot ledge and traverse right for 40 feet to a two-bolt anchor at the base of Sky Streak (alternate first pitch for the Last Unicorn—see below). While some of this lengthy approach is often scrambled, a belay may be prudent for its entire length.

Route: Pitch 1, original route (90 feet, 5.10b): From the Sky Streak anchor, traverse right for another 30 feet and ascend a somewhat blocky, broken section of holds and flakes (there may be pitons) to a stance. Above, a puzzling set of shallow, parallel corners will give you pause (and a bolt), which will bring you to a small belay ledge with two bolts.

Pitch 1a, Sky Streak (80 feet, 5.10b): Many climbers are now using part of Sky Streak as an alternate first pitch. The belay is better situated and the climbing is of equal quality and difficulty. Step left, climb past two bolts (crux) to easier climbing and another bolt on a ledge, then trend up and right to join the Last Unicorn at its first belay.

Pitch 2 (100 feet, 5.10b): Climb up and slightly left, passing two bolts, to a flake and then a steep headwall with three more bolts that lead to the left end of an obvious overlap. Undercling and face climb right along the overlap to a hanging belay from two bolts.

Pitch 3 (80 feet, 5.10b): Climb straight up from the belay, up an open groove with four bolts and a piton to a crescendo finish at the very top of the wall.

Descent: By far the easiest is to rappel. From the top belay, traverse 30 feet left to another two-bolt anchor (the top of Science Friction Wall). From that anchor, two rappels get you back to the tree ledge (there are several intermediate rappel station options).

To walk off, thrash straight up from the final belay for several hundred feet to the climbers trails at the top of the cliff, then bear right (north), continue for 500 feet to the top of the slabs, and descend trails as for Sliding Board (climb 67).

69. Hotter than Hell, Inferno, and Atlantis   II, 5.9–5.10b

Although Hotter than Hell, Inferno, and Atlantis are all great routes in their own right, combining their best pitches gives a grand tour de force of South Buttress climbing that requires about every move in the book. From thin face climbing to finger and hand jams to wild stemming, these pitches provide an eclectic adventure that should make just about your whole body sore the next day. On a fine autumn day with a bright blue sky above and red maples below, there is no finer place to be in all of New Hampshire.

The choice to combine pitches on these routes stems, at least in part, from various epics of my youth. Hotter than Hell was a nemesis for me, requiring several attempts. On my first, I took way too long to get to the crux and by the time I got there, I was a quivering mess. I was standing on tiny holds trying to figure out how to bail with my ego intact when I heard my wife honking at me from way down on the road. "Oh gosh," I said, "Look at how the time has flown. I gotta go. Sorry. Lower me." "But what about the gear and the rope and, well, me?" my irritated partner asked. Fortunately, some other climbers were waiting for the route and she was able to join them.

My first ride up Inferno's first pitch was on an appropriately baking summer day in the high 90s. Black rock, poor protection, dripping sweat, and absolutely no

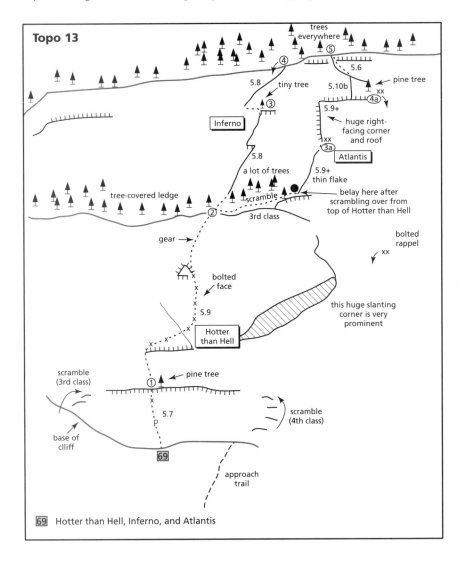

Topo 13

trees everywhere

5.6
pine tree
5.10b
5.8 tiny tree
5.9+
huge right-facing corner and roof
Inferno
Atlantis
5.8
5.9+ thin flake
a lot of trees
belay here after scrambling over from top of Hotter than Hell
tree-covered ledge
scramble
3rd class
bolted rappel
gear
bolted face
this huge slanting corner is very prominent
5.9
Hotter than Hell
scramble (3rd class)
pine tree
base of cliff
5.7
scramble (4th class)
69
approach trail

69 Hotter than Hell, Inferno, and Atlantis

Hotter than Hell, Inferno, and Atlantis on Whitehorse Ledge. Photo by S. Peter Lewis

idea of where to go all came together near the top of the pitch. I stared, blinking salty tears from my eyes, for many long minutes before finally committing to one slimy 5.8 move. We rappelled off and went swimming in the river.

In one of the early guides for the area, Atlantis is described as destined to be a classic, with a wild traverse on its fourth pitch that was "amazingly only 5.7!" Well, that sounded too good to be true, so my close friend Dave and I headed over that way one summer day long ago. We avoided the first pitch (it is like the first pitch of Inferno, only worse) by climbing Hotter than Hell (no problem for me; I was seconding). The third pitch brought me (literally) to my knees, but I managed to squirm up it. And then there we were, 300 feet off the deck staring at that cool traverse. Dave chimneyed the big corner, then headed right, leading the traverse and the finger crack at its end in fine fashion (he can make anything look 5.7).

Whistling away on the dull end, I scampered up the chimney and then smacked my head into the roof at the start of the traverse. All scampering stopped. Yikes. I stared at 40 feet of yawning death. I lost my nerve completely, hemmed and hawed, and finally asked Dave to count to three. "Why?" he asked, from out of sight. "Just do it," I said. On three I jumped and took a huge pendulum across the face.

But really, these epic adventures were nothing more than the early wanderings of a child climber trying to sort out life at the end of the rope. You will do fine. Oh, and the traverse on Atlantis? Amazingly, it is only 5.9.

First ascent: Hotter than Hell, Matt Peer and Craig Stemley, May 29, 1980;

Inferno, Bob Anderson and Wayne Christian, August 1972; Atlantis, Ed Webster and Doug Madara, September 1976.

Equipment: For Atlantis add some extra cams, including very small ones; two ropes for rappel.

Start: From the right-hand corner of the upper hotel parking lot, follow a path straight toward the cliff for 50 feet, then turn left on a well-maintained trail. The trail parallels the cliff for 1,000 feet, then turns right and steepens, reaching the base

Conrad Yager dancing the crux moves on the top pitch of Atlantis. Photo by S. Peter Lewis

of the South Buttress after another 500 feet. Hotter than Hell begins 50 feet left of where the approach trail intersects the cliff, below a tree ledge 45 feet off the ground and in the center of the steep slab that forms the cliff's left (south) side.

Route: Pitch 1, Hotter than Hell (45 feet, 5.7): Climb a nice 5.7 pitch up the slab (piton, bolt) to the tree ledge.

Pitch 2, Hotter than Hell (165 feet, 5.9): Climb up to the obvious bolt, then trend right and up, following more bolts, to a niche (possible belay), short finger crack, and more face climbing to the obvious tree ledge. Here is where your mix-and-match options begin.

Pitch 3, Inferno (100 feet, 5.8): Slightly right of the huge pine tree that marks the end of Hotter than Hell is a crack/flake that slants right up the upper wall, passing a 5-inch-diameter pine tree about 20 feet up. Climb this, then the obvious twisting finger and hand crack above to a nice small ledge with a stunted tree.

Pitch 4, Inferno (50 feet, 5.8): Step left from the ledge and climb a series of short, weird cracks to another huge tree ledge.

Pitch 3a, Atlantis (50 feet, 5.9): From the end of Hotter than Hell, scramble up to another little tree ledge 40 feet to the right and belay. Climb a steep, strenuous, right-leaning flake to a fixed belay at the base of a huge corner.

Pitch 4a, Atlantis (100 feet, 5.9+–5.10b): Stem the huge corner (loose block) and then make a wild traverse right under the roof. Near the end, you can either climb straight up a finger crack (5.10b; tricky gear) or continue traversing right to the two-bolt anchor at the top of Lost Souls.

Pitch 5, Atlantis (60 feet, 5.6): Climb easily up and left to a final little overlap and the woods.

Descent: You can either rappel the route or walk off. To walk off: From the tree ledge at the top of the final pitches of Inferno and Atlantis, hike up to the next short cliff band, traverse left under it, and then up and right on slabs to the top of the cliff. From here there are two options. (1) If you have all your stuff, hike north to the top of the slabs and go down the Bryce Path, as for Sliding Board (climb 67). (2) Descend along the left edge of the South Buttress back to the base of the route (steep, nasty, and often wet).

Or rappel (two ropes) either from the top of Inferno or from the top of pitch 4a of Atlantis—go all the way to the right end of the traverse and do not do the last easy pitch, then make one rappel (two ropes) down and left to a bolted anchor with big chains and then again to the base.

Cathedral Ledge

Just 0.25 mile north of Whitehorse, Cathedral presents an entirely different nature. Universally steep, it has almost no friction climbs and far fewer face climbs, but is loaded with cracks. Over the years, this impressive 450-foot cliff has played an impressive role in the history of Northeast climbing, with many standard-pushing ascents being made on its steep walls. While the pitches we chose for Whitehorse are typically delicate and thought provoking, many of the pitches on Cathedral require you to have your guns ready. Fortunately, the pitches are usually short and the belay ledges comfortable enough to hang out on and let the lactic acid drain out.

Special Considerations

Cathedral Ledge is located in Echo Lake State Park. There are no climbing restrictions except for raptor closures, which are possible in the spring; check the information kiosk by the road under the center of the cliff. The road at the north end of the cliff has a gate that may be closed at night; if you drive down from the top after it has been locked, do not try to drive around it. You are stuck there until morning (it is only about a half hour's walk into town, so you will not starve).

Standard Equipment

A generous selection of nuts, Tricams, and cams to 3 inches.

Approach

On the west side of Route 16 in the north end of North Conway Village is a town park. At the second traffic light north of the park, turn left onto River Road. Follow it over the Saco River and continue straight for about 0.5 mile, then turn right onto a small side street with a little brown "STATE PARK" sign. The road heads straight in toward the cliff and then turns north under it—the information kiosk is here—before curving around and up to the top. This road makes access to the bottoms and tops of the routes here incredibly easy. You may park at any of the pullouts under the cliff, and there is ample parking at the top of the cliff too. See map 16.

70. Funhouse and Bombardment   (ratings below)

If Funhouse, Bombardment, Black Lung, and Upper Refuse (climb 70) were strung out end to end, you would arguably have the best intermediate climb on the East Coast. But because of their patchwork layout on the left side of Cathedral Ledge, you can pick a mix of pitches to suit your tastes. Feeling strong? Do the Bombardment/Black Lung combination. Want a mellow day? Do the Funhouse/Upper Refuse combo. Want a pretty full day? Do them all.

Over the last twenty years, I have climbed these pitches so many, many times, almost always while working as a guide, that saying I have them "wired" is a gross understatement. And yet I never get tired of them. The moves are pure fun, the protection automatic, the belays second nature. It sounds boring, but it is not. This very familiar ground allows me to kick back into auto mode, watch the new folks on the end of the rope, help them over the sticky bits, put them at ease, find out about their lives and dreams, and grow to like them. As we near the top of the cliff and the trees recede far below, the most beautiful valley I know stretches out behind us.

Start: From the state park kiosk below the center of the cliff, bear left at a huge granite block and follow a trail that parallels the cliff for several hundred feet. Eventually the trail turns right and ascends steeply uphill to the base of the cliff, intersecting it at a distinctive right-leaning arch. Funhouse begins right of this; Bombardment begins left of it.

Funhouse   I, 5.7

On a cliff known for its verticality and exposure, Funhouse provides a moderate and sheltered adventure. Great corners and cracks and ample belay ledges (with shade

Topo 14

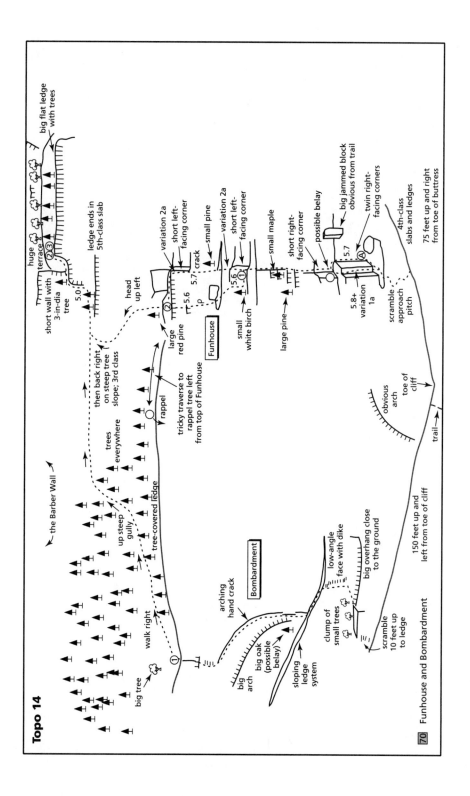

the Barber Wall →

big tree

walk right

①

tree-covered ledge

arching hand crack

Bombardment

big arch

big oak (possible belay)

sloping ledge system

up steep gully

trees everywhere

rappel

tricky traverse to rappel tree left from top of Funhouse

then back right on steep tree slope; 3rd class

head up left

large red pine

②

5.0

ledge ends in 5th-class slab

short wall with 3-in-dia tree

huge terrace ②③

big flat ledge with trees

5.6

5.7 crack

variation 2a

short left-facing corner

small pine

variation 2a

short left-facing corner

Funhouse

5.6

①

small white birch

small maple

large pine

short right-facing corner

possible belay

big jammed block obvious from trail

twin right-facing corners

5.7

Ⓐ

variation 1a

5.8+

scramble approach pitch

4th-class slabs and ledges

75 feet up and right from toe of buttress

obvious arch

toe of cliff

trail

clump of small trees

low-angle face with dike

big overhang close to the ground

scramble 10 feet up to ledge

150 feet up and left from toe of cliff

70 Funhouse and Bombardment

Dave Kelly on Funhouse, Cathedral Ledge. Photo by S. Peter Lewis

trees) mean that you climb a little, then relax, then climb some more, then relax and eat, and . . . well, you get the idea.

First ascent: Joe Cote and Larry Poorman, 1969.

Approach pitch (75 feet, 4th class): From the arch, follow a series of dirty ledges 75 feet right to a flat ledge at the base of a pair of very distinct right-facing corners.

Route: Pitch 1 (75 feet, 5.7): Climb the right-hand corner to a ledge at 20 feet (possible belay), then climb another short, right-facing corner, and climb a crack on a slab to easy rock fins and a big ledge.

Pitch 1a (75 feet, 5.8+): Climb the overhanging right-facing corner 5 feet left of the normal first pitch.

Pitch 2 (75 feet, 5.7): Climb an awkward bulge 8 feet left of an obvious hand crack, step around a bulge on the left, then back right onto a ledge at the base of a steep wall with a crack; climb the crack to a big ledge with an obvious red pine.

Pitch 2a (75 feet, 5.7): Climb the hand crack on the right (technically this is the second pitch of a route called Pooh, although it is often mistaken for Funhouse) to a ledge, then continue up the cracks and weakness above, stepping left at the top on a foot ledge that leads to the red pine.

Pitch 3 (100 feet, 5.0): Climb up a slab directly above the ledge, then head up and left on easy ground, then back right on an obvious tree ledge. Climb a final short wall past a 3-inch-diameter tree, then step right onto a huge terrace with a lot of trees. The low-angled ramp of Upper Refuse is directly above.

Descent: There are three options. You can climb to the top of the cliff via the Book of Solemnity (climb 73) or Upper Refuse/Black Lung (climb 72). You can hike the tree ledge left (south) and then follow a steep gully up and around to the top of the cliff. Or you can rappel (two ropes) from a huge pine on the tree ledge 50 feet left (south) of the top of pitch 2 of Funhouse (tricky getting to it).

Bombardment   1, 5.8

This is perhaps Cathedral Ledge's finest hand crack. If you hang from the edge of this arching crack and blindly paddle your feet, your forearms will burn and your fingers will slowly uncurl; but if you jam efficiently and look for the good footholds, it is a

Blair Foltz on the classic hand crack of Bombardment. Photo by S. Peter Lewis

cruise all the way to the end, where the sting in the tail greets you: the crux face move.

First ascent: Dave Cilley (rope-solo), October 6, 1972.

Start: From the point where the approach trail meets the cliff, walk uphill to the left for about 150 feet to where the cliff appears to end at a blocky little wall. Above you is a distinctive left-trending arch. Bombardment follows the obvious hand crack above and parallel to the arch. Scramble 10 feet up onto an obvious flat ledge and belay at a clump of small trees on the right.

Route: Pitch 1 (140 feet, 5.8): Climb right across a clean slab to a faint dike (5.6 R) that leads up and left to a wide ledge; traverse the ledge up and left (remember to protect your second) until you reach a big oak tree (possible belay), then climb the obvious left-arching hand crack above to the tree-covered ledge.

Pitch 2 (200 feet, 5.0): Walk 50 feet right along the edge of the cliff (taking care not to knock stuff off), turn uphill following an obvious dirty gully with trees (climbers path), turn right at its top and walk until the trail ends at a steep slab, climb the short wall on your left (5.0) past the 3-inch-diameter tree mentioned on Funhouse's third pitch, and walk right onto the huge terrace below Upper Refuse.

Descent: If you choose not to continue up the cliff on pitch 2, hike 100 feet right (north) to a large pine and rappel with two ropes (same as for Funhouse).

71. Lichen Delight   I, 5.11a

On September 21, 1972, the upper left wall of Cathedral was a quiet place. The air was crisp, the autumn colors were near peak, and the climbing season was winding down. On this near-vertical wall that stretches left from Upper Refuse (climb 72) for 400 feet, seven obvious cracks shoot up the granite from the tree-covered ledge to the top of the cliff. In previous years, six of them had been climbed, always on aid—they were great practice aid cracks for aspiring big-wall climbers.

But that was all about to change. In the coming days and weeks, a young climber named Henry Barber and his partners, Bob Anderson and Al Rubin, would rewrite New Hampshire free-climbing history. Theirs would be a spate of first free ascents of classic routes that would never again be equaled in New Hampshire. In the space of just a few hours on September 23, Chicken Delight (5.9), Double Vee (5.9+), and Nutcracker (5.9+) were all promoted to free climbs by Barber and Anderson. On the very next day, Layton's Ascent (5.9+) and Nomad (5.10a) were each ticked. After a few days' rest, the pair then set their sights on the Grim Reaper (5.10+ R/X), and the route nearly lived up to its name when Barber fell just before the top. Fearing a ground fall (from 135 feet), Barber grabbed the nearby rappel rope that the pair had fortuitously left in place. (The route has only had a handful of ascents since.)

Finally, late in October 1972, Barber and Rubin free-climbed our chosen classic here, Lichen Delight. This stunning and strenuous crack line was the first 5.11 in the area and has since been a benchmark lead for many aspiring crack climbers. In the coming years, Henry would go on to set new free-climbing standards around the world, earning himself the nickname "Hot Henry." He still lives less than 5 miles from Cathedral Ledge, and it is not unusual to see him climbing (with apparent ease) up Lichen Delight and his other routes on the upper left wall.

Oh, and the name of that section of the cliff? The "Barber Wall," of course.

First ascent: Dave Cilley and Sibylle Hechtel (with some aid), July 22, 1971; first free ascent: Henry Barber and Al Rubin, October 21, 1972.

Equipment: A cam of at least 4 inches.

The wall at Cathedral Ledge in Mount Washington Valley. Photo by S. Peter Lewis

Dave Rose on the finger-jamming crux of Lichen Delight. Photo by S. Peter Lewis

Start: Climb either Bombardment or Funhouse (climb 70) to reach the tree-covered ledge. About 60 feet left of the start of Upper Refuse and just left of an obvious buttress (30 feet high) is an obvious diagonal crack system that shoots up and right on the steep wall. About 40 feet left of this crack, scramble up to a slightly higher ledge below a left-facing corner with a hand crack in it that leads to an obvious alcove 50 feet up.

Route: Pitch 1 (110 feet, 5.11a): Stem up the dihedral to the alcove, place the big cam, then step out right and climb finger cracks (strenuous) up the wall to a great ledge.

Pitch 1a, Lichen It a Lot (110 feet, 5.10d): At the alcove, undercling a move or two left and climb a small, left-facing corner (small wires) to the same belay ledge as the regular first pitch. Popular.

The upper wall at Cathedral Ledge. Photo by S. Peter Lewis

Pitch 2 (50 feet, 5.6): While it is possible to climb a groove on the left or a finger crack straight up (both about 5.10 and not overly well protected), the quality of the climbing is not terrific. Our suggestion is to get off quick (so you can climb another classic in this book) by walking to the right on the ledge for about 30 feet and finishing up an easy crack.

Descent: Walk north for 300 feet to the tourist lookout at the top of the cliff and walk down the road.

72. Upper Refuse and Black Lung   (ratings below)

I vividly remember standing below Cathedral one day a couple of decades ago and watching over Tom Vinson's shoulder as his finger traced the ramp on Upper Refuse. "It goes up a big inside corner, and it's only 5.6," he said. Sure, I thought to myself, but it is *three hundred feet off the ground.* I was just a kid from Connecticut and my feet had barely dangled higher off the earth than Ragged Mountain's paltry 105 feet (see chapter 4). I knew I could do 5.6, but could I do it as far off the ground as a thirty-story building? Well, it turned out I could. I do not even remember my first time up Refuse. But I do remember many of the subsequent trips up that route.

Three routes converge at the top of Upper Refuse—The Book of Solemnity (climb 73), Black Lung, and Upper Refuse—and the last little pitch leads to a tourist lookout complete with a steel-pipe railing. On almost every ascent, there is a collective gasp when the tourists see our heads appear above the void, then inane questions follow: "Did you really climb up this?" ("No.") "How long did it take?" ("Um, is this Tuesday . . . ?") "Were you frightened?" ("No, but I've had surgery for that.") A couple of years ago, I decided that I had answered just enough dumb questions, thank you very much, and decided to have some fun.

I made a grappling hook out of some huge landscaping spikes, a roll of duct tape, and an old rope. One of my favorite clients and I headed up Upper Refuse. I belayed just 20 feet below the top and brought Alison up quietly. I could hear the din of tourist chatter above. Alison and I whispered and stifled giggles as I took out the grappling hook. She put me on belay and with great flair and drama I stepped up and poked my head into view. Someone from New Jersey pointed. "Look, there's one now," they shouted.

I scanned the railing, waiting for the crowd to pile up. "Please stand back!" I yelled theatrically. Then I swung the grappling hook around and around my head and gave it a great fling. It rattled over the fence but when I pulled, it came off. I swung and tossed again and over it went a second time. A kindly gentleman said, "I can hook it on for you if you'd like, son." I replied, "Thanks, but that wouldn't be sporting," and tried again. This time it hooked and I pretended to pull on the rope as I smeared up the last few feet to the railing. There was great applause and pats on the back and, no kidding, I heard an elderly man say to his wife, "See, I told you that's how they do it."

Upper Refuse   I, 5.6

This fine face route climbs the obvious right-trending, low-angled ramp above the terrace on the right end of the tree-covered ledge.

First ascent: Yale University climbers R. S. G. Hall, Walter Spofford, and someone named Merrill, 1935.

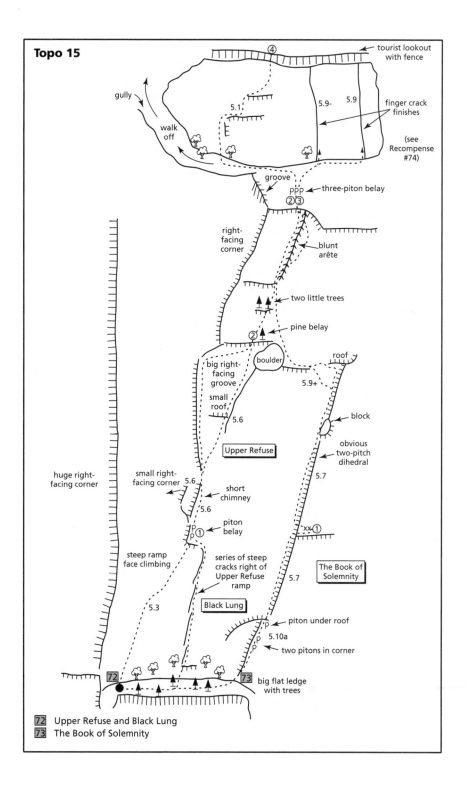

Topo 15

tourist lookout with fence

gully

walk off

5.1

④

5.9- 5.9

finger crack finishes

(see Recompense #74)

groove

ppp ← three-piton belay
②③

right-facing corner

blunt arête

two little trees

② pine belay

boulder

roof

big right-facing groove

5.9+

small roof

5.6

block

obvious two-pitch dihedral

Upper Refuse

5.7

huge right-facing corner

small right-facing corner 5.6

short chimney

5.6

piton belay

steep ramp face climbing

P ①
P

xx ①

5.7

The Book of Solemnity

series of steep cracks right of Upper Refuse ramp

5.3

Black Lung

piton under roof

P

5.10a

P
P ← two pitons in corner

72

73 big flat ledge with trees

72 Upper Refuse and Black Lung
73 The Book of Solemnity

Jeremiah Lewis on Cathedral Ledge's Upper Refuse ramp. Photo by S. Peter Lewis

Start: Climb either Funhouse or Bombardment (climb 70) to the big tree ledge. The start of this climb is at the far left edge of the ramp.

Route: Pitch 1 (75 feet, 5.3): Climb up and right on perfect rock to a ledge in a niche with two pitons.

Pitch 2 (60 feet, 5.6): Climb the obvious V-groove chimney above (5.6) to easier climbing up a groove and either pull the little roof at its right side (fun 5.6) or continue up the groove (easier). Both variations end at a great ledge with a pine tree and several cracks.

Pitch 3 (40 feet, 5.5): Climb the steep wall directly above, pass a pine tree and a birch stump, then go up and right to a crack on the arête, or stay in the right-facing corner above. Both variations end on a big ledge with a piton anchor.

Pitch 4 (75 feet, 4th class–5.1): Scramble up the gully above to the short upper wall. From its left edge, step out right and follow the easy face up to the tourist lookout at the top of the cliff. Alternatively, after the initial scramble you can walk off left and up an obvious gully (thereby sneaking around the tourists).

Descent: From the tourist lookout, walk straight back from the cliff and walk down the road.

Black Lung   I, 5.8

A perfectly protected finger and hand crack up a steep wall.

First ascent: Henry Barber and Dave Cilley, October 1, 1972.

Start: Climb either Funhouse or Bombardment (climb 70) to the big tree ledge. The start of this climb is 15 feet right of the start of Upper Refuse.

Route: Pitch 1 (60 feet, 5.8): Climb a series of steep cracks to the crux at a bulging hand crack and belay at the top of the first pitch of Upper Refuse. Continue on that route to the top of the cliff.

Descent: From the tourist lookout walk straight back from the cliff and walk down the road.

73. The Book of Solemnity   I, 5.10a

Solemnity means "the ceremonious observance of an occasion or event." In the case of this stellar two-pitch dihedral (aka "open book"), there is abundant reason for a ceremony. Nowhere on Cathedral is there a brilliant corner so wonderful, so perfect, and so deserving of recognition. Now, if you are not the sort who would enjoy 200 feet of jamming, stemming, and liebacking, skip on to the next climb.

Yup, I knew you would stick around.

Of all the routes that I have done in New Hampshire, "the Book" is perhaps the one that I climb the most consistently. By that I mean that it is absolutely certain that I will do the same thing on the first pitch—fall once on the second pin and then get the move. I have never climbed the pitch clean. Never. But I always get the moves on the second try. Always.

The first time I did the Book, more than twenty years ago now, I got myself into a bit of a jam at that second piton and I think it set the stage for my troubles ever since. This was back in the old days of EBs, swami belts, and chalk-in-a-stuff-sack-on-a-sling-over-the-shoulder. And I was not real good on my feet, either.

I scuffed my way up the corner past the first pin, clipped it, clawed my way up until the pin was at my feet (the horror), and then, hanging off a sickly tip lieback hold, I stretched a carabiner for the second pin. I tapped at the eye but just could not get the sucker in. I made one last try, banging frantically at the piton, but the 'biner slipped

Joe Lentini stemming pitch 1 of the Book of Solemnity on Cathedral Ledge (the top piece of pro is the piton in the story). Photo by S. Peter Lewis

out of my sweaty fingers, and in a moment of sheer innovation, just before launching for a 5-foot whipper, I stuck my middle finger through the eye of the pin.

Some of you may think this was a stupid move. At the time I thought it was brilliant. Now, with a good (albeit painful) handhold, I milked the stem a little, getting my feet in better position, let a little adrenaline evaporate, and took stock.

Wow, what a stupid move. I did not have the nerve to go for the next holds without the protection of the pin, but I could not clip it without taking my finger out of it. After a few moments of pondering, I did what any of the rest of you would do under the circumstances. I got another 'biner, positioned it right over the eye of the piton, pried the gate open, and after mentally counting to three, pulled my finger out of the piton and slammed the 'biner down at the same time. And it worked. I have the scar to prove it.

First ascent: Joe Cote and Steve Arsenault, September 1971.

Equipment: Nothing bigger than 2½ inches; double ropes helpful.

Start: Climb either Funhouse or Bombardment (climb 70) to the big tree ledge. The start of this climb is 40 feet right of the start of Upper Refuse, at a clean right-facing corner with two pitons in it and a roof at 25 feet.

Route: Pitch 1 (75 feet, 5.10a): Stem up the clean dihedral past two fixed pitons to a stance below the obvious roof (crux at second piton; fall once, then get it). Move delicately to the right around the roof (another piton) and lieback the corner to an obvious ledge on the right with two bolts.

Pitch 2 (125 feet, 5.9+): Continue stemming up the dihedral (5.7) to a stance below an obvious small roof. Climb left, either high (stretching for a hidden jug) or low (on small holds), both 5.10a, to a foot ledge. **Caution:** Unless you want your second to break a leg, *do not* place any protection after moving left at the roof; the climbing is easy (5.5) and your second will be protected from directly above while pulling the crux moves. Double ropes will help make this safer. Now climb a short wide crack to the junction with Upper Refuse (climb 72), which is followed to the ledge and piton belay at the top of its third pitch.

Pitch 3 (75 feet, 4th class–5.1): Scramble up the gully above to the short upper wall. From its left edge, step out right and follow the easy face up to the tourist lookout at the top of the cliff. Alternatively, after the initial scramble you can walk off left and up an obvious gully.

Descent: From the tourist lookout, walk straight back from the cliff and walk down the road.

74. Recompense   III, 5.9

Bold, sweeping cracks, airy flakes and corners, and a dramatic finish at the very highest point of the cliff make this *the* route at its rating in the area. The first ascent of Recompense in 1959 was one of the most stunning achievements in the history of Northeast climbing. Area historians Laura and Guy Waterman in *Yankee Rock and Ice* have called John Turner's ascent of Recompense the "climb of the decade" in the Northeast.

I have climbed Recompense many times over two decades, and every ascent has been accompanied by a certain amount of apprehension. While the final corner may be the technical crux, oh, how that chimney on the second pitch makes me quiver. I

Cathedral Ledge's Prow. Photo by S. Peter Lewis

always dawdle on the lower part of the pitch, fussing with gear, brushing twigs off the ledges, and glancing up at the dark maw. I know it is well protected. I know it is secure. I know it is short. I know I have never fallen out of it. And yet I still worry.

Recently I led the pitch, slowly welding protection every couple of feet, continually screeching "I'm in; take it up" as I clipped each piece. I finally ran it out the last 3 feet to the big ledge. My second, a dear friend and far better climber than I, sweated and grunted and worked and worked to get the gear out. When he arrived at the belay, he just glared at me, panting. A few weeks later, he queried me about the chimney. "Did you ever go back and redpoint it?" he asked caustically.

Visiting climbers often approach the nearest clot of climbers in the pullouts below the cliff, looking for advice. Hundreds of routes soar overhead—not the mere dozen back in Turner's time—and the choices are daunting. "What's the best 5.9 here?" Even now, decades after Turner danced his way up the cracks and corners, the same answer rings out. "You've just got to do Recompense."

First ascent: John Turner and Richard Wilmott (all but the last 40 feet of the final pitch), May 18, 1959; John Reppy and Harold May (the complete line), July 5, 1963; Paul Ross and George Meyers (the Beast Flake variation), July 5, 1972.

Equipment: Cams to 4 inches; a lot of slings.

Start: From the state park kiosk below the center of the cliff, walk straight toward the cliff through a short bit of talus, bear left, and enter the woods. After 100 feet, turn right and uphill to stairs in a steep gully, go up and slightly right for 50 feet

Alison Osius in the maw on pitch 3 of Recompense with Roy Goldstein and Jim Ewing.
Photo by S. Peter Lewis

to a second set of stairs, then scramble left and 10 feet to a ledge with trees.

Route: Pitch 1 (150 feet, 5.7+): Climb straight up an easy crack, passing a couple of small trees, then continue up steeper cracks above for about 50 feet where a step around left into a finger crack leads to a short, steep, right-leaning corner (crux, piton), then another step left to an excellent ledge with two bolts.

Pitch 2, original route (100 feet, 5.8+): Climb straight up a series of short corners and ledges, past a birch tree, and into the obvious chimney (big cam in the lower section). Continue up the squeeze chimney above (crux, good, small gear) to a sloping ledge below the final corner.

Pitch 2a, the Beast Flake (80 feet, 5.9): An outstanding (and out there) pitch. Climb 20 feet up pitch 2 to an iron-cross move left into bottom of the Beast Flake (crux, well protected). Climb the cool flake to the top and a sloping, uncomfortable belay 5 feet around to the right. (**Caution:** The slings at the top of the flake may not be safe.)

Pitch 3a, the Beast Flake (25 feet, 5.9-): Step down to the right, then curl yourself under and around an alcove (crux, well protected) until you can stem into the upper squeeze chimney at the top of the original pitch 2, then up the chimney to the belay.

Pitch 3, original route (100 feet, 5.9): Lieback and stem up the superb dihedral, with the crux where the corner jogs right about 20 feet up, to a large, flat ledge on the left.

Pitch 4, Little Feat (35 feet, 5.9-): Climb the thin crack directly above the corner to the tourist lookout. Alternatively, you can climb another finger crack 10 feet left (Lookout Crack, 5.9-) or walk off left (with caution) and up to the top of the cliff.

Descent: Walk back down the auto road.

75. The Prow   III, 5.6 A2 or 5.11d

There is probably no route on all of Cathedral with a more perfect name. The Prow climbs a 350-foot nose of rock that sweeps up to the highest point on the face. At no time are you more than 15 feet from the very edge. This climb was done early enough to have had a complete metamorphosis: long aid climb with pitons, a great mixed clean aid and free route, a desperate free climb. In each stage it has been unquestionably classic. With perfect rock, clean cracks, a spectacular roof, and a lot of fixed protection, the Prow is a wonderful adventure no matter how you do it.

My first experience on the Prow was as a big aid climb. It was the early 1980s and I was fairly inexperienced, timid, and easily frightened. My friend John Tremblay was equally inexperienced, bold, and fearless. He led.

We started early one morning with an enormous rack of clunky 'biners, hexes, 1-inch slings, and a butt-bag I sewed myself (we had heard about the hanging belays). I do not remember much about the early pitches except that it took us a long time. Noon found us at the top of the third pitch, hanging our butts out over the Big Flush, a nasty gully filled with crumbling granite, trees, and car parts. Because of the circuitous nature of those early pitches, we were still only a long pitch off the ground, but in my mind we were *three pitches up* and I was on edge.

Louise Shepherd and Alison Osius on the first all-female free ascent of the Prow, in 1985. Photo by S. Peter Lewis

John, however, was stoked, both physically and mentally. He had a gleam in his eye and kept rolling cigarettes at the belays. By the roof pitch, I was just plain scared. Too young and stupid to have ascenders, I was following every pitch on aid and scaring myself silly on every placement. The traverse into the corner below the roof was horrid. Oh, those tiny stoppers. They must call them stoppers because they can stop your heart from beating. An hour before dusk, we topped out and staggered down the road. I thought I had climbed El Cap. My shoulders were shot.

Over the years I did the route several more times, even freeing some of the harder bits. I never did get the bulge on pitch 4 or the roof pitch; there is sort of an informal club here in North Conway Village of folks who share the same frustration—the "Yeah, I've freed everything but the bulge and the roof pitch" club.

One afternoon in the late 1980s, I went to the top of the cliff with the young local star Jimmy Surette. I lowered him all the way to the top of the first pitch on two very long ropes and then top-roped him back up. He just climbed and climbed and climbed, and I could barely keep up with him. He paused only once, for me to pass the knot, and was on top in 20 minutes. My shoulders were shot.

First ascent: British expatriate Paul Ross with Hugh Thompson, April 1973; partial free ascents: Michael Hartrich, Jeff Pheasant, Rick Mulhern, and John Bragg (freed the slab on the first pitch variation), 1973; Rick Fleming and Mark Bon Signor (freed the last pitch), April 1976; John Bragg and Joe Lentini (freed the second and third pitches), May 1976; first continuous free ascent: Jim Dunn with Jay Wilson, July 14, 1977.

Equipment: Small stoppers and cams, nothing over 2½ inches; quite a bit of fixed gear.

Start: From the state park kiosk below the center of the cliff, walk straight toward the cliff through a short bit of talus, bear left, and enter the woods. After 100 feet, turn uphill to stairs in a steep gully, go up and slightly right for 50 feet to a second set of stairs, scramble left and up 10 feet to a large ledge with trees.

Route: Pitch 1 (75 feet, 5.7): Climb straight up a series of cracks (same start as Recompense, climb 74) and then trend right to a belay from two bolts on a ledge at the very base of the obvious overhanging second pitch.

Pitch 1a (75 feet, 5.9 R): Climb up a few feet, then traverse for 40 feet to the right, reaching a belay at the base of a slab (possible belay). Climb the slab past widely spaced bolts to the same ledge. This was the original line.

Pitch 2 (50 feet, 5.11+ or A2): The free version climbs either from right to left on jugs to reach the crack (easier) or straight up to the overhanging prow. The crack soon fades to thin face moves and a belay at a horizontal crack. The pitch is mostly fixed. If aiding, take the straight-up variation.

Pitch 3 (50 feet, 5.10 or 5.7 A2): Head horizontally right around the prow and then follow a flake to a hard pull back onto the left side of the face into cracks, which are followed to a hanging belay.

Pitch 4 (50 feet, 5.11+ or A2): The notorious bulge pitch. Climb the bulging face above either from the left (easier but scary) or straight up to a finger crack (5.11), which is jammed to another hanging belay on the very edge of the prow.

Pitch 5 (60 feet, 5.11+ or A2): The famous roof pitch traverses left with great difficulty into a tiny left-facing corner, which is followed (extremely technical) up to the obvious roof. Pull around and then over the roof (hang in there; there is a jug) and follow a short crack to a good ledge.

Pitch 6 (75 feet, 5.9 or 5.6 A2): Climb a thin crack up a slab to either a wide crack on the right (5.6) or a thin finger crack up the wall to its left that finishes at an obvious pine tree (5.9).

Descent: Walk down the auto road.

76. Mordor Wall   IV, 5.7 A3 or 5.12c (summer) or WI 5 (winter)

The Mordor Wall is one of the most impressive sweeps of granite in New Hampshire. Standing under its smooth, water-streaked start, you could swear you are in Yosemite. And although it is short, just five pitches, it is complicated enough to usually take a very long day. I have even seen portaledges hanging from the anchors on the third pitch. The climb has also been done as a mixed aid/ice climb—a huge fang of ice drips down over the roof and coats part of the third pitch.

I have never been much of an aid climber. I can count my list of big aid routes on one finger, and even on that route I never led a pitch harder than A2. I find standing in aiders absolutely terrifying—even if it is a bomber piece. When I am free climbing, I always have some warning before I am going to fall, often in the form of several seconds to several minutes of whimpering and drooling on myself while the terror slowly builds. But standing in aiders is like driving a car whose brake lines have quietly leaked all their fluid out just as you come upon a stalled logging truck; one second you are just cruising along and the next the whole world has cracked open under your feet.

Several years ago my friend Dave and I were working on a film project and we needed to fix a rope on an overhanging wall. We schlepped all our stuff up to the base of the Mordor and in a moment of sheer stupidity I offered to lead the first

pitch. It was only A2, after all, and I was solid on that (at least I had been in 1984). Time was of the essence so I hurried a bit, placing a string of cams and creaky nuts under the expando flake that led to the hanging corner. After a bunch of time-bomb placements in the wiggly flake, I found myself at the base of the corner and shoved a cam into the now-solid crack. Full of confidence, I stood up and was fiddling in the next piece when the cam popped. In the next millisecond air whooshed, gear clinked, odd pinging sounds rang out, and tree roots rushed up at my face.

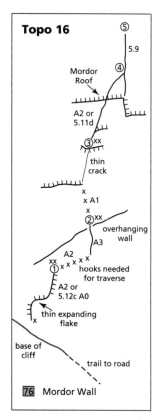

Dave caught me and quickly lowered me to the ground. I stood up and felt myself all over. Whew. I was okay. Then I looked up at him.

No, I was not okay. Everything was twisted, warped, and blurry. Dave looked worse than normal. I wondered why there was no pain. I grabbed my skull in case brain was oozing out and stumbled toward Dave. "My *head,* my *head,* what's *wrong* with my *head?*"

Dave gave me the same disgusted look he has been giving me for two decades, reached over, straightened out my skewed glasses, and gently pushed them back onto my face.

First ascent: Joe Cote and John Merrill (pitch 1, with no thoughts of going any higher), 1967; Joe Cote and Steve Arsenault (to the sidewalk on pitch 3), 1970;

Steve Arsenault and Scott Brim (rappelled down and climbed the roof on pitch four), later that summer of 1970; Ed Webster (the whole route from the ground, freeing the roof pitch), August 1979; Jim Surrette (freed all but the last move on pitch 1), 1985; first winter ascent: Bryan Becker and Alain Comeau, January 1979.

Equipment: Usual hard-aid trinkets; add a lot of small nuts and cams, hooks (including pointed ones), a few small bashies, ascenders, belay seat, etc.; pitons not needed—much of the hard aid is fixed.

Jim Surette heel-hooking the roof on an early free ascent of the Mordor Wall in 1985. Photo by S. Peter Lewis

Mordor Wall on Cathedral Ledge. Photo by S. Peter Lewis

Start: From the state park kiosk below the center of the cliff, walk north (to the right) along the road for about 300 feet, then turn left into the woods and hike past a huge boulder (in about 100 feet), then up the obvious trail to the base of the wall. The approach takes 5 minutes. The start is an obvious, terribly thin, right-curving arch/flake about 50 feet right of a mossy chimney.

Route: Pitch 1 (75 feet, A2 or 5.12c A0): A hook move and bolt connect to the wafer-thin flake, which is aided right to a shallow dihedral with a bolt anchor at the top.

Pitch 2 (100 feet, A3): Hook your way across the wall to the right, clipping the occasional bolt, and then follow a line of fixed bashies up a faint seam to a bolted belay over the crest of the wall.

Pitch 3 (125 feet, A1): Follow a bolt ladder lead to an A1 crack and a comfortable fixed belay on the left end of "the Sidewalk."

Pitch 4 (75 feet, A2 or 5.11d): Climb a thin crack to a bolt and then continue up and over the Mordor Roof, then head up and right to another fixed and hanging belay.

Pitch 5 (150 feet, 5.9): Climb the crack system above to the top.

Descent: From the tree ledge at the top of the route, walk straight back into the woods and follow any number of trails out to the summit road, turn right, and walk down. (A more aesthetic trail also follows the top of the cliff down the right side.)

77. Thin Air   II, 5.6

I could climb Thin Air by rote. As I can walk through my house in the depths of night and turn every corner, miss every creaking floorboard, and reach perfectly for every door latch, so too can I climb Thin Air. I can hit the cross-through smear on pitch 2 while chatting with a neighbor on another route, slot the hand jam in the chimney as if I were flicking a familiar light switch, and make the outrageously high step above the stacked flakes on the third pitch as though I might hop up on my grandfather's porch.

I could climb Thin Air by rote—but I do not. Instead, I savor every smear, every jam, each pinch and wonderfully familiar lieback. At the belays, I tie in without measuring, lean back as a sailor leans into a friendly wind, and smile. Thin Air is magic.

One blue and brittle October day not long ago, I was leaning back in my harness far out at the end of the second-pitch traverse when a sound caught my ear. I turned, looked across the valley, and saw a mighty wind rustle the pines like grass and head my way. It rushed to the base of the cliff, grabbed a hundred-hundred-thousand crimson maple leaves and heaved them up at me. They leaped up the cliff, brushing past like a crowd of butterflies, and soared overhead into an incredible firework display in the blue sky. Then they fell and fell and fell, tumbling back down head-over-heels and seeming to laugh, caressing my smiling face, skittering and ticking down the granite with the sound of vast applause. It was as if the last wind of autumn were congratulating itself for a season well done.

The next day it snowed.

First ascent: John Turner and Craig Merrihue, August 1956.

Equipment: Small rack to 2½ inches; there is a lot of fixed gear.

Start: From the state park kiosk below the center of the cliff, walk north (to the

Dave Kelly on his umpteenth trip across the Thin Air traverse. Photo by S. Peter Lewis

right) along the road for about 300 feet to an obvious trail on the left. Take this trail; in 100 feet pass a humongous boulder. Continue on the trail until under the huge, blank Mordor Wall (climb 76), turn left, and follow the trail steeply along the cliff base for 250 feet to a flat, worn area.

Route: Pitch 1 (50 feet, 5.5): Climb straight up on excellent holds (5.5; 5.3 if you start 15 feet to the left) to easier climbing, protection, and a shattered pillar, which is climbed on its left side, to a comfortable ledge with a fixed belay off pitons.

Pitch 2 (75 feet, 5.6): Step down off the shattered pillar, then traverse right and slightly up (protect your second) to an obvious horizontal crack; step up into the crack and continue traversing right, passing two bolts and a piton, to another comfortable foot ledge and belay with two bolts. (You can rappel 165 feet to the ground from here.) Pitches 1 and 2 may be combined—bypass the pitch 1 belay to the right.

Pitch 3 (60 feet, 5.5): Climb up and right, then up and left to a hidden flake that takes you to the obvious chimney with an ash tree; squirm up the chimney to a huge ledge with a double-bolt anchor. Have lunch.

Pitch 4 (125 feet, 5.6): Climb off the right side of the ledge and follow the obvious weakness straight up the steep wall above. At 60 feet you encounter very steep flakes where trending left helps ease the strain. Easier climbing leads to a ledge with a red pine tree. (It is hard to see or hear your second while he or she follows this pitch; do not run the rope out up the dirty groove above.)

Pitch 5 (40 feet, 5.0): Scamper up the dirty groove above to the obvious ledge and trees (there is a 5.8 bouldery finish on the right). An incredible finger crack,

Topo 17

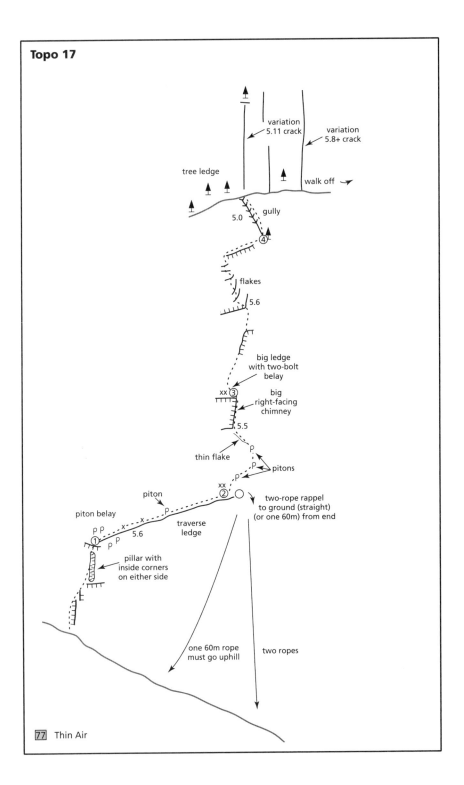

variation
5.11 crack

variation
5.8+ crack

tree ledge

walk off

5.0   gully

④

flakes

5.6

big ledge
with two-bolt
belay

xx ③

big
right-facing
chimney

5.5

thin flake

P

P   pitons

P

xx

piton

②

P

two-rope rappel
to ground (straight)
(or one 60m) from end

piton belay

P P   x   x   P

P P   5.6

traverse
ledge

pillar with
inside corners
on either side

one 60m rope
must go uphill

two ropes

Airation (5.11), rises 50 feet straight above to an obvious pine tree—a great challenge if you are up to it. Two cracks to the right is a great 5.8+, Pine Tree Eliminate.

Descent: Walk right (north) for about 100 feet on tree ledges (with caution), turn left uphill, and follow obvious climbers paths out to the auto road; turn right and walk down the road back to the cliff base.

78. Repentence II, WI 5

The season after the historic first ascent solo of Cannon's Black Dike by John Bouchard saw several new routes by another leader of the era, John Bragg. In 1973 Bragg repeated the Black Dike as well as adding Dracula and Smear at Frankenstein Cliff (see the next section) in Crawford Notch—the former route being steeper than the Black Dike but much shorter and less committing. But Bragg's real plum of the season came in the relatively urban setting of Cathedral Ledge in North Conway Village when he and Rick Wilcox climbed Repentence. Northeast climbing historians Laura and Guy Waterman wrote in *Yankee Rock and Ice:* "The route that had made history as a bold rock climb by [John] Turner in 1959 thus reentered history as a pivotal ice climb of the new era fourteen years later. Repentence was technically an advance over the Black Dike. It was the first climb that probably could not have been done without wrist loops."

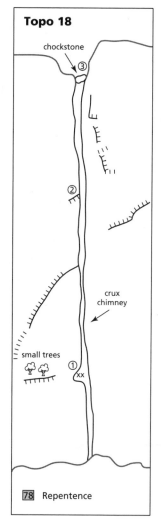

Topo 18

chockstone

③

②

crux chimney

small trees

①

xx

78 Repentence

Turner had rock-climbed the 350-foot chimney of Repentence at a time when people thought such things were not possible. Now, armed for the first time with leashes connecting their ice tools to their wrists, Bragg and Wilcox stood at the bottom of the same chimney in its winter garb and choked with ice. Today's climber armed with the latest (and much superior) boots, ice axes, and crampons may well wonder what all the hype was about when Bragg and Wilcox walked down the road after the first winter ascent of Repentence. Our suggestion is to go borrow some period equipment from Rick and climb the route.

My first experience with Repentence came in the mid-1980s. Never ahead (or even level with) the technology curve, I approached the first pitch with leather boots, hinged SMC crampons, crude (even for the day) ice tools, and much trembling. I was certainly out of my league. A mossy but not too steep groove with adequate, if thin, ice led for 75 feet to a comfortable belay ledge. I scratched my way up a few feet, found a bit of a stance, and looked for a screw placement. It was too thin. I looked up and licked my lips. The ice was friendly (plastic), but it did not look like it would get much thicker for a while.

My partner suggested putting a piton in a horizontal crack a few feet higher and off to the right. I made a few more tentative moves, reached out, banged in a solid Lost

Kurt Winkler styling the steep last pitch of Repentence. Photo by S. Peter Lewis

Arrow, threaded a sling through it so that two loops hung down, and clipped in. Back in control, I confidently continued, got in a good screw higher up, and was soon at the belay. While seconding, my partner found that I had clipped only one loop of the sling on the piton and was actually facing a ground fall for most of the pitch.

Well, that was it; my nerves were shot. My partner struggled for a while on the crux pillar on the second pitch while I huddled in a cave and whimpered. We went down. Repentence would have to wait.

First ascent: John Bragg and Rick Wilcox, 1973.

Equipment: 6–10 ice screws; a smattering of rock gear, including one 4-inch or bigger cam for last pitch.

Start: Follow the Cathedral Ledge auto road north for 5–10 minutes until just past the central part of the cliff. Turn left into the woods onto what is usually a well-packed trail and hike 300 feet to the base of the cliff. Repentence is the left-hand of two obvious chimney systems that run the length of the cliff about 100 feet right of a huge looming cavern. The right-hand route is Remission, another area classic (WI 5+ M4 and much more committing).

Route: Pitch 1 (75 feet, WI 4): Climb the mossy, often thin groove to a comfortable ledge on the left with two bolts.

Pitch 2 (150 feet, WI 5—can feel much harder in lean conditions): The crux ice pitch climbs a free-standing pillar off the right side of the ledge and continues up a long, very narrow chimney to another ledge on the left. In lean conditions with the ice far back in the chimney, this pitch can be rather desperate.

Pitch 3 (125 feet, WI 5 M4): Continue up the wider chimney above on typically thicker ice to a huge chockstone at the very top. Place the big cam and then climb out the left side of the chockstone into a thin corner, which is dry-tooled for several moves to the top. This 10-foot section is considered by many to be the crux of the entire route.

Descent: From the top of the climb, continue up a snow gully for 75 feet, then turn right and follow the top of the cliff down around its right end and back to the road. This trail is usually packed but is easy to figure out even if not packed.

Frankenstein Cliff

Frankenstein, New Hampshire's most well-known ice-climbing playground, is roadside climbing at its best. What are towering drippy walls, waterfalls, and slimy gullies in the summer turn to dozens of blue-ice rivulets when the thermometer bottoms out. Paralleling US 302, the entire Frankenstein Cliff area is only about a mile long, and yet there are more than seventy-five routes recorded here. As you can imagine, with that many things to choose from, our job was a tough one. We finally decided to start at WI 3 and, with the highest quality in mind, ratchet things upward to WI 5. The result is a selection of five routes providing more than 850 feet of classic New Hampshire ice. If you come here on a busy Saturday in February and every drip seems to have someone clad in the latest Gore-Tex clawing up it, do not despair; there are a lot of alternatives and the locals are very friendly.

I have been to Frankenstein so many times that I have lost track, but some linger in my memory. I remember the joy of pure adventure as I opened "the Window"

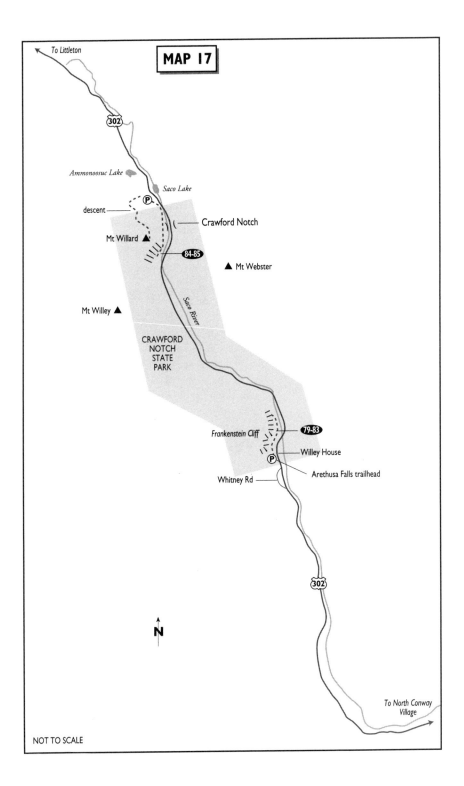

MAP 17

To Littleton

302

Ammonoosuc Lake

Saco Lake

P

descent

Crawford Notch

Mt Willard ▲

84-85

▲ Mt Webster

Saco River

Mt Willey ▲

CRAWFORD
NOTCH
STATE
PARK

Frankenstein Cliff

79-83

P

Willey House

Arethusa Falls trailhead

Whitney Rd

302

N

To North Conway
Village

NOT TO SCALE

with my ax on the variation to the Standard Route and squirmed through. There was a cocksure day on Dracula when the ice was warm and plastic, everyone was a hero, and I followed the climb with just one tool. A week later the route was cold and brittle; I broke a crampon and just managed to scrape up the route with my life.

The history of Frankenstein is linked inexorably to the steep-ice revolution sparked by Yvon Chouinard in the Adirondacks in 1969. Before then, Frankenstein Cliffs was just an area along US 302 in Crawford Notch covered with unclimbable frozen waterfalls. After the revolution, Frankenstein became the Promised Land. Of the routes highlighted here, three—Chia, Pegasus, and Standard Route—were climbed in the winter of 1970–71, and the harder two, Dropline and Dracula, were climbed just a few years later. In 1969 climbers thought long stretches of steep ice were impossible; less than eight years later, long vertical pillars were almost routine.

While it is true that the ice revolution was sparked by a jump in technology— rigid crampons, drooped picks, better protection—a brave soul is still required to confirm the new definition of the possible. The early history of Frankenstein is full of such brave souls who have helped advance standards for decades, not only here but throughout the Northeast. In recent years, with the next revolution (mixed climbing) upon us, young visionaries have redefined what is possible on the walls and overhangs between the older drips.

Special Considerations
Frankenstein Cliff is located in Crawford Notch State Park; there are no climbing restrictions. Please be nice to the folks who own the house at the end of the dirt road.

Standard Equipment
A standard rack of eight to ten ice screws.

Approach
About 0.25 mile after entering Crawford Notch State Park (a small sign is on the right-hand side of the road), turn left onto a dirt road and then turn immediately right into a parking lot (room here for about fifty cars).

Walk up the road for several hundred yards to its end (additional parking here), then turn right onto railroad tracks (usually well packed) and hike north to your intended route. See map 17.

79. Pegasus   I, WI 3+–4 M5.6
This is the big, 160-foot-high blue flow in the sunny amphitheater called, well, the Amphitheater. Pegasus has a steep lower wall, a low-angled midsection, and then a nearly vertical pillar on the left. A fun variation tackles the shorter right-hand pillar and rock corner on the right.

I have never been as cold as I have been at Frankenstein. It is 1982 and I am tied to a big birch tree at the base of Pegasus. My partner is somewhere above, hacking at iron-hard ice with a pathetic ice hammer that was obviously AWOL during the technology revolution. It is ten below zero; I am wearing leather boots, wool pants, and a windbreaker; we are alone; I have not moved in a long time; it will be dark in a mere six hours; and I am scared.

Following the pitch, I have to watch my feet to make sure they strike the ice—they are long since dead-cold. I beat and beat and beat my ax at each placement,

Part of Frankenstein Cliff in Mount Washington Valley. Photo by David Stone

Nick Yardley on Frankenstein Cliff's classic route Pegasus. Photo by S. Peter Lewis

never getting any purchase at all, and then move on it anyway. At the belay I stare bug-eyed at my partner, he nods, and then we stumble left below the upper pillar, skid down the snow gully, and get the heck out of there.

These days, with modern clothing and tools, Pegasus can be just plain fun at ten below zero.

First ascent: Dennis Merritt and Sam Streibert, winter of 1970–71.

Start: Walk along the railroad tracks for about 10 minutes until you see the railroad trestle over a prominent gorge. Turn left about 50 feet before the trestle and follow a steep trail up to the base of the cliff band. The first climb you approach on the trail is Pegasus; Chia (climb 80) is about 150 feet to its right.

Route: Pitch 1 (100 feet, WI 3): Climb the lower wall and then scamper up the easy middle part of the climb to a belay near the base (and off to the side of) the pillar.

Pitch 1a (50 feet, WI 3+ M5.6): After the lower wall, trend up and right, passing another pillar, to a two-bolt anchor on a ledge to the right.

Pitch 2 (60 feet, WI 4): Climb the pillar to easier bulges and the woods.

Pitch 2a (40 feet, WI 3 M5.6): Climb the shorter pillar just left of the belay to a ledge, then tackle the rock corner above that is well protected by fixed pitons.

Descent: Hike right (north) past Chia and then down around to the right, arriving shortly at the base of that route. Traverse back over to Pegasus.

80. Chia
I, WI 3–4+

This classic route located high in the back of the sunny Amphitheater is the right-hand of two prominent icefalls here—Pegasus (climb 79) is the other. Chia features a left-to-right-trending ramp.

Kitty Calhoun on the steep Direct variation to Chia. Photo by S. Peter Lewis

First ascent: Sam Streibert and Dennis Merritt, winter of 1970–71.

Start: Walk along the railroad tracks for about 10 minutes and turn left about 50 feet before the railroad trestle over a prominent gorge. Follow a steep trail up to the base of the cliff band. The first climb on the trail is Pegasus (climb 79); Chia is about 150 feet to its right.

Route: Pitch 1 (150 feet, WI 3–4+): The standard line of ascent begins at the lower-left corner of the flow and follows the ramp up and right to the top. It can be climbed in one long pitch or broken in half (avoid doing it as a multipitch climb on busy days).

Pitch 1a (150 feet, WI 4+): A much more difficult line can be had by starting 50 feet to the right on a vertical pillar, climbing that, then crossing the ramp to the left and tackling another vertical pillar.

Descent: Follow the obvious trail to the right (north), which curves back to the south and the base of the route.

81. Standard Route   II, WI 3+

At 300 feet long, this is the biggest, fattest, most crowded climb at Frankenstein Cliff—and one of the most often climbed intermediate routes in all the Northeast. Pick a weekday or start early and be prepared to have a blast.

Frankenstein Cliff. Photo by S. Peter Lewis

Brad White climbing above the cave on Frankenstein's Standard Route. Photo by
S. Peter Lewis

First ascent: Sam Streibert and Dennis Merritt, winter of 1970–71.

Start: About 20–25 minutes from the parking lot and 10 minutes north of the trestle, this huge blue flow almost reaches the tracks.

Route: Pitch 1 (100 feet, WI 3): Climb the center of the flow to a cave on the right and fixed anchors.

Pitch 2 (100 feet, WI 3+): Climb out the cave's left side, then up a steep wall, then up a series of bulges (do not run the rope out—you will never hear your partner).

Pitch 2a (100 feet, WI 3): This fun variation, "the Window," climbs through a hole in a curtain off the cave's right side (you may have to do some excavation) and then climbs up and left on bulges to rejoin the regular line.

Pitch 3 (100 feet, WI 2+): Climb more bulges up and left, following the line of least resistance, to the woods (a steep wall can be climbed on the right for added spice).

Descent: Hike right (north) on a packed trail for several hundred feet and then turn right down a steep gully that leads to woods and the tracks.

82. Dropline — I, WI 5

This dramatic icicle is probably Frankenstein's most famous hard route—a dead-vertical 150-foot yellow drip down a blank wall high above the railroad tracks. Did I say I have been really cold at Frankenstein?

One February day long, long ago, I trudged up and around Dracula to the top of the cliff and tossed a rope off Dropline. I eased over the edge, gulped my heart back into my chest, and then quietly rappelled down the blank wall next to the route. At the bottom I put my ascenders on the rope, got my cameras out, and prepared to climb back up the rope, taking pictures as a friend climbed the route.

My friend soon scampered out onto the drip and started swinging. Big, powerful swings, one with each hand, then high, strong kicks, one with each foot; up and up and up. I hurriedly jumared, snapped a photo, and then hauled on the jumars again. I could hardly keep up. Swing, swing, kick, kick, jumar, jumar, click, click.

"Gosh, slow down, Dave, I can't jumar as fast as you can climb!" Years before

New Hampshire's Frankenstein Cliff. Photo by S. Peter Lewis

David Breashears cranking Frankenstein's Dropline in the early 1980s. Photo by S. Peter Lewis

NOVA, Everest, or IMAX, Dave Breashears was just a really good ice climber. He just smiled at me and kept on kicking. I hauled and hauled and struggled with my ascenders, occasionally getting a shot off, and becoming more and more winded.

I have never been as hot as I have been at Frankenstein.

First ascent: Rainsford Rouner, Peter Cole, and Rick Wilcox, February 1976.

Start: Walk about 20–25 minutes from the parking lot and 10 minutes north of

Frankenstein Cliff. Photo by David Stone

the trestle, continue about 100 feet right (north) of Standard Route (climb 81), and walk steeply into a shallow amphitheater.

Route: Pitch 1 (100 feet, WI 3): Climb a left-trending ramp, often very thin,

Conrad Yager on Frankenstein's best Grade IV, Dracula. Photo by S. Peter Lewis

up little walls and past shrubs to a belay 20 feet left of the obvious upper drip.

Pitch 2 (70 feet, WI 5): Now get down to business. Traverse right along a break; place a screw, and then battle your way onto the drip (it often overhangs for a few feet). The ice above is unrelentingly steep and the tracks are *very* far below, and, as if to add insult to injury, the trees at the top try to push you off backward just when your gas tank nears empty.

Descent: Hike right (north) on a packed trail for several hundred feet and then turn right down a steep gully that leads to woods and the tracks.

83. Dracula   I, WI 4+

This is perhaps Frankenstein's most aesthetic route, a series of dark blue columns stacked 140 feet high in the back of a steep black corner.

First ascent: John Bragg and A. J. LaFleur, 1973.

Start: Follow the tracks north from Standard Route (climb 81) for about 400 feet and look for this dramatic climb high up and around to the left. A steep snow slope leads 300 feet to the base.

Route: Pitch 1 (140 feet, WI 4+): Climb a short initial bulge to a ledge and then forge up the long central column, stemming occasionally to minimize the pump factor, to a rest ledge on the left with a pine tree (possible belay/retreat point); the final steep curtain, often undercut, is considered the crux.

Descent: Hike right (north) on a packed trail for several hundred feet and then turn right down a steep gully that leads to woods and the tracks. If you have left gear at the base of the route, when you reach the bottom of the snow gully, traverse right and follow the cliff back to the climb.

Mount Willard

No one knows who first climbed Cinema or Hitchcock Gully first. Pity—it would be great to have your name next to these. In an area filled with wonderful moderate winter climbs, these two routes are perhaps the most wonderful. More like alpine adventures than ice climbs, Cinema and Hitchcock gullies can be linked together for a grand 800-plus-foot tour de force of snow, ice, and good old New Hampshire bush-whacking. And for added measure, the approach is a snap (walk along the railroad tracks, put your crampons on, and start climbing) and the descent a piece of cake (two rappels and a 500-foot glissade back to the tracks).

Be warned, however: the south face of Mount Willard loads fiercely after a big snow and often slides. Back in the old days when they used to run the trains in the winter, I have seen a wall 20 feet thick where the plow train came through.

My first foray onto Cinema was just at the tail end of a really big storm. We sloshed up through deep snow for two pitches to a tree belay on the left (we could not dig down far enough to find any ice). As my friend Tom led out to the right on a big arcing traverse on the third pitch, I could not look up without the driving snow stinging my face.

Then I heard something odd. It sounded like distant applause or bacon frying, neither of which made a whole lot of sense. Then I heard Tom yelling something. I looked up and saw a wave of snow about 18 inches thick hissing down at me from the tree ledge above. My first (and, as it turned out, only) thought was stupid: "Wow, this is just like being on a real climb, and if I just stand here and brace myself, the avalanche will pass gently around my legs."

My next recollection is being upside down below the belay tree with snow crammed into every possible orifice. I could not see because snow was packed tightly between my glasses and my eyeballs. But I was not hurt. I stumbled upright and was delighted to see my brake hand still on the rope and that the rope still led uphill to Tom. And now I could finally make out what he was yelling. "For goodness sake, stop yanking on the rope; I don't have any screws in."

Standard Equipment

Six to ten ice screws, including some short ones. Two ropes for rappel.

Approach

At the very top of Crawford Notch on US 302 is a very obvious road cut with a pond, an old train station, and an Appalachian Mountain Club hostel. Park at the pullout just south of the train station. See map 17.

84. Cinema Gully   II, WI 2–3

Cinema Gully to Upper Hitchcock Gully climbs the center of the expansive slabs that cover the south face of Mount Willard, giving three to four delightful pitches of easy snow and ice. Often thinly iced, the climbing can be delicate and the line wandering as you poke around for stuff thick enough to sink a screw into. Upon gaining the tree ledge at the top of the route, you are faced with a long traverse around to the north that can vary from scratchy crawling through scrub and saplings in low snow conditions to a packed trench during a good winter.

Once on the east face, you find the antithesis of Cinema's wide-open climbing in the narrow, shadowed cleft of Upper Hitchcock. With the rock wall hanging over your head, you can pretend the climbing is harder and more serious than it is, really adding spice to the day.

First ascent: Unknown.

Special considerations: Cinema Gully can be avalanche prone and should be avoided after or during a big storm.

Start: From the pullout, hike the railroad tracks south for about 15 minutes (in typical snow conditions) to the base of the obvious south face of Mount Willard. Cinema Gully starts up a shallow snow groove in the very center of the face and begins almost at the tracks.

Route: Pitch 1 (180 feet, WI 2): Climb up the shallow groove (often thin) to steep snow, and belay wherever the ice is thick enough below bulges.

Pitch 2 (100 feet, WI 2): Climb the bulge and continue up the shallow bowl in the face, mostly on steep snow, to another belay at bulges.

Pitch 3 (150 feet, WI 2–3): Climb up and left along the obvious line of weakness to reach the trees above; or, more difficult, climb straight up to the woods.

Pitch 4 (500 feet, 3rd class): Traverse the tree ledge north (steep and brushy) and around the corner, passing an obvious bulgy wall, until below an aesthetic, right-slanting gully in a rock wall.

Pitch 5 (125 feet, WI 2–3): This is Upper Hitchcock Gully. Climb the gully to the woods.

Descent: Although it is possible to hike west from the top of the gully to intersect

New Hampshire's Mount Willard (climbers circled to show scale). Photo by Brian Post

a trail leading from the summit of Mount Willard back to the top of the notch, a far easier option is via rappel. Rappel once with two ropes to the big ledge below Upper Hitchcock. Below Upper Hitchcock and in line with it is a white birch tree that hangs over Lower Hitchcock. Rappel from this tree into Lower Hitchcock and glissade its lower portion back to the tracks.

85. Across the Universe   II, 5.9- (5.5 R) A0 or 5.10c

The routes in this book are full of superlatives. Some are on perfect rock or ice. Others played a pivotal role in the history of Northeast climbing. Others are delightfully easy or tremendously challenging. And then there are routes like Across the Universe, with average-quality rock, only minor historical significance, and of decidedly moderate difficulty. But the view—oh, the view. This route could be an absolute pile of choss and it would still be high on my list of routes to do.

Pick a fine day in late September or early October, a good friend or two, a light rack, and a camera and head up to Mount Willard. The walk along the old Maine Central railroad tracks is dead flat and in just 15 minutes or so you will find yourself at the very toe of the slabs that grace the south face of Mount Willard. Pitch 1 starts off squirrelly on a dirty little headwall, but soon the rock improves and you find yourself padding delicately at 5.9- past two old bolts.

The next pitch, the technical crux, climbs out the right side of the big overlap that hangs over the belay. I remember working the crux moves above the bolt over and over again way back in the 1980s until I finally got that one 5.10c move. Ever since, I have clipped the bolt, pulled on the draw, and coasted past the crux move without even a twinge of guilt.

The open slabs of Mount Willard. Photo by S. Peter Lewis

Topo 19

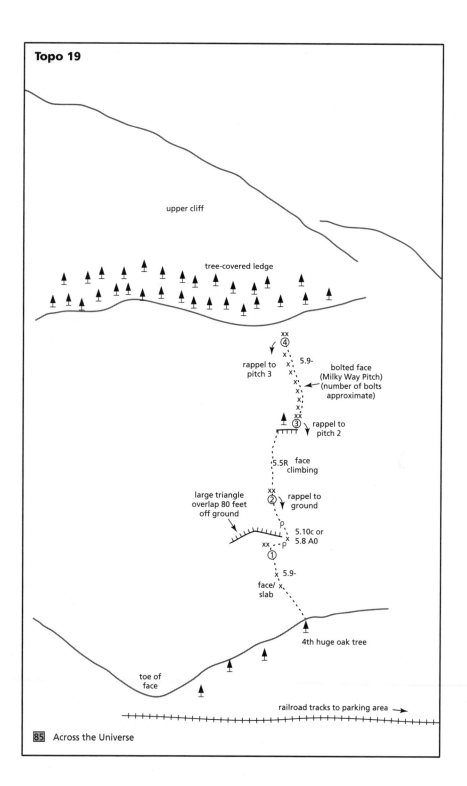

upper cliff

tree-covered ledge

xx
④

rappel to
pitch 3

x
x
x
x
x
x
x
x
xx
③

5.9-

bolted face
(Milky Way Pitch)
(number of bolts
approximate)

rappel to
pitch 2

5.5R face
climbing

large triangle
overlap 80 feet
off ground

xx
②

rappel to
ground

p

5.10c or
5.8 A0

x
xx
①

p

x 5.9-

face/
slab

x

4th huge oak tree

toe of
face

railroad tracks to parking area →

Brian Johnston enjoys the view from the Milky Way on Mount Willard's Across the Universe route. Photo by S. Peter Lewis

Pitch 3 is nothing special. The angle lessens, the difficulties diminish, and the rock gets funky. After a full pitch of runout 5.5, you find yourself at the base of a grand sweep of white granite, the aptly named "Milky Way Pitch." This is the pitch to savor. The rock is immaculate, the moves consistent and hard enough (5.9-ish) to keep you focused, and the bolts far enough apart to keep you alert.

The problem is that view. Every time I am up there, I find myself pausing after each clip to turn around and simply gaze. The entirety of Crawford Notch lies below with the 2,500-foot west wall of Mount Webster dominating on the left and the bulk of Mount Willey on the right. The Saco River winds hundreds of feet beneath; the trees are orange, yellow, and red; a cool breeze blows and peacefulness just hangs in the air. Someday I am going to sew sticky rubber onto the seat of a pair of climbing pants so that I can stop in midpitch, turn around, sit down, and just soak it all in.

First ascent: Todd Swain, Mike Cody, and Dick Peterson, August 30, 1982.

Special considerations: The railroad below the cliff is in use during the summer; take special care when walking the tracks.

Equipment: A very small rack of nuts, cams, and Tricams; much of the route is fixed.

Start: From the pullout, hike the railroad tracks south for about 15 minutes to the base of the obvious south face of Mount Willard. From the toe of the face, hike the crumbly groove for 50 feet right, then traverse the base of the cliff up and right, passing huge oak trees. Belay at the fourth tree, directly below the obvious overlap 80 feet above (you see the overlap as you hike the base, but it is out of site from the belay tree).

Route: Pitch 1 (60 feet, 5.9-): Climb a steep wall directly behind the belay tree to a sloping face, traverse left for a few feet, and then step up to an old bolt. Climb past the bolt on difficult smearing to another bolt (one of these bolts has no hanger and you need to neck-tie it with a wired stopper) and then up to a good ledge with two bolts directly below the big overlap above.

Pitch 2 (80 feet, 5.8 A0 or 5.10c): Head up and right to the right edge of the overlap, then clip a piton and then a bolt on the steep headwall. Either pull on the bolt or make the move (5.10.c) to holds up and left and another piton. Climb up the easy face above for 60 feet to a two-bolt anchor in a shattered hole. (You can belay just above the overlap in a flake; this may be a good option if you need to see your second.)

Pitch 3 (175 feet, 5.5 R): Climb up the low-angled face above, aiming for an obvious tree clump up and right. Climb around the left side of the tree clump, then traverse right above it to a bolted belay below a smooth white slab with bolts.

Pitch 4 (125 feet, 5.9-): Pad your way up the "Milky Way Pitch" past widely spaced fixed protection to another bolted anchor. This is some of the most satisfying climbing anywhere and the view is just stunning (if you can turn your head while making the moves).

Descent: Make two double-rope rappels to the top of pitch 2 and then one more to the ground (do not even think of walking off from the top).

Mount Washington

At 6,288 feet, "Crystal Hill," as it was first called, ranks as just a mere bump in the western part of our country. I lived out West for several years and frequently bragged to friends about our mighty mountain back home. The typical response was a little chuckle, a pat on the head, and some sarcastic comment like, "Shoot, we got Wal-Marts out here that high."

One winter while I was living in Denver, a western guide made a trip out East to run an avalanche seminar in North Conway Village. While there, he got a chance to climb Pinnacle Gully, a moderate climb on Mount Washington's east side. One day after he returned to Denver, we were with a group of friends and the subject of Mount Washington came up. I made some comment and, as predictable as sunrise, there was a chuckle, a pat on the head, and the beginning of a demeaning comment. "*Mount* Washington, um, isn't that a little like calling. . . . "

The comment was swiftly stifled by a wave of the hand and a stinging look from my friend who had just been on the mountain. "Have you ever been there?" my friend asked. "Well, no." "Then shut up, because you don't know what you're talking about." It took everything I had to keep from chuckling.

Mount Washington is one of the nastiest places on the planet. The average temperature is 44 degrees and the wind blows 25 miles per hour 24 hours a day. Whoops, hold on; those are the June averages; sorry. In January it is typically 4 degrees and blowing 46 miles per hour every minute of every day. In April 1934, the wind blew 231 miles per hour—the highest wind speed ever recorded on the surface of the earth. And oh yeah, the mountain gets 254 inches of snow each year. Maybe Wal-Marts are okay at 6,000 feet out West, but they could not hack it at that altitude out here.

On this, the highest peak in the Northeast, we have included three winter routes and one summer route (Pinnacle Buttress). The technical portions of these routes

Climbers on the summit cone of Mount Washington on a perfect winter day. Photo by
S. Peter Lewis

start at timberline and climb up into an environment comparable to Labrador's—a
land of rock, wind, tiny alpine plants, and snow that falls sideways, even in the summer. These are grand adventures that will take your breath away.

Special Considerations
The area is on U.S. Forest Service land. There are no climbing restrictions. A voluntary sign-in/sign-out is at the AMC's Pinkham Notch visitor center.

Be prepared for bad and quickly changing weather (see below). Be prepared to

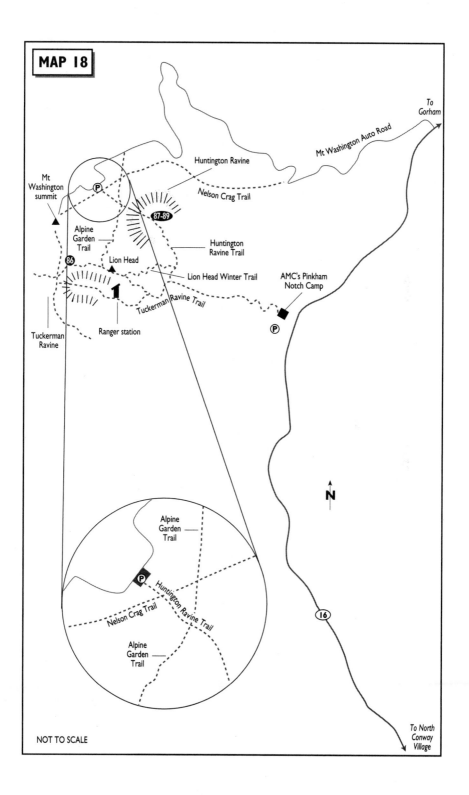

MAP 18

Mt Washington Auto Road

To Gorham

Huntington Ravine

Nelson Crag Trail

Mt Washington summit

Alpine Garden Trail

87-89

Huntington Ravine Trail

Lion Head

86

Lion Head Winter Trail

AMC's Pinkham Notch Camp

Tuckerman Ravine Trail

Ranger station

Tuckerman Ravine

N

Alpine Garden Trail

Nelson Crag Trail

Huntington Ravine Trail

Alpine Garden Trail

16

NOT TO SCALE

To North Conway Village

navigate the descent with map and compass. Be willing to turn back when things are not right.

Avalanches are common here in the winter and the danger is rated and posted every day: at AMC Pinkham Notch visitor center, at the base of Tuckerman Ravine, at the Harvard cabin below Huntington Ravine, and at *www.tuckerman.org*. Please take this information seriously; climbers have died here even under "moderate" avalanche conditions. These are big-mountain routes with all the accompanying dangers.

At the summit there is a parking lot, some buildings (including the famous Mount Washington Observatory), and not much else. Though there are people working in the bowels of some of the buildings, in winter there are absolutely no open facilities of any kind on the summit. Life-or-death emergencies are the only thing the summit folks will respond to, so do not pound on the doors if you are just cold and hungry.

Weather and Seasons
Winter season: late November through April. Summer season: mid-June through early September. Even a typical summer day has temperatures of 55–60 degrees, winds of 20–40 miles per hour, and low visibility.

Standard Equipment
Winter climbs: six to ten ice screws; a smattering of rock gear to 2 inches (a few small to medium pitons); mountaineering crampons; alpine ice ax; two ropes (in case the need to retreat—not at all uncommon—arises); clothing for arctic conditions, including 100-percent coverage for face and eyes; avalanche transceiver; headlamp; map; compass; signal whistle; food; water; extra clothing; bivy sack.

Rock climbs: See the Equipment paragraph for Pinnacle Buttress.

Approach
On the left (west) side of Route 16 at Pinkham Notch, park at AMC's Pinkham Notch Camp and find the trailhead for Tuckerman Ravine Trail.

An alternate approach for Pinnacle Buttress only (the road is closed in summer) involves driving up the Mount Washington Auto Road (toll road), which heads west from Route 16 at 5 miles north of Pinkham Notch, and continuing to the 7-mile marker to park on the left. See map 18.

86. Right Gully
I, 3rd–4th class snow

This is a classic route up the tallest and, arguably, the coldest, windiest, and snowiest mountain in the Northeast. Mount Washington has been climbed in winter for more than 150 years. If you tag the summit and return safely, you can congratulate yourself on 8 miles of travel and almost 8,000 feet of elevation change—a good day. But keep in mind that the rating for the climb itself does not take into account the non-technical approach and descent (4-plus miles each way). Mount Washington can be one of the most beautiful, enchanting places on earth. And sometimes it is just weird.

In the early 1990s I took a pair of folks up on a two-day mountaineering trip to Mount Washington. We camped at Hermit Lake, just below timberline on the east side, and temperatures that clear night dropped to minus 27 degrees. I was testing a new sleeping bag that was supposed to be rated to 30 degrees below, and I froze my butt off. After chattering and squirming all that frigid December night, dawn had us up and *moving*.

Clad in every bit of clothing we had, we trudged into the base of the ravine to find the temperature a balmy minus 15 degrees and the wind picking up. It had been a lean winter so far, and Right Gully was bony and very alpine looking. Fortunately, I had brought some technical gear and we were soon short-roping and short-pitching our way up the gully, burning calories and finally getting warm.

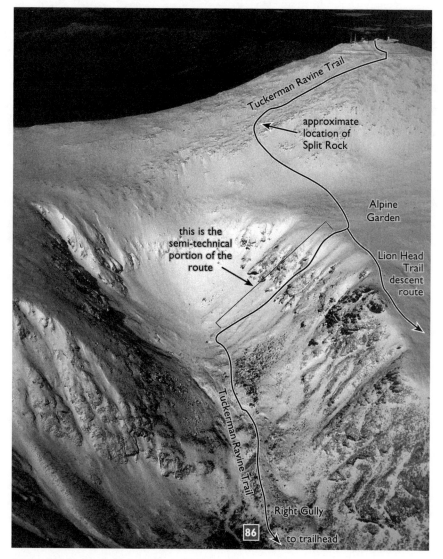

Mount Washington's Right Gully in Tuckerman Ravine. Photo by S. Peter Lewis

Mount Washington's Huntington Ravine from across the valley. Photo by S. Peter Lewis

It was eerie, though. In the gully we were on the lee slope and quite sheltered; it was breezy, to be sure, but we were not getting jostled. But I swear we could feel the dull pulsing of the wind through the mantle of the mountain, pounding, sweeping, and roaring its way toward the Atlantic 90 miles away. I wondered if it was shoving rocks around up above the gully and was mentally preparing myself to tell the guys we would have to bail on a summit attempt.

Sure enough, we poked our skinny little necks up into the jet stream and nearly went bald. One of the guys leaned against me and put his lips up to the side of my head. "Whatdyathink?" he shouted. It was early, it was clear, we felt strong—it was just really, really windy. But I had a strange hunch. I motioned them in close and we tucked our heads together. "Letsgivitashot," I yelled. Thumbs up. We turned west, leaned crazily into the gale, and scratched our way slowly toward the summit cone.

Twenty minutes later we stood at the base of the summit cone, in the lee of the wind again, hoods down, goggles off, talking without raising our voices. I took out a lighter, flicked it, and the flame stood straight up without a waver. To our south we watched as a pair of poor slobs actually crawled toward us from near the top of our climb.

Odd place, Mount Washington.

First ascent: Unknown.

Special considerations: In typical conditions, this is a straightforward, 3rd- to 4th-class snow climb rarely requiring belays. However, be forewarned: early season conditions may make this a scratchy ice climb, and heavy snowfall or high wind conditions can make it extremely avalanche prone. Avalanche danger can be high in the gully as well as the surrounding area; check the avalanche bulletin and forecast. People have died on this easy climb because they failed to heed conditions or warnings.

Start: From directly behind the AMC visitor center, follow the Tuckerman Ravine Trail for 2 miles to the Huntington Ravine Fire Road; continue straight on the Tuckerman Ravine Trail for another 0.4 mile to the Hermit Lake Shelter at the base of the Tuckerman Ravine (4,000 feet elevation). Check with the AMC's caretaker about the weather and avalanche forecasts for the ravine. Continue west on the trail for another 0.5 mile or so to the very base of the headwall. An emergency cache marks the end of the hiking and the beginning of the climb.

Route (800 feet, 3rd–4th snow): From the cache, the route makes a straight line up the obvious snow gully to the north, the second gully to the right of the right edge of the obvious smooth bowl formed by the headwall itself. Climb moderate to steep snow for about 800 vertical feet to a sudden transition to perfectly flat ground at the Alpine Garden.

Once you reach the Alpine Garden, you have two basic choices: try for the summit or bail out and head down. If you still have time (for most folks, this means it is no later than 1:00 P.M.), you still have gas (your butt is not dragging), and weather conditions are good and projected to stay good (reasonable visibility, no approaching storms, low winds), then a summit attempt is not unreasonable. If the route is out of condition, you may be able to make an ascent of the mountain by climbing up the winter Lion Head Trail—the normal descent route for this climb (see below). But if you answer "no" to any one of the conditions listed above, the prudent climber will call it a day.

Assuming all is well, head west toward the southeast slope of the summit cone and then turn northwest to the landmark "Split Rock." Now head straight north from Split Rock, following cairns on the upper stretch of the Tuckerman Ravine Trail to the summit. The summit cone can seem endless.

Descent: Retrace your climb down past Split Rock and across the Alpine Garden to the top of Right Gully. You are on the Lion Head Trail at this point (although in the winter it is almost impossible to tell); continue east on level ground to the rocky promontory of Lion Head itself and then drop down, following the trail, to the junction with the Lion Head summer trail. If the summer trail is still open (till mid-December most seasons), take that back down to Hermit Lake. If not, bear left (northeast) and follow the Lion Head winter trail down steeply to the junction with the Huntington Ravine Fire Road, turn right for just a couple hundred yards, and then turn left on the Tuckerman Ravine Trail and head back down to Pinkham Notch.

87. Pinnacle Buttress   III, 5.8

On many a sweltering day while I am padding up the blistering slabs of Whitehorse Ledge, my thoughts often run north 20 miles and up 3,000 feet to the soaring arêtes and corners in Huntington Ravine on Mount Washington. The air is crisp, maybe

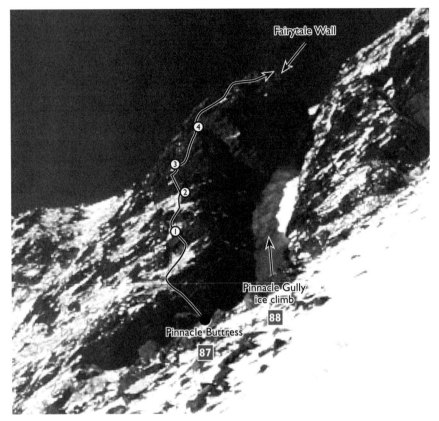

Pinnacle Buttress on Mount Washington. Photo by S. Peter Lewis

even cold, the wind is whispering, the clouds and mist are curling about the walls—sometimes overhead, sometimes underfoot—and they occasionally spit ice pellets that bounce off the lichen-speckled granite.

In the hike up to the Pinnacle Buttress, you pass through the northern hardwood forest, quickly dash through the spruce-fir zone, and soon find yourself roping up where the last of the dwarfed, twisted spruces (called "krummholz") cling to the thin soil. When you top out into the Alpine Garden, you are in the subartic zone, where lichen and tiny alpine plants fight the wind just like their cousins thousands of miles to the north.

If the day is fine, the sun shines and the wind keeps the blackflies at bay as you stem up the corners and reach for the quartz and feldspar holds on the spine of the Pinnacle. Above the short cruxes, high on the ridge, if you are lucky, you will find the hidden traverse that leads around to the right and onto a smooth green face with a crack shooting sideways across it. This fairytale face hangs in the sky, undercut below by the black gash of Pinnacle Gully, with nothing above but sky. As you tiptoe across the wall, with the hiss of the slapping waterfall echoing off the walls, dawdle, take your time, and occasionally just close your eyes and listen—this is a wondrous place indeed.

First ascent: William P. Allis and Robert Underhill with Dana Durand, Kenneth A. Henderson, and Jessie M. Whitehead, October 14, 1928.

Equipment: A modest rack to 3 inches plus a lot of slings; two ropes (in case bad weather forces you down—it can snow here in July); fleece jacket, hat, gloves, rain shell, headlamp, food and water, a map and compass (know how to use them).

Start: From directly behind the AMC visitor center, follow the Tuckerman Ravine Trail for 2 miles to the Huntington Ravine Fire Road; bear right and follow the fire road for about another mile to the base of Huntington Ravine. Continue on the Huntington Ravine Trail up the bowl of the ravine until you reach the base of the headwall proper. The deeply notched Pinnacle Gully (climb 88), and its accompanying waterfall, are on the left; Pinnacle Buttress is the obvious ridge that forms the left (south) wall of the gully. Step across the waterfall and belay at the base of the obvious left-trending ramp/groove. Most parties take 2–2½ hours to reach the base by hiking from Pinkham Notch.

An alternate approach and descent involves driving up the Mount Washington Auto Road to the 7-mile marker. From here, hike southeast on the Huntington Ravine Trail, cross the Nelson Crag Trail, and continue to the junction with the Alpine Garden Trail, where there is a huge cairn (this takes less than 10 minutes). Now continue on the Huntington Ravine Trail down the headwall of the ravine to the base of the route (the trail down the headwall is *very* steep in places). Though much shorter (45 minutes), this approach is not nearly as sporting.

Pinnacle Buttress is the obvious ridge on the left. Photo by S. Peter Lewis

Route: Pitch 1 (160 feet, 5.5): Follow the obvious, left-leaning ramp/groove (5.2) to a grassy ledge, then head up and right to a left-facing corner (5.5) and ledges above.

Pitch 2 (100 feet, 4th class): Scramble up and slightly left on bushy terraces to a ledge below a steep corner.

Pitch 3 (100 feet, 5.8): Lieback up a right-facing corner, the "Laundry Chute," with a crack on its left wall (piton) to a ledge. Continue up the short, steep wall above past fixed gear to a hard move over an overhang and belay at the crest of the wall above.

Pitches 4–6 (350 feet, 5.2–5.6): Follow the ridge crest as closely as you can over ledges and the occasional steep wall. There are many variations. For a great adventure, keep poking your head around to the right where an incredibly exposed traverse across the Fairytale Wall (5.5; great gear) rewards you with one of the most spectacular positions east of the Rockies.

Descent: From the top of the buttress, bushwhack straight up for several hundred feet to reach the flat Alpine Garden. Hike west about 200 feet to the Alpine Garden Trail, then bear left (south) and hike to the junction with the Lion Head Trail, then bear left (east) and follow that trail steeply downhill to the junction with the Tuckerman Ravine Trail. Turn left (northeast) and follow it back down to Pinkham Notch. This return, like the approach, takes 2–2½ hours.

For the return to the Mount Washington Auto Road, from the top of the climb bushwhack straight up for several hundred feet to the Alpine Garden. Hike west about 200 feet to the Alpine Garden Trail, then bear right (north) and hike to the junction with the Huntington Ravine Trail at the huge cairn. Turn left (northwest) and follow the Huntington Ravine Trail back to the 7-mile mark on the road. This return takes 20–40 minutes.

88. Pinnacle Gully   III, WI 3

Pinnacle Gully is the quintessential mountain route in New Hampshire, and it is fitting that it has been drawing mountaineers for more than seventy years. Robert Underhill and Lincoln O'Brien first attempted the climb in 1929, getting up the crux pitch and sparking interest from the best climbers of the era. As recounted by Laura and Guy Waterman in *Yankee Rock and Ice,* Underhill called it "incomparably the most difficult and dangerous winter or spring climb in the White Mountains." With the likes of Brad Washburn, Ad Carter, Bob Bates, and Charles Houston coveting the first ascent, an unlikely pair—Samuel Scoville and Julian Whittlesey ("we were both novices")—simply walked into Huntington Ravine in February 1930 and did it. When the first ascent was made in their step-cutting epic, it was among the most difficult climbs in the country. Fifty years after the first ascent, when asked if it was the hardest climb he had ever done, Whittlesey answered, "It was the only one."

In 1970, when Jim McCarthy, Bill Putnam, Rick Wilcox, Rob Wallace, and Carl Brandon "walked up into Huntington Ravine and marched straight up Pinnacle Gully without chopping a single step," as noted in *Yankee Rock and Ice,* the ice revolution that Yvon Chouinard had started the previous year in the Adirondacks went into full swing. This route has been, and will continue to be, a measuring stick for many climbers regardless of their generation, and a successful ascent of Pinnacle Gully is still coveted.

I coveted the route myself back in the early 1980s, so it was with great excitement

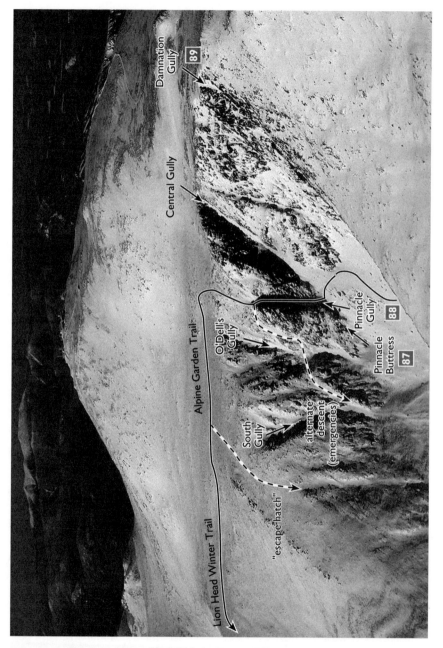

Huntington Ravine on New Hampshire's Mount Washington. Photo by S. Peter Lewis

(and some trepidation) that I hit the trail with my dear friend Ray one January morning long before first light. This was a big deal, and I felt as if we were marching directly into the opened jaws of frozen death. The first pitch went slowly as we hacked our way up the bulges with our straight-shafted tools and kicked repeatedly with our leather boots and hinged crampons. The rest of the climb was easier because it was mostly snow, and we kept the scratching and sparking to a minimum. We bashed our way to the Alpine Garden and, with little light left, decided to saunter down the snow gully of the Escape Hatch and return home as conquerors.

Well . . . it had been a lean snow year. The gully was just a tangle of head-high brush. After falling over for the fiftieth time, I started crying. Things ripped. It got dark. At the bottom, I fell into a stream up to my waist. It got darker. We stumbled down the trail. Ray carried my stuff. I fell asleep in the snow outside the Harvard Cabin. I vaguely remember Ray kicking me in the butt repeatedly. My next clear memory is waking up late the next morning face down on the floor of my living room, in a puddle of drool, fully clothed including harness, boots, and crampons. A conqueror indeed.

First ascent: Samuel Scoville and Julian Whittlesey, February 8, 1930.

Special considerations: Avalanche danger is rarely a problem. This route is dangerous when crowded (falling ice funnels right down the gully).

Equipment: 60-m rope (to do the route in three stretched pitches).

Start: From directly behind the AMC visitor center, follow the Tuckerman Ravine Trail for 2 miles to the Huntington Ravine Fire Road; bear right and follow the fire road for about another mile to the base of Huntington Ravine. Continue on the Huntington Ravine Trail up the bowl of the ravine until you reach the base of the headwall proper. The deeply notched Pinnacle Gully and its accompanying waterfall are on the left; Pinnacle Buttress (climb 87) is the obvious ridge that forms the left (south) wall of the gully. When the trail is well packed, the approach usually takes 2–3 hours. If not packed . . . well, just make sure you are not first on the trail after a big storm. The climb ascends the obvious dark slot to the left of Central Gully.

Route: Pitch 1 (150 feet, WI 3): The crux pitch. Begin on the left side of the gully and traverse up and right over a series of bulges and belay above the top of the swell.

Pitch 2 (150 feet, WI 2): Follow the center of the gully, often snow, to a stance below the next bulge.

Pitch 3 (150 feet, WI 2+): Climb moderate bulges for another rope length.

Pitch 4 (150 feet, WI 2): One more pitch of moderate ice and snow leads to the top of the Pinnacle.

Descent: From the top of the buttress, bushwhack straight up for several hundred feet of steep, brushy hillside (may require belays under certain conditions) to the flat Alpine Garden. Bear left (south) on the Alpine Garden Trail and hike to the junction with the Lion Head Winter Trail, then bear left (east) and follow that trail steeply downhill to the junction with the Huntington Fire Road. Bear right for several hundred feet, then turn left (northeast) on the Tuckerman Ravine Trail and follow it back down to Pinkham Notch.

There are two alternate descents. From the very top of the route, you can head left and down along the steep, brushy south side of Pinnacle Buttress, eventually crossing Odell's Gully (the next gully left of Pinnacle Gully looking up) and then traversing left to South Gully and descending its lower reaches. This is often a nasty and technically dangerous option.

The second descent option, and the fastest when there is a deep snowpack, is to climb to the Alpine Garden and then traverse left (south) along the south rim of the ravine until you come to the top of a broad snow gully, the "escape hatch," which can be glissaded back to the floor of the ravine. The escape hatch can be tough to find in bad weather and is a terrible option if there is little snow.

89. Damnation Gully   II, WI 3
"Nelson Crag Gully," as Damnation was once referred to, is the longest climb in Huntington Ravine. Unlike nearby Pinnacle Gully (climb 88), which is narrow, dark, and brooding and ends with 300 feet of brushy wallowing, Damnation is open, basks in the sun most of the day, and ends crisply at the very brow of the north wall of the ravine. Sometimes it even boasts a jaunty little cornice.

Damnation Gully in Mount Washington's Huntington Ravine. Photo by David Stone

The first people in this gully, legendary climbers Robert Underhill and Lincoln O'Brien, climbed 985 of the gully's 1,000 feet but never got proper credit for it. It was late in the winter of 1929 and the pair had hiked into Huntington in hopes of being the first ever up Pinnacle Gully. After chopping steps for 2 hours on the first pitch (the crux), they found themselves on a shelf under the brooding roof of the overhanging ridge. Though they were past the major difficulties, what lay above was still unknown to the world. They looked up, looked back at their watches, and headed down.

But they did not go all the way down. They traversed north and started up a sinuous line of ice and snow up the north wall of the ravine. Moderate ice led to steep snow, then a steep ice wall. They skirted right, then back left above the wall and continued up pitch after pitch of snow to the top. Remarkably, there was still time for the pair to "stroll" (Underhill's word in Laura and Guy Waterman's account) to the summit. On that one day, Underhill and O'Brien had climbed the hardest pitch on Pinnacle Gully and 96 percent of Damnation Gully—yet they were not credited for the first ascent of either climb. Still, a good day in the ravine.

First ascent: Robert Underhill and Lincoln O'Brien (all but crux 15-foot bulge), 1929; Andrew Kaufman and William Putnam (complete ascent), 1943.

Special considerations: The standard descent for Damnation includes traversing the desolate Alpine Garden; in bad weather be prepared to navigate with map and compass and to rappel the route and leave gear. The route can have high avalanche danger.

Start: From directly behind the AMC visitor center, follow the Tuckerman Ravine Trail for 2 miles to the Huntington Ravine Fire Road; bear right and follow the fire road for about another mile to the base of Huntington Ravine. Continue on the Huntington Ravine Trail up the bowl of the ravine until you reach the base of the headwall proper.

Route (1,000 feet, WI 3): From the base of the ravine, head up the talus slope (the Fan) toward the big Central Gully (the obvious right-diagonalling snow gully in the center of the ravine), then cut right for about 500 feet to the base of the second gully in from the right. A lot of snow and that one steep bulge lead for many pitches to the top. Be aware of the possibility of a cornice and wind-slab conditions near the top—this gully has avalanched with people in it.

Descent: Traverse the rim of the ravine west and then south until you are above the top-out for Pinnacle Gully (climb 88). Follow the descent options for that route.

PART V
MAINE ────────────────────

Opposite: *Tyler Stableford topping out on Mount Katahdin's classic alpine rock route the Armadillo.* Photo by Peter Cole

255

I f all of the United States except Maine were as flat as Kansas, climbers would still be happy. While Maine is not host to a marquee climbing area like the Gunks in New York or Mount Washington Valley in New Hampshire, Maine's mountains and forests and rocky coast have tucked into them places that deserve more than just cameo recognition. If Maine were the only place to climb in the country, you would still find cutting-edge sport routes, scores of traditional climbing crags with routes up to five pitches long, and winter ice climbs and alpine routes to rival anything else in the Northeast.

Maine is the third most rural state in the nation, and its crags and mountains are spread out in an area almost as big as the rest of New England combined. Climbing here means solitude, long scenic drives, some arduous approaches (as well as some just minutes long), sometimes scarce amenities, the occasional moose, and absolutely no "scene."

For this book, we focus on Maine's two unique contributions to the Northeast climbing experience: the incredible alpine climbing on Mount Katahdin and the coastal granite crags of Acadia National Park. The routes in these areas run the gamut from 5.5 to 5.13, from warm granite to brittle ice, from 50 feet high to 2,000 feet, and from the crown of the Appalachian Mountains—Mount Katahdin—to the only sea-cliff climbing in the country.

But be assured that these routes will give you only a taste of what can be found here. Much of Maine's diverse climbing information is tucked between the ears of the state's few local climbers. You are likely to run into some of them as you climb the routes here and, being a friendly lot, they should be happy to direct you to other places where you can enjoy brilliant climbing in the wilds of Maine.

CHAPTER 9. MOUNT KATAHDIN _____

Climbing type ▲ Rock, alpine/ice
Rock type ▲ Granite
Elevation ▲ Base, 2,914 feet; summit, 5,267 feet
Number of routes ▲ 6 in this book

This mountain is in the wrong place—it really belongs in Alaska. Poking its ridges and gullies almost a mile above the surrounding forest, this great granite massif was called Katahdin, "the Greatest Mountain," by the original people of the region. And great it is.

In a sea of trees that extend in unbroken waves as far as the eye can see, Katahdin is a great break in the landscape of Maine's North Woods, a mountain that appears out of nowhere without foothills or rivals. Though almost 1,000 feet lower than its more famous cousin in New Hampshire, Mount Washington, Katahdin is by far the less polished. It is steeper, more jagged, more deeply cleaved by glaciers, and far more barren, and its famous "Knife Edge" is narrower and more precipitous than most similarly named features in the Rockies.

Katahdin's remoteness and inaccessibility are partly responsible for its charm. While hundreds of people may be found on the flanks of Mount Washington on a late winter day, Katahdin may have only a handful of brave souls, or maybe none at all, struggling up its flanks. This is a place you can really feel (and be) alone.

It should come as no surprise, given its geology and remoteness, that Katahdin is the home of the longest, most difficult, most serious climbs in the Northeast. Soaring ridges, steep gullies, and flying buttresses, some 2,000 feet high, are found on all sides of this mountain that is webbed with dozens of technical climbs.

Picking just a handful of plums for this book was no easy task. In the end we chose two rock climbs (one that also makes a wonderful winter mixed route) and four alpine/ice climbs. Climb these routes, and you will have no questions about why this is the best alpine playground in the East.

Special Considerations

Mount Katahdin is in Baxter State Park; travel and climbing here are highly regulated—especially in winter.

In summer, day users must register at a park entrance station, and camping is by reservation only (you should call *months* in advance). Summer climbing trips can be done in 2 days or so. Day use is regulated by parking areas' vehicle capacity. During peak summer season, the park often fills for day use—get to a park entrance early. Climbing or mountain hiking may be restricted at the discretion of the park director. Park users must be reasonably well prepared and equipped, and must take reasonable precautions against endangering themselves or others. Hikers must wear appropriate footwear and clothing and must carry a working flashlight. No children under the age of six years are allowed above timberline.

Winter climbers must apply to the park well in advance, meet strict requirements about group size and experience, and bring an extensive list of required equipment. Before planning a trip to Katahdin, contact the park (207-723-5149; *www.baxterstateparkauthority.com*). A trip to Katahdin is a small expedition and climbing here is serious, so you must be prepared in every way. Because of the extensive ski-in approach, most winter climbers spend at least several days to a week at Chimney Pond. The bunkhouse at Chimney Pond can accommodate twelve people—but space is limited, so be prepared to camp.

Emergency Information

Call local police and fire departments (911) or the Maine State Police (*77), who will in turn contact the proper authorities at Baxter State Park. Self-rescue capabilities are critical here—response time by a trained rescue team is many hours to a day away.

Note: Cell phone reliability on the mountain is based primarily on location—up high works fairly consistently; down low does not. Ask park officials at Abol Bridge or Roaring Brook ranger stations about other emergency contact options.

Weather and Seasons

Summer: May through September; winter: December through March.

Standard Equipment

Winter climbs: six to ten ice screws, a light rock rack, several pitons, a lot of slings, two 60-meter ropes; a good four-season tent; sleeping bag rated to at least minus 20

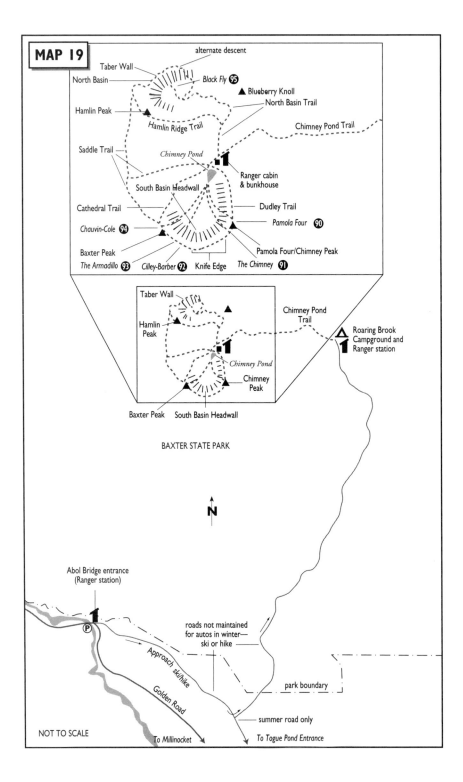

MAP 19

alternate descent

Taber Wall

North Basin

Black Fly **95**

▲ Blueberry Knoll

North Basin Trail

Hamlin Peak

Chimney Pond Trail

Hamlin Ridge Trail

Saddle Trail

Chimney Pond

Ranger cabin
& bunkhouse

South Basin Headwall

Cathedral Trail

Dudley Trail

Chauvin-Cole **94**

Pamola Four **90**

Baxter Peak

Pamola Four/Chimney Peak

The Armadillo **93**   *Cilley-Barber* **92**   Knife Edge   *The Chimney* **91**

Taber Wall

▲

Chimney Pond
Trail

Hamlin
Peak

△🏠 Roaring Brook
Campground and
Ranger station

🏠

Chimney Pond

Chimney
Peak

Baxter Peak   South Basin Headwall

BAXTER STATE PARK

N

Abol Bridge entrance
(Ranger station)

🏠

Ⓟ

roads not maintained
for autos in winter—
ski or hike

Approach ski/hike

park boundary

Golden Road

summer road only

NOT TO SCALE

To Millinocket   To Togue Pond Entrance

degrees F; clothing for arctic conditions, including goggles and face mask; headlamp, compass, first-aid kit, avalanche beacons, other winter survival gear for a long winter camping trip; sleds for the ski in.

Rock-climbing: Helmets required; also see each climb description's Equipment paragraph.

Getting There

Katahdin is way out in the boonies, about a 6-hour drive from the southwestern tip of Maine. Take Interstate 95 north up through the center of the state until about an hour past Bangor. Take exit 56 at Medway and then follow Route 157/11 west to the mill town of Millinocket (the last place to buy supplies); you must check in before your climb, and you can do that at the park headquarters in Millinocket.

Winter access: From Millinocket follow the winter road northwest to Baxter State Park (it is well marked) for another 20 miles or to Abol Bridge ranger station, the winter access point for Katahdin.

Summer access: From Millinocket follow the road northwest to Baxter State Park's Togue Pond entrance, 2–3 miles before (southeast of) Abol Bridge, and continue to Roaring Brook Campground.

Approach

In the winter, from Abol Bridge it is at least a 12-mile ski to Roaring Brook Campground. Check in before your climb at Roaring Brook ranger station if you did not do so in Millinocket. You will also go through an equipment check at Roaring Brook.

From Roaring Brook Campground, lug your stuff up the 3.5-mile trail to Chimney Pond, where there is a bunkhouse and tent camping nearby. The latest condition reports and route updates are also available here—check with the ranger.

South Basin Headwall: From Chimney Pond (summer or winter), walk directly south to the north side of the headwall to reach the base of the headwall.

North Basin: From Chimney Pond, hike, ski, or snowshoe 0.2 mile back toward Roaring Brook Campground to the North Basin Trail. Head north on the North Basin Trail, passing the Hamlin Ridge Trail on the left, and proceed to Blueberry Knoll. Take the trail to Blueberry Knoll. Just before reaching the knoll, take a left and bushwhack into the North Basin.

90. Pamola Four   III, 5.5–5.9 (summer) or 5.5–5.8 WI 2+ (winter)

Gazing south from Chimney Pond, you cannot miss the ridge of Pamola Four. It stands silhouetted against the sky as an almost 2,000-foot crest of granite that reaches within throwing distance of the 4,902-foot summit of Pamola Peak (also called Chimney Peak on maps). And if the light is right and your timing is good, you can even watch climbers work their way up the ridge—a tantalizing lure that you may not be able to resist. The rock is quite good (though this is an alpine peak that constantly shrugs its shoulders) and the route is clean all the way up to the ridge on Pamola, where a quick hike south puts you on the summit of Katahdin.

While many of the classic climbs in this book can be done as summer or winter routes, perhaps none offer as splendid a mixed bag as the grand ridge on Pamola Four, the route known early on as "Cook's Climb." In summer the route offers a pleasant romp up slabs, cracks, and corners on one of the longest ridge climbs in the East. The days are long, you can take your time, the rock is dry and warm, and your pack is light with just the bare essentials for a day in the mountains.

In February the route becomes one of the best alpine adventures in the East. You start early because the days are short and you must move fast. The rock is cold, the cracks are often choked with winter's detritus, and the ledges are packed with snow. Your pack is still fairly light (because you are wearing most of your clothes) and the day is scrappy with a hand jam one minute, a tool placement the next, and often the scratching of crampons on rough granite. Pamola Four is a route to savor no matter what the season.

First ascent: Unknown, although undoubtedly done in 1920s or 1930s; first winter ascent: Landon Fake and Kevin Slater, February 1986.

Equipment: Summer, a light rack of gear up to 3 inches and plenty of slings; winter, add a handful of ice screws.

Start: This route climbs the ridge seen in profile from Chimney Pond. Hike across Chimney Pond to the base of the headwall and then head right (to the base of the buttress for the variation given below) to the base of the Chimney.

Route (about 1,500 feet, 5.5–5.9 summer or 5.5–5.8 WI 2+ winter): From the base of the Chimney, climb a buttress on the left. (*Variation:* Starting at the base of the

Maine's Baxter State Park. Photo by Brian Post

buttress itself, down around and left from the Chimney, and climbing a green slab gives several alternate pitches.) From either start, climb to the crest of the ridge. Now follow the ridge for a half dozen or more pitches, weaving back and forth to either increase or decrease difficulty (in winter, most people look to decrease the difficulty).

Descent: From the summit of Pamola Peak, take the Dudley Trail back down to Chimney Pond. This is an exposed hike that can be difficult in bad weather.

91. The Chimney   II, WI 2

A century ago, when alpinism was in its infancy in this country, mountains were traditionally climbed via their most obvious weaknesses—gullies and ridges. If ever there was an obvious weakness on a mountain, it is Katahdin's Chimney. More a gully than a chimney, this route slashes up the west flank of Pamola Peak from just above Chimney Pond to the crest of the Knife Edge just a couple hundred feet shy of the summit.

The first ascent of this route was led by Willard Helburn in 1923, although the route had been done as a summer rock climb some years earlier. Laura and Guy Waterman note in *Yankee Rock and Ice* that, in a 1916 Boston newspaper account, journalist Allen Chamberlain wrote, "And as for stunts to satisfy the nerviest of climbers there are enough and to spare on the walls of Chimney Pond basin itself, including the ascent of the Pamola chimney, in the climbing of which one may readily imperil his neck and all his limbs at one and the same time." Forty years later, when alpinism was in full swing in this country and much harder routes were being climbed, the Chimney still had its devotees—many now viewing it as a great winter training route.

Regarding the climbing clubs, organizations, and college groups of the 1950s and 1960s, the Watermans tell us in *Yankee Rock and Ice* that "every once in a while a party from one of these various coteries would make the long trip north and climb Katahdin's snow-filled chimney, thereby acquiring great prestige in winter climbing circles." If you climb the Chimney today, you will likely not risk much in the way of life and limb, and a successful ascent will certainly not bring you much "prestige." Nevertheless, this unmistakable line, with its great length, beauty, and rich history, still beckons.

First winter ascent: Willard Helburn, Henry Chamberlain, Roger Holden, Owen Kennedy, Margaret Helburn, Jesse Dow, and Margaret Whipple, March 1923.

Special considerations: Large slab avalanches are not uncommon here and the Chimney provides a perfect funnel—avoid this climb whenever evidence points to unacceptable risk.

Equipment: A very light rack of screws and rock protection.

Start: Hike across Chimney Pond to the South Basin Headwall and then head right, passing Pamola Peak; the bottom of the Chimney is obvious after several hundred yards.

Route (about 2,000 feet, WI 2): Since this climb is mostly steep snow, it does not break naturally down into pitches. Many pitches of snow lead up the gully, under and around chockstones, and through the "Eye of the Needle" for added spice. The route is not technically difficult and can be climbed using the techniques of

Katrina Yeager and Larry Robjent on Katahdin's Chimney route, as classic today as it was in 1928. Photo by Brian Post

moving together, short pitching, and short roping. At the top of the gully, head left for several hundred feet to the summit of Pamola Peak.

Descent: Take the Dudley Trail back down to Chimney Pond. This is an exposed hike that can be difficult in bad weather. If route conditions allow, you can down-climb and glissade the gully itself.

92. Cilley-Barber Route   IV, WI 4

In 1973 you could easily count the number of technical winter climbs at Katahdin on one hand—and none of those climbs were hard. This was long before the use of bent-shafted ice tools, screws you can put in with one hand, plastic boots, and the rigid crampons that snap on to them. Dave Cilley and Henry Barber hoofed the 12 miles into Chimney Pond, spied the perfect line up nearly 2,000 feet of Katahdin's steep South Basin Headwall, and went for it.

"We knew we had to go fast and light," Barber said, telling me about the ascent almost thirty years later—and this was years before "fast and light" became an alpine

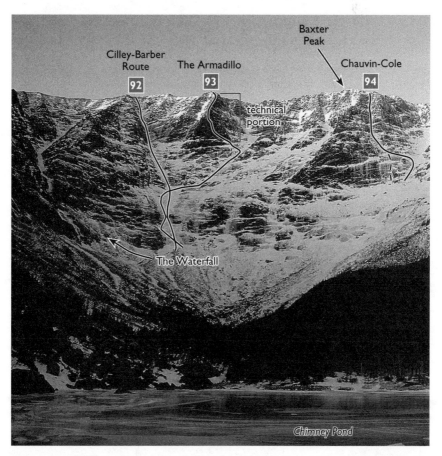

Mount Katahdin's South Basin headwall above Chimney Pond. Photo by Brian Post

climbing mantra. They wore all their clothes and took one rope, one pack, and no wrist loops. Above the 3-inch-thick crux bulge, Barber found poor ice. "I drove my ax and alpine hammer into the turf" and called it a belay, Barber said.

Cilley, who did not know the precarious nature of the anchor, slipped on the crux and according to Barber "went winging into space, zipping across a roof." The fall yanked Barber off his stance and the load came onto the two poorly placed tools. Barber's long ax, pounded in shaft first, tore most of the way out, but held. Barber

The Cilley-Barber route is one of the most coveted long routes on Maine's Mount Katahdin. Photo by Brian Post

dug in his heels and hauled. "That was pretty exciting," he said with a chuckle.

Today if you want excitement, we suggest you just climb this incredible route, one of the most coveted hard routes at Katahdin, and skip the aerial drama.

First ascent: Henry Barber and Dave Cilley, February 1973.

Special considerations: This is a very long route with variable difficulties. Move very quickly on the easier terrain via simul-climbing, short pitching, or short roping and save the 5th-class belays for the steep ice sections. Speed is essential. The route can have significant avalanche danger.

Start: Hike across Chimney Pond to the headwall and head right to the bottom of the climb, which is very obvious: on the right side of the big buttress to the right of the Waterfall.

Route Pitches 1–12 (2,000 feet, steep snow, ice up to WI 4): Experience and conditions will determine how you break this climb up into pitches. Climb an obvious break on the left side of the lower cliff band for two pitches, then climb steep snow for several hundred feet and a series of steep ice bulges to reach a right-facing corner. Climb the steep ice in the corner and continue either to the left or straight up, eventually reaching the summit ridge. The crux ice lead does not always form, but do not let that deter you—it is a fine mixed pitch.

Descent: On a very good day you can head left (southeast) to Pamola Peak and then descend the Dudley Trail—this is a scrappy, semitechnical descent.

An easier and less technical descent is to head right (northwest) to the very top of Katahdin at Baxter Peak (15–20 minutes in good weather) and descend the Saddle Trail.

93. The Armadillo   IV, 5.7–5.9

The route up the huge buttress of the Armadillo is the most spectacular alpine rock climb in this book. The buttress is a great triangular sentinel high on the South Basin Headwall almost 2,000 feet above Chimney Pond, and the base of the route lies at 4,700 feet—a point even with the *summit* of Maine's second-highest mountain, nearby Hamlin Peak. Poking its head into the clouds way above Chimney Pond, the Armadillo looks mysterious. And it is not just looks; this big granite thing *is* mysterious.

The first ascent of this route is hidden in the misty past. While the formation of the Armadillo was first climbed by a party of five led by Herbert (Hec) Towle in 1935, no one is quite sure what route they took. In 1954 two variations went up, both likely about 5.6; one was led by Bob Kruszyna and the other by John Reppy. The standard route described here was likely first climbed around 1950, but no one is certain who did it. Northeast historians Laura and Guy Waterman recount in *Yankee Rock and Ice* that they set out with friends in the summer of 1985 to chase the "ghosts of earlier giants up cracks and chimneys on the Northeast's most spectacular rock wall." Their goal was to explore the various routes up the buttress and, specifically, to repeat the 1935 ascent based on a six-sentence written description.

After "two and a half hours of bushwhacking through dew-laden brush" and up rock slabs, they climbed one chimney pitch and then traversed 80 feet to the north. "We had already used up almost five sentences of the six-sentence paragraph," they muse in their classic climbing history book. Following their noses, they poked

The climbing route on Katahdin's Armadillo. Photo by Peter Cole

around, occasionally finding an old piton along the way. High on the climb, they finally determined that they were at the junction of the three earliest routes on the mountain: the 1935 route and the two 1954 routes.

Try as they might to stay on the 1935 line, they soon found themselves off route again on harder "although most pleasant" terrain. "The remaining three or four pitches of class 4 and 5 climbing along one of the most alpine ridges in the East, the party agreed, offered as classic a ridge as anyone would find in the Tetons or Cascades. It was a delightful situation: high in a glacial cirque surrounded by other steep ridges and gulleys hundreds of feet below on either side, overlooking sparkling Chimney Pond." Alas, the 1935 route was nowhere to be seen—oh, the joys of being off route.

First ascent: Herbert (Hec) Towle (with four others), 1935; Bob Kruszyna (variation), 1954; John Reppy (variation), 1954; standard route: unknown.

Special considerations: The approach is very long and semitechnical, including more than 1,500 vertical feet of (often wet) slabs, bushes, drainages, ledge systems (including dead ends), and loose rock. Be prepared to move quickly and safely on sketchy 3rd-class terrain. This is a long mountain route complete with all the alpine hazards of rockfall, bad weather, exposure, loose rock, and tough routefinding. Do not be lulled into complacency by the climb's modest technical rating (expect runouts on easier terrain and in chimneys).

Equipment: A medium-sized rack of stoppers and cams, including a couple to 4 inches; helmets.

Start: Hike across Chimney Pond to the South Basin Headwall and then head right to ascend the steep slopes below and left of the bottom of an obvious drainage that runs the length of the headwall—this is the line of the Cilley-Barber Route (climb 92). Take the line of least resistance (often following the beginning of the Cilley-Barber Route) for several hundred feet and then head right across low-angled terrain, then bear up and right, aiming for the depression that is to the right of and above the Armadillo. The exact line you take on this approach depends on conditions, weather, visibility, and your routefinding skills. The complicated approach gains 1,500 feet in elevation—you may be able to zoom up there in just over an hour, or it may take three. Study the photo carefully. When nearly level with the base of the huge triangular flake that leans against the wall of the Armadillo, traverse left along ledges to the start of the route.

Route: Due to the alpine nature of this route, there are many belay options and variations along the way, so a pitch-by-pitch description is not helpful. If you have successfully navigated the complex approach to this route, you are now on the right side of the base of the Armadillo buttress.

Chimney pitches (130 feet, 5.5–5.7): On the front of the buttress, at its base, lies a huge detached flake with a chimney crack on each side. Move up and left on a grassy ledge (tricky; consider roping up) to the base of the wide chimney on the flake's right side. Boulder up (pin) to a ledge and then left (old pin) and enter the chimney proper. Stem, jam, and wedge yourself up the chimney for 100 feet (5.5) and then make a choice: continue up the chimney for another 30 feet to a belay or move left onto the front face of the detached flake and make harder moves (5.7) up to the belay.

Left-Side Variation (80 feet, 5.8): According to longtime Katahdin climber Bob Baribeau, "occasionally someone climbs the left side of the flake . . . *solid* 5.8 off-width, hard, not easy to protect . . . with the occasional loose flake." This brings you to the base of the 4- to 6-inch crack above the chimney.

Wind in the Willows Variation (80 feet, 5.9): To the left of the 5.8 off-width of the

Tyler Stableford leading the Wind in the Willows variation on the Armadillo.
Photo by Peter Cole

Left-Side Variation, a right-arching finger crack climbs steeply to a junction with the off-width crack, which is then followed to the top of the flake. Highly recommended.

Crack pitches (180 feet, 5.6–5.7): Climb the obvious 4- to 6-inch crack (5.7; perfect for winter toe jams in plastic boots) to a great ledge (potential belay). Now move slightly left, then back right again, stemming and jamming (5.6) to the very spine of the Armadillo. Most parties climb the crack in two pitches.

Vertebrae pitches (450 feet, 4th–5th class): Take the line of most pleasant resistance along the vertebrae of the Armadillo (mostly 4th-class climbing with the occasional 5th-class move sprinkled in) until you come out on top of the Knife Edge, the ridge between Baxter and Pamola Peaks. The summit of Katahdin at Baxter Peak is just 15 minutes away to the right (northwest).

Descent: Hike the Knife Edge south (left, looking up from the Armadillo) to Pamola Peak and then take the Dudley Trail back down to Chimney Pond.

Alternatively, you can hike north to the summit of Baxter Peak and then down the Cathedral Trail or the Saddle Trail.

94. Chauvin-Cole   III, WI 3+ M2

Alpine starts are overrated. Sure, getting up at midnight may be the key to getting you to the summit on a new route—but not always. In the winter of 1982, longtime Northeast climbers Peter Cole and Marc Chauvin were among the climbers hunkered down at Chimney Pond waiting for a storm to clear. Rain and sleet had whipped in the night before and the trails and climbing routes had taken a beating.

At ten o'clock the following morning, Cole and Chauvin were hanging around the

Route detail of the Chauvin-Cole route on Katahdin. Photo by Brian Post

cabin when one of them looked out and saw blue. "Peter had been intrigued by a line on the South Basin Headwall," Chauvin told me twenty years later. "It topped out right at the summit." And when Cole saw the sky clearing, he said just two words: "Let's go."

Moving quickly, the pair climbed more than 1,000 feet of low-angled ground to reach the steep snow at the base of a prominent headwall. The snow was perfect for cramponing (one benefit of the previous night's rain) so they continued up the lower pitches of steep snow unroped and eventually traversed left to the base of the gully proper.

Just then, Chauvin realized that in his haste to get going he had forgotten his harness. But "it wasn't that long after swami belts," Chauvin said, "so it was no big deal. I just took a long sling and made a harness." For the next couple of hours Cole and Chauvin climbed pitch after pitch of steep snow with the occasional ice bulge thrown in for spice on this aesthetic route, and finally pulled over the top almost within spitting distance of the summit cairn.

The next day Chauvin took it easy and was hanging around the cabin when one of the rangers came in. Unable to get in the day before because of the previous storm, he was now concerned about another bout of bad weather that could wash out the trail. "You guys are going to have to leave, there's another storm coming," he said. "It's too bad you didn't get any climbing in," he added, consolingly. "Actually, we did a new route yesterday," Chauvin said with a grin. "You guys went climbing yester-day?" the ranger asked, his brow furrowing. (The weather had still been unstable, and leaving at ten in the morning is absolutely not allowed here.) "You wouldn't have gone out if I had been here," he said sternly. "Well, then it's a good thing that you weren't here," Chauvin said.

Or . . . at least he may have said it. "I remember thinking it, and I was young

Marc Chauvin on the first ascent of the Chauvin-Cole route on the South Basin headwall in 1982. Photo by Peter Cole

enough at the time that it's pretty likely I said it," Chauvin recalled with a chuckle. Having known Marc for more than twenty years, I'm betting he said it.

First ascent: Marc Chauvin and Peter Cole, 1982.

Start: Cross Chimney Pond and head right to the base of the awesome South Basin Headwall, passing the start of the Chimney (climb 91), until below the center of the headwall. To the right of the Armadillo buttress is a large basin high on the face with a very large buttress on its right side. In the center of this buttress is the obvious weakness of the Chauvin-Cole route. Climb low-angled ice and snow for many hundreds of feet up the so-called Shelf Route, a ramp that begins several hundred feet past the start of the Cilley-Barber Route (climb 92) and gives quick access to the right side of the South Basin Headwall.

Route: Pitches 1–8 (800–1,000 feet, steep snow, ice up to WI 3+, climbing to M2): Like many of Katahdin's classic alpine routes, the exact breakdown of pitches varies depending on the experience of the party, the conditions of the route, and the weather. Begin to the right of the buttress and climb up several pitches of steep snow and then traverse left to reach the main groove/gully in the center of the buttress. (A two-pitch direct start to the left of this start goes up the center of the buttress at WI 3+ M2.)

The route up the groove/gully varies in difficulty and terrain; under normal conditions, expect a lot of steep snow interspersed with sections of steep ice and mixed climbing. This is a sustained, long, and classic high mountain route that ends less than a rope length from the summit of Katahdin at Baxter Peak.

Descent: Take the Saddle Trail to the right (north) back down to Chimney Pond.

95. Black Fly   IV, WI 4+

Katahdin's North Basin in winter is about as far from anywhere as you can get in the Northeast. While the South Basin Headwall may be big and alpine, at least you can usually see Chimney Pond and are often within earshot of other climbers. The North Basin is located north of Chimney Pond on the other side of Hamlin Ridge, out of sight and rarely visited. If there was climbing on the moon, the North Basin would be on its dark side.

While many of the long, easy snow routes in the North Basin were climbed in the 1800s, the route we have included here, Black Fly and its variations, epitomizes adventure climbing at Katahdin, combining remoteness, difficulty, and variety in more than 1,000 feet of snow, ice, and granite.

The original line of Black Fly was climbed in the 1980s by Dave Getchel Jr. and Doug Carver; it was a landmark climb of its time—really "out there." After climbing the steep ice and snow of the lower portion of the route, Getchel and Carver skirted the upper wall to the left and finished up (relatively) easy mixed ground.

Bob Baribeau told me that, late in the decade, he and Kurt Winkler headed up with other plans. "Look at this thing over here," Baribeau said to Winkler, referring to a weakness in the wall directly above the lower section of Black Fly. "I've always wanted to do it. Let's straighten Black Fly out." Just right of the snowfield atop the lower gully, the pair found three pitches of stemming, 5.5–5.6 chimney moves, crack climbing, and dry tooling on slabs that led them right to a cairn on the crest of the ridge. Their line is now referred to as the Baribeau Direct Variation.

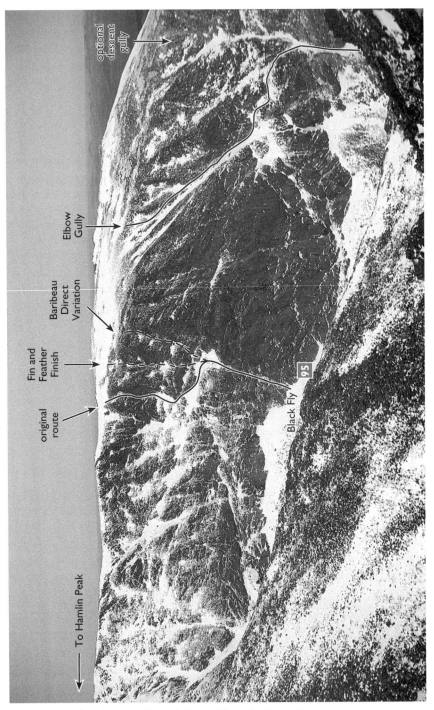

Mount Katahdin's less-visited North Basin. Photo by Brian Post

Another Baribeau variation, the Fin and Feather Finish, climbs out a cave on the left edge of the snowfield above the lower gully via "20 feet of very difficult underclinging with ice tools" and then climbs more straightforward ground for another 400 feet to the ridge. Heading over the day before the climb, Baribeau "stashed gear and scoped the route." Leaving the next morning at three o'clock, he remarked that "we could see the lights at the mill in Millinocket."

Whether you climb the original line of Black Fly or one of the newer variations, be prepared for a long, perhaps arduous, and certainly solitary adventure. And just

Bob Baribeau on the first ascent of the Baribeau Direct Variation to the classic Black Fly. Photo by Kurt Winkler

hope that you see the lights in Millinocket at the beginning of your day instead of the end, or you may be in trouble.

First ascent: Dave Getchel Jr. and Doug Carver, early 1980s; Kurt Winkler and Bob Baribeau (Baribeau Direct Variation), 1988; and Bob Baribeau and P. Marten (Fin and Feather Finish), 2002.

Special considerations: Climbing in the North Basin is very committing—even by Katahdin standards. The approaches and descents are lengthy. A high level of fitness and expertise, a very early start, and an excellent weather forecast give you the best chances of having an adventure instead of an epic.

Equipment: A generous rack of screws and rock gear; a double rope system is a good idea; be prepared for a very long day (and part of a night).

Start: The North Basin is dominated by the huge Taber Wall, perhaps the largest alpine cliff in the East. On its right side is an obvious 400-foot trough that runs with ice—start here.

Route: Pitches 1–10 (1,500+ feet, steep snow and sustained ice to WI 4+): Three pitches up the 400-foot ice trough (among the most sustained at Katahdin) bring you to a snowfield. The original route traverses left for several pitches along an obvious snow shelf and then shoots up another trough in the upper wall via mixed rock, ice, and snow. There are two variations.

Baribeau Direct Variation (600 feet, WI 4, 5.6): From the obvious snow shelf, this carries the lower line straight up the cliff via some great mixed terrain—mostly rock.

Fin and Feather Finish (600 feet, WI 4): This goes left a bit on the snow shelf to a difficult exit out a cave and then climbs straight up the wall. An ice-choked crack low down is the crux of this variation, and if you do not see ice from below, you may want to pass—it is reported to be a desperate mixed pitch when dry. Several pitches of ice and steep snow lead to the top.

Descent: Go left to the summit of Hamlin Peak, then make a short hike to the Saddle Trail, which then leads back to Chimney Pond (best option).

Or head right, passing Elbow Gully (a prominent snow gully on the far right side of the North Basin) to the next gully north, which can be down-climbed (or glissaded in good conditions) for 2,000 feet back to the base of the basin.

CHAPTER 10. ACADIA NATIONAL PARK ———

Climbing type ▲ Multipitch
Rock type ▲ Granite
Elevation ▲ 0–500 feet
Number of routes ▲ 9 in this book

Salty air, bald mountain summits, clear lakes, the crashing North Atlantic, seals, eagles, the only fjord on the American East Coast, and—for the rock climber—soaring pink granite faces, cracks, and corners. Though Acadia National Park is one of

Opposite: *Steve Nichipor and Alden Strong on Maine's seaside classic Morning Glory.*
Photo by S. Peter Lewis

the most visited places in the national park system, with more than 3 million visitors annually, most visitors stick to the typical tourist stops and rarely turn their engines off. If you walk just 5 minutes from the popular overlooks or a few feet off a trail, you will often find yourself alone with nothing but the smell of fir and the sound of distant surf and raucous seagulls.

The rock climbing at Acadia, though limited compared with many of the areas found in this book, makes up for lack of scale by its beauty and diversity. The granite is impeccable, tipped up at a comfortable angle (steep, but not too steep), fractured frequently into gear-eating cracks, and interspersed with nice, flat belay ledges. And to top it off, some of the crags literally hang over the churning sea.

Acadia climbing tradition has always been that the routes are more important than the names of the first-ascent party, so many of the area's classic first ascents are anonymous. Acadia climbers also eschew bolted routes.

Our romp across Acadia gives us a grand tour of the ratings and the settings as we travel from multipitch climbing on the big cliff (the Precipice) on Champlain Mountain to the overhanging (and intimidating) sea cliff at Great Head, where you can feel as if you are rappelling right into the perfect storm, to the top-rope crag of Otter Cliffs at the very edge of the restless sea.

Special Considerations

This is a national park; travel on the Loop Road, parking, and climbing are strictly regulated. Please park only where designated—in parking areas or in the right lane of the Loop Road where allowed (clearly marked).

Climbing at Otter Cliffs and especially at Great Head can be hampered, or even made dangerous, by high tides. Please consult a tide chart before climbing at these areas and give yourself plenty of time to get back to the top of the cliff. The ocean can be rough and people have been trapped by the rising tide. Trees cannot be used for top-rope anchors at Otter Cliffs (Park Service regulation) and should not be used at Great Head. The Park Service has provided stainless-steel staples as anchors (bomber) for some routes and bolts for others; for still others, you will have to build gear anchors.

Emergency Information

Call local police and fire departments (911) or Acadia National Park (207-299-3369).

Weather and Seasons

May through October; autumn months are particularly spectacular.

Standard Equipment

A standard selection of nuts, Tricams, and cams to 3 inches.

Getting There

Acadia National Park is on Mount Desert Island on the coast of Maine about two-thirds of the way between the New Hampshire and Canadian borders. From the southwestern

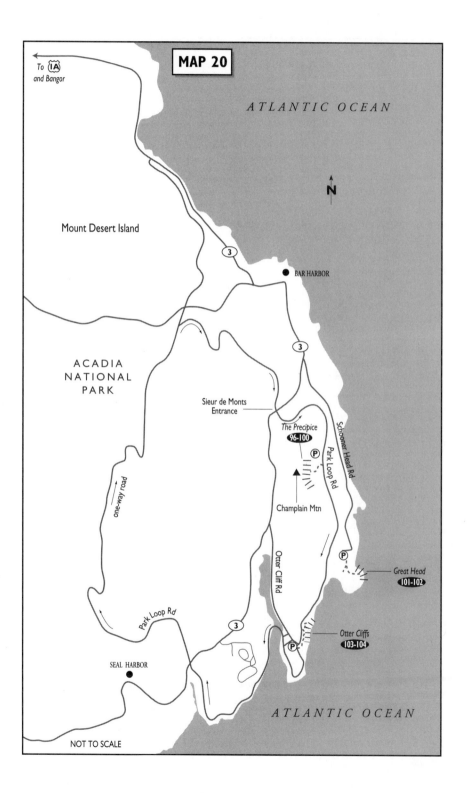

MAP 20

To **IA** and Bangor

ATLANTIC OCEAN

N

Mount Desert Island

3

● BAR HARBOR

3

ACADIA NATIONAL PARK

Sieur de Monts Entrance

The Precipice
96-100

one-way road

P

Schooner Head Rd

Park Loop Rd

Champlain Mtn

P

Great Head
101-102

Otter Cliff Rd

Park Loop Rd

3

P

Otter Cliffs
103-104

● SEAL HARBOR

ATLANTIC OCEAN

NOT TO SCALE

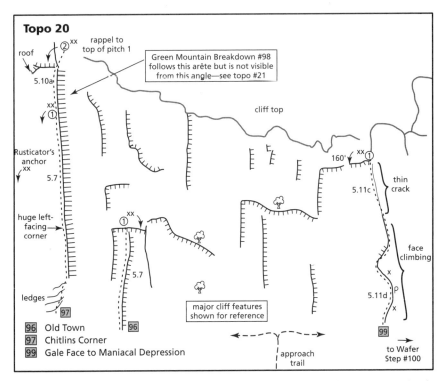

tip of Maine, the drive to Acadia takes about 3½ hours. From southern New England, take I-95 northeast to Bangor. Get off at exit 45A and follow I-395 for just a few miles east to US 1A. Take US 1A southeast into Ellsworth, where it meets Route 3. Take Route 3 south onto Mount Desert Island and the town of Bar Harbor.

For the Precipice: Take Route 3 south out of Bar Harbor and in just a few minutes turn right for the Park Loop Road's Sieur de Monts entrance. Take a right at the stop sign onto the Loop Road (one way) and drive for about 2 miles to the Precipice Trail parking area on the right.

For Great Head: From Bar Harbor, take Route 3 south for about 1 mile, then turn left onto Schooner Head Road and follow it for 2.4 miles to a stop sign. Continue straight ahead for 0.3 mile to the Great Head Trail parking lot on the left.

For Otter Cliffs: From Bar Harbor, take Route 3 south for 3-4 miles to a left turn onto Otter Cliff Road. When Otter Cliff Road dead-ends on the Park Loop Road, turn right and park at the first parking lot on the right. After climbing at Otter Cliffs, continue on the Loop Road for just 0.25 mile and then turn right, drive through a picnic area, and turn left onto Otter Cliff Road to return to Route 3.

The Precipice

The South Wall of Champlain Mountain—called the Precipice—is the stunning home of dozens of climbs up to three pitches long. Many of the routes on this big cliff at Acadia follow wonderful cracks—although there are some good face climbs too—and most pitches end at flat, spacious belays.

If I had to pick just one climbing day, one chain of pitches, one endless string of jams, stems, and smears, it would be a day twenty years ago on the golden granite of Acadia. I was young, pretty fit, and climbing with a good friend—and though I never was a particularly talented rock climber, for some reason I was "on" that day. We

The Precipice at Maine's Acadia National Park. Photo by Peter Cole

climbed many of the routes listed here, as well as others, and when the sun dropped we had covered about 750 feet of perfect granite from 5.5 to 5.11.

My friend Mark was my tour guide, offering me the sharp end on the island's best. I still remember the absolute delight of the Precipice's Wafer Step—it was so wonderful that I scampered up it again, sans rope, as soon as my feet touched down on rappel after leading it. I can still feel the perfect friction on the stems up Old Town and the wonderful feeling of reaching one of those big buckets that we came to call "Acadia jugs."

The toughest spot of the day was on the second pitch of Chitlins Corner. There is a little foothold up under that big roof, and I milked it for more than a half hour as I fiddled with gear and glanced right at the looming void. This was long before micro cams, and my silly straight-sided stoppers and wired hexes just would not stick in the little slot under the roof.

Realizing I could never down-climb the corner below me without skidding off and landing in Mark's lap, I finally just went for it—with the last gear way below my feet. I can still picture the moves, feel my pounding heart, and see the cerebral video—darting image-bursts as my eyes frantically searched for something, anything, for my hands to grab. There was a stretch, a reach, a long Wiley Coyote air-hanging moment, and then a flash and it was over and I was at the belay, panting.

I will let you guess whether I was at the belay at the *top* of the pitch or the one 30 feet below me.

Approach
From the the Precipice Trail parking lot, walk south along the road (with traffic) to the climbers trail on the right (not marked but obvious). Hike straight in toward the cliff (past a kiosk) and in just 2 minutes you come to a little cliff. Turn left and follow the cliff's base for 50 feet to its end and then climb talus up and around the left side of the cliff to the base of the main cliff above. The approach takes 5 minutes to the center of the wall.

96. Old Town   I, 5.7
Old Town may be the finest inside corner on the island. It is clean, steep, and well protected. But believe me, it is no stroll. I well remember jumping on the route full of confidence but running low on ammo. The day was almost over and I had just polished off nearby Connecticut Cracks, a tricky 5.11a, with just one fall. I figured I would scamper up Old Town to round things out.

A few moves into it, I realized that 5.7 can still be stout and that perhaps I had underestimated this little gem. Though the years have fogged things a bit, I remember running it out a bit, then a stem skidded off briefly and a bit of panic welled up. I got my act back together, made another move, and there it was, the king of all in-cut holds. With my feet suddenly stable, I tossed in a piece of gear and casually strolled to the top.

First ascent: Unknown.

Equipment: Two ropes for the rappel.

Start: Walk left (south) and uphill along the base of the Precipice for about 150 feet. Look for two left-facing corners about 50 feet right of Chitlins Corner (climb 97).

The Precipice's Old Town route. Photo by S. Peter Lewis

The left one has a wide crack in it and a series of discontinuous finger cracks on the face to its left (Connecticut Cracks, great 5.11). The corner to its right is Old Town.

Route: Pitch 1 (80 feet, 5.7): Stem and lieback up the immaculate corner with perfect protection to a flat ledge and a two-bolt anchor.

Descent: Rappel the route.

Kevin Hand on the classic corner of Old Town. Photo by Peter Cole

97. Chitlins Corner   I, 5.10a

Okay, you want a line, this is it. Chitlins Corner looks as though it has been cut out of the golden granite with a cleaver. Up and up it stretches until blocked by an enormous roof, where the route skips right and jumps into another corner to the top. The first long 5.7 pitch is an exercise in sheer jamming, liebacking, and stemming pleasure, and it goes and goes and goes.

But just inches above the belay for the second pitch, the route changes character. The crack in the back becomes a seam, the wall steepens, and the roof above your head juts farther and farther out into space. This is where I was trapped for many long minutes one day way back in my youth, fumbling with useless stoppers and hexes up in the maw of that roof. I related the tale to my friend Jeff recently, and he chuckled, nodded in agreement about the terrors of the "old days," and then said simply, "Now I just plug in a little cam, step down to the right, and it's over in a snap."

Next time I go up, I am going to leave the little cams behind out of a sense of nostalgia and just bring old gear. No, really, I am going to leave the cams in my pack; I might even leave them in the car.

Well, I might bring just one little one.

Chitlins Corner on the Precipice. Photo by S. Peter Lewis

First ascent: Unknown, though certainly sometime in the 1950s; first free ascent: Doug Madara and Paul Ross, 1977.

Equipment: A few very small wires and cams.

Start: Walk left (south) and uphill along the base of the Precipice for about 200

Mark Arsenault at the roof on Chitlins Corner during the marathon day (note the ancient gear). Photo by S. Peter Lewis

feet to the base of a dramatic left-facing corner that soars the full height of the cliff and is capped by a large roof.

Route: Pitch 1 (170 feet, 5.7): Climb easy, blocky rock to the left of the corner, enter the corner itself, and jam and stem the spectacular corner for a very long pitch to a nice, small ledge with two bolts.

Pitch 2 (45 feet, 5.10a): Continue stemming up the corner above (small gear) to a tiny stance at the big roof above, move right below the roof, and climb up into a short, right-facing corner then move right to a two-bolt belay.

Descent: Make three short rappels: The first is down and left to a two-bolt anchor at the top of the first pitch. Make a second rappel down and left on the face left of the corner to another bolted anchor (Rusticator's anchor). Make one last rappel to the ground.

98. Green Mountain Breakdown   I, 5.9

There is just something about an inside corner; it begs to be climbed. A wall on either side, often a crack in the back, pushing, pulling. Corners just make sense. So a sensible climber will start up the stunning Chitlins Corner (climb 97) and stay in it, right?

A sensible climber maybe, but an adventurous climber might also strike out up the right wall partway up the first pitch and follow a series of steep cracks to a small ledge on the corner of the arête. There may not be a more wonderful place to hang out in all of Acadia. Above, on the blade of the ridge above, is a tiny inside corner that stretches up the spine to a roof. If you are quiet here and put your ear to the rock, you can hear the corner, whispering, begging to be climbed.

First ascent: Unknown, probably late 1970s or early 1980s.

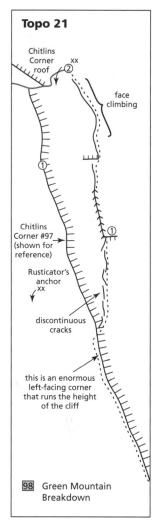

Topo 21

Start: Walk left (south) and uphill along the base of the Precipice for about 200 feet to the base of the dramatic left-facing corner that is Chitlins Corner (climb 97); Green Mountain Breakdown shares this first pitch.

Route: Pitch 1 (90 feet, 5.7): Climb easy, blocky rock to the left of the corner, enter the corner itself, and climb it for about 60 feet. Move onto the right wall and follow discontinuous cracks to a belay on a small ledge perched right on the arête—spectacular.

Pitch 2 (80 feet, 5.9): Follow the clean corner above to the crux moves over the right side of a small roof, climb the crack above for several feet, then move right and face climb to a two-bolt anchor.

Descent: Same as for Chitlins Corner (climb 97).

Tyler Stableford and Kevin Hand on Green Mountain Breakdown in Acadia National Park. Photo by Peter Cole

99. Gale Face to Maniacal Depression   I, 5.11d

One day more than twenty years ago, a chance meeting between Ed Webster and John Harlin III at the old Norumbega Mountain Shop led to the first ascent of seven new routes in about as many days, including the Gale Face direct start to one of the island's

The Precipice's Gale Face to Maniacal Depression. Photo by S. Peter Lewis

most difficult climbs. After a free ascent of Maniacal Depression, with its notorious (5.11) tips crack at the top, Webster and Harlin prepared to rappel down. "Wow, look at this amazing open face down here," Webster exclaimed. Why this, the most prominent piece of unclimbed granite at Acadia, remained virgin was obvious to Webster. Long a bastion of the traditional style, Acadia was a place where climbers simply did not put in bolts.

But Webster, an accomplished New Hampshire climber with many classic first ascents to his credit (see the Last Unicorn, climb 68) in the nearby White Mountains, felt the face deserved a route and was committed to as pure a style as possible—but the route would need bolts. The tactic was simple: Clean the route but do not top-rope it; then lead as high as possible; place a bolt either from a stance or by hanging gingerly from a hook, poor piton, or bashie; then lower off and pull the rope; then relead past the bolt, climb as high as possible, and repeat the process. While this was an accepted practice in North Conway Village, "I felt moderately sinful putting in bolts this way," Webster told me in a recent interview. "But the climbing was absolutely superb."

In the end, after 125 feet of sustained, hard climbing, Gale Face was born, equipped with just two bolts and a fixed piton. The route proved very controversial and within a year it was chopped.

Today you can enjoy the Gale Face to Maniacal Depression combination as it was first conceived. The route was reestablished long ago and has since gained a reputation as one of the island's finest 5.11s (though it remains one of the only routes in the area with bolts). "It's a lovely piece of granite and looks right out over the ocean," Webster said. "I feel a certain sense of redemption."

First ascent: Ed Webster and John Harlin III (Gale Face), October 1981; first free ascent: Jeff Achey and Mark Sonnenfeld (upper fingertip crack of Maniacal Depression), 1977.

Equipment: Two ropes for rappel.

Start: From the point where the trail reaches the base of the main wall, turn right and hike uphill. In less than 100 feet, you come to an open area of talus with a large rectangular boulder at the base of the cliff and a clean face above. This is the start for Gale Face.

Route: Pitch 1 (160 feet, 5.11d): In the center of the buttress, climb carefully up to a bolt. Climb the steep face above to a piton, then move left past a second bolt to a thin flake. At the top of the flake, traverse right into a corner and follow it up to a steep slab to the final headwall split by a very thin seam/crack (the crux of Maniacal Depression). There is a two-bolt belay at the top.

Descent: Rappel the route.

100. Wafer Step   I, 5.5

This neat little route may be the most pleasant 5.5 in the world. It is located at the far right end of the Precipice. Wafer Step begins with a short, steep jam crack that gives way to a curving flake that leads left across a golden wall.

Once while soloing the route (back in my young and foolish days), I noticed a tour bus below me on the road with a cluster of folks staring up at me. Safely gripping a pair of huge buckets, I let out a little screech, let my feet skid out from under

Wafer Step on Maine's Precipice cliff. Photo by S. Peter Lewis

me, and then flailed them around a bit—all the time looking down at the bus over my shoulder. I swear I saw a couple of camera flashes go off, then the cluster piled back on and the bus belched off down the Park Loop Road.

First ascent: Unknown.

Start: From the point where the trail reaches the base of the main wall, turn right and follow the cliff's base for a couple hundred feet to a stone staircase. Climb the staircase and then continue contouring the base of the cliff for another 150 feet or so until you come to an obvious flat area. There is a detached, 12-foot-high spike of rock next to the cliff and behind it is a low-angled wall with two vertical cracks about 15 feet apart. The crack on the right is Wafer Step.

Route: Pitch 1 (75 feet, 5.5): Jam the right-hand crack to a stance, then follow it left to where it merges with the crack on the left (Recollections of Pacifica, a fine 5.9). Belay at the ledge above with a fixed anchor.

Descent: Rappel the route.

Great Head

Sea-cliff climbing at Acadia has been a tradition since Fritz Wiessner first visited Otter Cliffs in the 1930s, and yet the treasure trove of routes at Great Head was not unburied for another fifty years as climbers focused on the nearby Otter Cliffs and the sea cliffs at Hunters Beach. Tucked around a cove away from the cosmopolitan Otter Cliffs, the big knob of granite at Great Head was assumed to be

Heather Butterfield on the best 5.5 route on the planet: Wafer Step. Photo by Jeff Butterfield

junk. "The area was long ignored by climbers, who imagined the rock suspect. I looked closer at Great Head in 1985 and discovered we had all been wrong," writes longtime local Jeff Butterfield in his guidebook to the area, *Acadia: A Climber's Guide.* Jeff had discovered the most spectacular sea-cliff climbing on the East Coast, and with various partners, he pioneered many of the routes on the crag in the early 1990s.

I went back to Acadia in 2002 to shoot some photos at Great Head for this book. Great Head is an intimidating place. Unlike at Otter, where its typical apron of flat granite at the bottom keeps the sea a bit at bay, at Great Head you just rappel into the drink. When the shooting was done, my friend Steve lowered me down for a lap on Morning Glory, perhaps one of the best 5.8s in Maine.

It was magnificent, if a little intimidating, with the ocean churning beneath my feet (this cliff makes Otter Cliffs feel as though it is miles from the water). For the rating, I found the climbing stout and very thought-provoking—even on a top rope. With my feet perched above the water, I worked my way into the corner and with great care sorted out the contorted moves needed to get to the upper, easier arête. It was wonderful, and I spent as much time looking over my shoulder at the blue Atlantic as I did looking for holds. I was a bit disappointed to reach the top.

A visiting western climber whom I had just met took the top-rope ride after me and scampered up the route in about 30 seconds. Perplexed at the need to hurry, I asked him, "Why did you climb that so fast? What's the rush?" He looked me up and down a bit pathetically, shook his head, and finally said, "Dude, look at yourself; you're a dying ember."

I prefer to think I climbed slowly not because I am old but because I was savoring the moment.

Approach

From the parking area, follow the wide Great Head Trail for about 200 feet and then turn left (at a sign for Great Head) and hike about 10 minutes until the trail breaks out onto the open summit of Great Head near the ruins of a stone tower.

101. Morning Glory   I, 5.8+

If you are lucky, the tide will be low and the sea mellow and the rock will be dry all the way down to the belay at the base of Morning Glory. But on other days, you may only be able to top-rope the upper two-thirds of the route, unless you have scuba gear. The pitch starts off a small shelf with the ocean licking at your heels—the route is accessible only by rappel.

Move up the ramp on the right and then make a tricky stem left into the base of the dihedral. Now the business starts. Even with three bolts in quick succession, the route maintains an air of seriousness—perhaps it is the ocean growling below. The moves are odd and off balance and you would be wise to search up and right for a funky handhold. Above the last bolt, big holds lead left to an arête and one of the most stunning positions you will ever find yourself in.

First ascent: Jeff Butterfield (with various partners), early 1990s.

Special considerations: Climbing at Great Head can be extremely dangerous during storms, big waves, or very high tides. Bring two ropes and leave one fixed on the rappel in case of emergency—there is no walk-off from the base of the route. The climb can easily be top-roped.

Equipment: A light rock rack to 2 inches; a couple of larger cams for belay.

Start: From the tower ruins, Morning Glory is located near the left (north) end of the cliff (looking out to sea), but it is only accessible by rappel, so walk right about 50 feet on the Great Head Trail, turn left near the first spruce tree, and follow a vague climbers trail down a broken slab to a drainage and notch just above a large terrace. Climb down to the terrace and walk to its far left end, where an exposed move around a bulge brings you to the two-bolt rappel station at chest height. Please take extra care getting to this anchor; the consequences of a slip would be disastrous.

Make one 80-foot rappel from the bolts to a small stance just above the water. (When stormy weather, high seas, or a very high tide bury this stance in the ocean, top-roping the route is the only option.) Build a gear anchor (big cams) at a small stance a few feet above and to the right of where the rappel lands you.

Route: Pitch 1 (80 feet, 5.8+): Climb up and right on a ramp, then step left into the base of a left-facing corner. Climb the corner past three bolts trending left after the

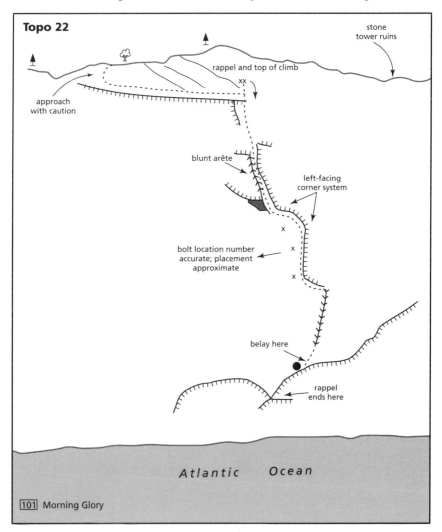

Topo 22

stone tower ruins

rappel and top of climb

approach with caution

blunt arête

left-facing corner system

x

bolt location number accurate; placement approximate

x

x

belay here

rappel ends here

Atlantic Ocean

101 Morning Glory

Steve Nichipor and Alden Strong above the Atlantic on Great Head's Morning Glory.
Photo by S. Peter Lewis

third bolt to a blunt arête and gear placements that lead back to the rappel station.

Descent: Like the other sea-cliff routes here, the "descent" is off the top—a walk off from the base is not possible on this route.

102. Transatlantic   I, 5.13a
Going back to Acadia last year to refresh my memory and gather up-to-date information for this book, I headed out to Great Head with my friend Jeff Butterfield. We scrambled down along one edge and peered at the overhanging wall and into the black hole of the Cavern. The Cavern at Great Head is one of the most spectacular places to climb in the Northeast—and one of the most dangerous. Storm surges, storms themselves, or unusually high tides turn the Cavern into a maelstrom of pounding surf. Waves come into the cavern with such force that spray is sent more than 100 feet into the air, accompanied by a sound like two locomotives hitting head on. The sea was quiet this day, but Jeff pantomimed the roar and the blast of spray that ejects from the Cavern on a big-sea day. It was scary just thinking about it. Jeff's first forays here in the '90s, when bolting was not yet acceptable, were "both scary and limited" and "initially, climbing in the main Cavern gave me the creeps."

Transatlantic takes the most uncompromising line right out the maw of the Cavern, and its creation follows the tradition of many extreme routes—it was a community effort. Butterfield climbed high on the first pitch, but did not have a drill so did not put in an anchor. Later, Joe Terravecchia climbed the first pitch, installed a two-bolt belay, and then scooted right up his route, Maine Squeeze (5.12a). Butterfield

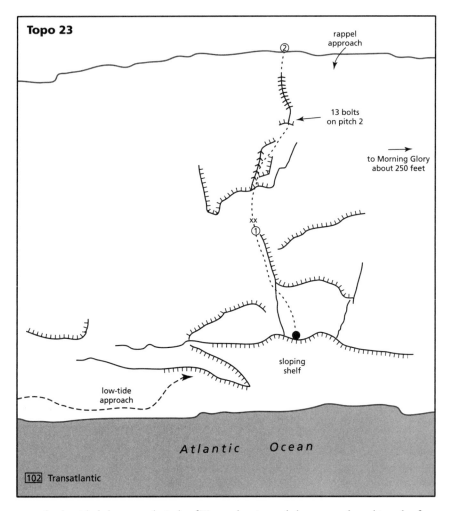

Topo 23

rappel
approach

13 bolts
on pitch 2

to Morning Glory
about 250 feet

xx

sloping
shelf

low-tide
approach

Atlantic   Ocean

102 Transatlantic

came back, aided the second pitch of Transatlantic, and then started working the free moves. After a summer or more of trying, he got the route down to one point of aid in the overhanging corner—giving it a 5.12d A0 rating. Pitch 2 has thirteen bolts—and according to Butterfield, "you want every one."

Two other longtime activists, Bob Parrott and A. J. Jones, both worked the pitch. But the climb stubbornly held on at 5.12d A0. Butterfield recounted the eventual first free ascent in a recent note to me. "Rob Frost called about arranging for some filming for [his video] *Uncommon Ground* and asked if there was anything new that we could sic Tim Kemple on [and] of course I thought of Transatlantic. Tim spent an afternoon working out the moves, then returned the next day. I had the privilege of belaying him while he sent it. Pretty damn impressive from my seat."

Very kind words from a guy who was just a letter grade away from getting the free ascent himself. But that is part of what makes Acadia so special. Whether you are cruising your way up a corner at the Precipice, jamming a perfect crack at Otter Cliffs, or hanging out over the roaring surf at Great Head, you will find friendly climbers who are quick to offer encouragement (and maybe even hand you a ripe plum).

First ascent: Jeff Butterfield, 1990s; first free ascent: Tim Kemple, June 2001.

Special considerations: The Cavern at Great Head is one of the most dangerous places to climb in the Northeast. Unless the day and the tide are perfect, stay out of the Cavern. At least one climber died here when he was unable to ascend a fixed line to the top of the cliff during a storm. Leaving a fixed rope from the rappel anchors (even if you plan to traverse in to the base of the route) is a good idea; bring ascenders (and know how to use them).

A. J. Jones on the first pitch of Transatlantic, with the 5.13a pitch looming above and the sea below. Photo by Jeff Butterfield

Equipment: A light rack with wires to 2½ inches.

Start: There are two ways to get to the base of this route: by rappel or by a traverse in from the side.

To approach by rappel, from the ruins of the stone tower walk right (south) for about 200 feet to a pair of bolted anchors. From the left-hand set of bolts (looking out to sea), rappel 90 feet into the Cavern, where you usually find dry rock above the high-tide mark. Transatlantic starts about 15 feet left of where you touch down on the rappel.

It is also possible to traverse in to the base of the climb, but conditions have to be just right. **Warning:** This semi-technical traverse is possible only if the rock is absolutely dry. Slimy one-celled animals on the rocks become grease factories if even one wave washes over them. In wet conditions, this traverse is extremely dangerous. Ideally, the day's low tide is around noon, giving you the most time to scamper across on dry rock (check a tide chart for the day of your climb).

From the tower ruins, walk right (north) for several hundred feet until you are at the far right end of the cliff (looking out to sea). Down-climb following vague climbers trails to a big ledgy slab that stretches down to the water. Scramble down the slab and head south (left, looking out to sea) under the cliff to a 50-foot traverse on ledges that lead you into the bowels of the Cavern and the belay.

Route: Pitch 1 (45 feet, 5.10a): Start on the left side of the Cavern and climb up to a large roof. Traverse left under it to a left-facing corner, which is climbed to a semihanging belay with two bolts. (This is a popular pitch in its own right.)

Pitch 2 (120 feet, 5.13a): Climb up and left through a very steep corner and roof system and then traverse right to a final overhanging headwall. This is one of the most spectacular pitches on the East Coast.

Descent: Like the other sea-cliff routes here, the "descent" is off the top—a walk off from the base (north along ledges; see Start, above) is possible only at low tide and in bone-dry conditions.

Otter Cliffs

Otter Cliffs is a magical place. Perfect granite drops straight onto a shelf at the edge of the sea, the air smells of balsam, seagulls hover and screech, and buoys clang in the distance. If the day is soft and foggy and the air is full of mist, do not despair. This is a perfect day to head to Otter Cliffs. If you are lucky, the crowds will be back in Bar Harbor sipping coffee.

Approach

Cross the Loop Road (watch for traffic), descend a set of stone stairs, then bear left (north) and walk an obvious trail for a couple hundred feet to an obvious climbers trail that turns right and heads about 50 feet down to the top of the cliff with the Sea Stack on the right.

103. Wonderwall   I, 5.6–5.7

As you look out over the ocean (incredible), the obvious landmark for the whole area is the Sea Stack, a detached granite pillar on your right (which you can hop onto if you are very brave). At Wonderwall, tie in to the bomber belay staple just back from the edge, lower into the swirling air above the surf, and take your time playing on this wonderful little wall. The friction is great, the holds ample, and hey, you are on a top-rope.

First ascent: Unknown.

Special considerations: This route is generally top-roped from above using the fixed belay staple provided by the Park Service.

Start: Looking out to sea and down from the top, 20 feet left (north) of the Sea Stack is an obvious inside corner; 20 feet farther is another obvious corner; and the wall to the immediate left (north) of this second corner is Wonderwall.

Route: Pitch 1 (50 feet, 5.6–5.7): On marvelous face holds, climb anywhere on this golden wall. The middle is easiest, while the left and right sides go at 5.7.

Descent: The "descent" is up. Finish the route and walk back up to your car.

104. A Dare by the Sea   I, 5.10c

This route's name is a play on words. It speaks cleverly of both the name of the first ascensionist, gifted Connecticut climber Jim Adair, and the pluck that he mustered to lead it—"a dare." In a classic photo by Ken Nichols, Jim is seen jamming and

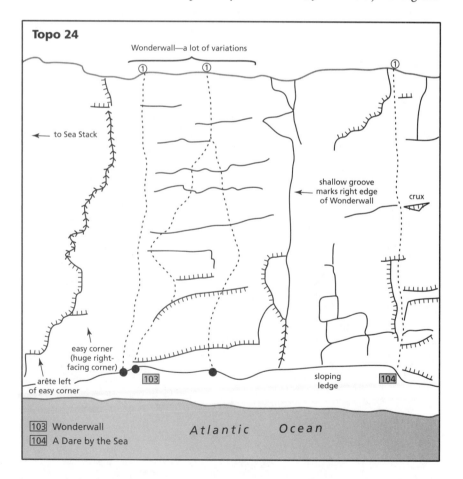

high-stepping low on the route. The day is misty and Jim is wearing cut-off jeans, a tee shirt, EBs, and a swami belt. The rope is casually draped across his thigh (bad form, usually), he has just a bunch of straight-sided stoppers, and there is not a cam or quickdraw in sight. And he looks really casual.

At Otter twenty years ago, I bravely racked up below A Dare by the Sea—a route rarely led back in the dark ages of the early 1980s—and started up. The rock was solid and the gear was good, and I soon found myself standing on a small hold above the roof

Tyler Stableford on the crux thin jams of Otter Cliffs' class hard route A Dare by the Sea. Photo by Peter Cole

contemplating the crux. I got a high nut, worked the key jam, smeared up on nothing apparent, and absolutely cranked for the jug. I latched it and then just danced up the final little headwall without a care in the world (or any protection, now that I think about it). Nowhere near as good a climber as Jim Adair, I just got lucky on this day.

Jump ahead twenty years, strap on the latest harness, lace on the newest suction-cup shoes, and grab a rack of curved stoppers, gee-whiz cams, and quickdraws—then get on the crux and see how casual you look. This spectacular crack is a hard lead, but it is a great one—although it is most often top-roped. Twenty years after I first led it, I still count A Dare by the Sea as one of the best 15 minutes of my climbing life. Sure, grabbing it on a top rope is easy, but if you want a memory that will last decades, take the sharp end on this sea-cliff classic.

First ascent: Jim Adair, late 1970s (Jim was killed in Yosemite in 1978).

Start: Looking out to sea and down from the top, 20 feet left (north) of the Sea Stack is an obvious inside corner; 20 feet farther is another obvious corner; and the wall to the immediate left (north) of this second corner is Wonderwall. Left (north) of Wonderwall is a series of stainless-steel belay staples. This route is located about 40 feet left (north) of Wonderwall, with a convenient staple (the second-to-last staple you see as you walk left/north from Wonderwall) at its top. When you look down from the top, you should see a distinct finger crack extending up from below and ending about 15 feet from the top.

Route: Pitch 1 (60 feet, 5.10c): Climb the face below the crack for about 20 feet, pull a small roof, power up the crack above, and finish on good face holds on a slightly overhanging wall to the top.

Descent: The "descent" is up. Finish the route and walk back up to your car.

APPENDIX A. RATINGS

Climbers love their numbers. All ratings systems are somewhat subjective and depend to a greater or lesser extent on the conditions of the climb and the skill of the party. These are the rating systems used in this book (sections below briefly explain each system):

To describe the time commitment of a particular route, we use the standard rating system (National Climbing Classification System, or NCCS) used in this country. Throughout the book, we use the Yosemite Decimal System (YDS) to rate rock climbs (both free and aid), the North American Water Ice Grading System to rate pure ice climbs, and the "M" system to rate mixed climbs. To describe a route's seriousness, we use the traditional "R" (potential for a long fall) and "X" (potential for a long, perhaps fatal, fall) ratings.

Examples of ratings found in this book:

- New York, Shawangunks, High Exposure (climb 13): I, 5.6+—a short route (a couple of hours) with moderate free climbing
- New Hampshire, Cathedral Ledge, the Prow (climb 75): III, 5.6 A2 or 5.11d— a midlength route (most of a day) with moderate free climbing and reasonably secure aid climbing, or an all-free route with very difficult free climbing
- New York, Chapel Pond, Chouinards Gully (climb 27): II, WI 3—a short route (2–4 hours) with moderate ice climbing
- New Hampshire, Cannon Cliff, The Black Dike (climb 62): III, WI 4–5 M3— a fairly long, difficult ice climb with moderate mixed climbing

Grade System

The NCCS system uses the roman numerals I through VII to measure the commitment of a climb, its overall nature, and how long it will take to get up it under typical conditions. This is the first rating number listed for each climb. It is used as a general guideline.

Grade I: 1–3 hours
Grade II: 2–4 hours
Grade III: 4–6 hours
Grade IV: 1 full day
Grade V: 1–2 days; most parties will bivouac
Grade VI: Several days
Grade VII: Many days, combined with extreme difficulties, length, and exposed alpine positions

Free Climbing Ratings (Yosemite Decimal System)

This system ranges from class 1 (hiking), class 2–3 (scrambling), class 4 (simple climbing; some climbers may opt for a rope), to 5th-class climbing (technical climbing requiring ropes and equipment for safety but is still "free climbing" in which the climber ascends with hands and feet on the rock and relies on equipment only to catch a fall). Class 5 climbing is further divided into fifteen categories expressed with decimal points,

UIAA	FRENCH	YOSEMITE DECIMAL SYSTEM	AUSTRALIAN	BRAZILIAN	BRITISH
I	1	5.2			
II	2	5.3	11		
III	3	5.4	12	II	
IV	4	5.5		IIsup	
V-		5.6	13	III	
V	5	5.7	14	IIIsup	
V+	5		15		
VI-		5.8	16	IV	
VI	6a	5.9	17 / 18	IVsup	
VI+	6a+	5.10a	19	V	
VII-	6b	5.10b	20	Vsup	
		5.10c	21	VI	
VII	6b+	5.10d	22	VIsup	
VII+	6c	5.11a	23	VII	
	6c+	5.11b			
VIII-	7a	5.11c	24	VIIsup	
VIII	7a+	5.11d	25	VIII	
	7b	5.12a			
VIII+	7b+	5.12b	26	VIIIsup	
IX-		5.12c			
	7c	5.12d	27		
IX	7c+	5.13a	28		
IX+	8a	5.13b	29		
		5.13c	30		
X-	8a+		31		
X	8b	5.13d	32		
	8b+				
X+	8c	5.14a	33		
		5.14b			
XI-	8c+	5.14c			
XI	9a	5.14d			
XI+	9a+	5.15a			
XII-		5.15b			

British technical grades (left scale): 3a, 3b, 3c, 4a, 4b, 4c, 5a, 5b, 5c, 6a, 6b, 6c, 7a

British adjectival grades (right scale): VD, HVD, MS, S, HS, VS, HVS, E1, E2, E3, E4, E5, E6, E7

from 5.0 to 5.15. Climbs of 5.10 difficulty and above are further subdivided by the letters *a* through *d*, or in some instances with the traditional Northeast subgrades of plus (+) or minus (-). This is the second rating number listed for rock climbs in this book. In general these ratings fall into the following categories:

5.0–5.5: Easy   5.9–5.11: Difficult to very difficult

5.6–5.8: Moderate   5.12–5.15: Extreme

Aid Climbing Ratings

The aid climbing rating system uses the prefix "A," followed by a number from 0 to 5. Aid climbing is used where free climbing is no longer possible and the climber must pull on protection points to make progress. The higher the rating number, the less secure the aid placements (can be any piece of gear) and the greater the likelihood for a fall. In this book, the aid rating is typically found after the free-climbing or ice rating.

A0: Pulling on a piece of protection or doing a rappel or pendulum on a free climb

A1: Straightforward climbing with consistently solid protection points, any one of which could hold a fall

A2: Less-secure placements; often steeper, more awkward climbing; but all protection points can easily hold body weight and most will hold a short fall

A3: Advanced techniques and gear are necessary to create a chain of often marginal pieces; if a piece pulls, there is the likelihood that others will rip and the possibility of a 30-plus-foot fall is real

A4: Each piece is just barely able to support body weight, and there are so many of these placements that pulling one may mean a breathtakingly long fall

A5: A dangerous pitch of pieces so marginal that the climber risks ripping most of them in a fall and would likely be injured (or worse)

Water Ice Grading System

This straightforward system rates pure ice climbs, using the prefix "WI" followed by a number from 1 through 8, based primarily on steepness. On ice climbs in this book, this rating follows the commitment grade.

WI 1: Low-angled ice and snow less than 50 degrees

WI 2: Ice up to 60 degrees

WI 3: Consistent 50-degree to 60-degree ice with short 70-degree to 90-degree bulges

WI 4: Short vertical columns with rests on 50-degree to 60-degree ice

WI 5: Long vertical sections with few rests (in this guide, no routes are rated higher than WI 5+)

WI 6: Sustained vertical or steeper columns with overhangs and essentially no rests

WI 7–8: Increasingly longer sections of vertical to overhanging ice culminating in multipitch horror shows

Mixed Climbing "M" System

This system evolved in recent years as more and more climbers have developed the art of connecting overhanging sections of ice by rock climbing with their crampons and tools. The basic idea is to give a reasonable comparison to how hard the mixed moves would feel if they were pure rock-climbing moves. Typically this number, which uses the prefix "M" followed by a number from 1 to 9, is listed after the pure ice rating. This system is very subjective, but in general:

M1 feels like 5.5	M6 feels like 5.10
M2 feels like 5.6	M7 feels like 5.11
M3 feels like 5.7	M8 feels like 5.12
M4 feels like 5.8	M9 and above feels ridiculous
M5 feels like 5.9	

APPENDIX B. RESOURCES

Access Fund (303-545-6772; *accessfund.org*) is a climber advocacy organization that works to keep climbing areas open. **Note:** A lot more information on the following areas can be found on the Internet.

New York
The Shawangunks
Climbing shops: Rock and Snow, downtown New Paltz (845-255-1311); Eastern Mountain Sports (small tech shop), on the way to the cliff (845-255-3280).

Supplies: New Paltz, 6 miles from the Mohonk Preserve, has it all; there is a deli (convenience store) at the intersection of Routes 299 and 44/55, just below the cliffs.

Camping: A multiuse camping area is on Route 299, less than a mile east of the intersection with US 44/55.

Websites: *www.newpaltzchamber.org, www.gunks.com.*

The Catskills
Climbing shops: Rock and Snow, in New Paltz (845-255-1311); Eastern Mountain Sports, in the Gunks (845-255-3280).

Supplies: Tannersville and Phoenecia have the basics.

Camping: The Department of Environmental Conservation (DEC) operates fifty-two campgrounds within the Adirondack and Catskills parks (*www.dec.state.ny.us*).

Websites: *www.neice.com.*

The Adirondacks
Climbing shops: The Mountaineer (also has area weather and ice conditions), on US 73 in Keene Valley (518-576-2281); Eastern Mountain Sports, on the main drag in Lake Placid, across from the movie theater (518-523-2505).

Supplies: A grocery in Keene Valley and one in Lake Placid close early; the Cliffhanger Cafe, on US 73 in Keene Valley (518-576-2009); the "Noonmark," a friendly diner on US 73.

Camping: The Department of Environmental Conservation (DEC) operates fifty-two campgrounds within the Adirondack and Catskills parks (*www.dec.state.ny.us*).

Websites: *www.rockandriver.com* (up-to-date ice conditions), *www.adksportsfitness .com, www.adirondacks.com, www.dec.state.ny.us.*

Connecticut
Ragged Mountain
Climbing shops: Eastern Mountain Sports, Corbin's Corner Shopping Parcade, West Hartford, about 20 minutes north of the mountain (860-561-4302); Country Sports, Albany Turnpike/US 44, Canton (860-693-2267).

Supplies: Meriden, 10 minutes south of Ragged on Route 71; New Britain, 10 minutes north on Route 71A.

Camping: No camping at Ragged; Black Rock State Park, less than 30 minutes away, Route 6 in Thomaston (860-283-8088).

Websites: *www.raggedmtn.org* (climbing info and a lot of links), *www.dep.state.ct.us /stateparks/camping/camping_info.htm, www.campconn.com* (Connecticut Campground Owners Association).

Vermont
Smugglers Notch
Climbing shops: Climb High Retail Shop, Shelburne, just south of Burlington (802-985-5055); Eastern Mountain Sports, South Burlington (802-864-0473).

Supplies: Burlington and its suburbs have everything; Jeffersonville and Stowe have the basics.

Camping: Available in Smugglers Notch; excellent sites are found between the high point in the notch and the Stone Hut (1-mile hike). Do not camp at the end of the plowed roads. The Stone Hut (an old stone building run by Vermont State Parks) is on Route 108 (802-253-4010).

Websites: *www.neice.com, www.6degrees.com/~alden/climbing/smugglersice.html.*

Mount Pisgah/Lake Willoughby Area
Climbing shops: See Smugglers Notch, Cannon Cliff/Franconia Notch, and Mount Washington Valley listings.

Supplies: Lyndonville; St. Johnsbury, 30 minutes south.

Camping: The Cheney House, an old Victorian home run as a state park by Vermont State Parks (camping, bunkroom, and cooking facilities available), is just down the road (802-525-6939).

Websites: *www.neice.com, www.6degrees.com/~alden/climbing/willoughby.html.*

New Hampshire
Cannon Cliff/Franconia Notch
Climbing shops: Outdoor Outfitters, Lincoln (603-745-4806); Lahout's Country Clothing, Littleton (603-444-5838); International Mountain Equipment, North Conway Village (603-356-6316); Eastern Mountain Sports, North Conway Village (603-356-5433); Ragged Mountain Equipment, North Conway Village (603-356-5950).

Supplies: Lincoln (10 miles south); Franconia (just north of the notch); Littleton (20 minutes north of the notch).

Camping: Lafayette Campground, part of Franconia Notch State Park, summer camping only (603-271-3628); Crazy Horse Campground, Littleton, private, winter camping available (800-639-4107); a lot of campgrounds in the White Mountain National Forest with both summer and winter camping (*www.fs.fed.us/r9/white/*).

Websites: *www.nhclimbs.com, www.neice.com, www.nerock.com.*

Mount Washington Valley

Climbing shops: International Mountain Equipment, North Conway Village (603-356-6316); Eastern Mountain Sports, North Conway Village (603-356-5433); Craggers, North Conway Village (603-356-8877); Ragged Mountain Equipment, 3 miles north of North Conway Village (603-356-5950).

Supplies: North Conway Village.

Camping: We cannot possibly list all the campgrounds in this area: White Mountain National Forest campgrounds (*www.fs.fed.us/r9/white/*); private camp-grounds (*www.ucampnh.com/index.html*); New Hampshire state park campgrounds (*www.nhparks.state.nh.us/*); Appalachian Mountain Club (603-466-2727), winter camping on Mount Washington or lodging at Pinkham Notch.

Websites: *www.nhclimbs.com, www.neice.com, www.nerock.com, www.mount washington.org.*

Maine

Mount Katahdin

Climbing shops: Eastern Mountain Sports, Maine Mall, right off I-95 on the way north (207-772-3776); see also Mount Washington Valley and Acadia National Park listings.

Supplies: Medway and Millinocket have essentials; Bangor has everything.

Camping: Camping at Katahdin in summer or winter is limited, requires reser-vations in advance, and is very competitive (people line up at park headquarters on January 1 each year to make reservations). Contact the camping office at Baxter State Park (207-723-5140).

Websites: *www.baxterstateparkauthority.com, www.nerock.com.*

Acadia National Park

Climbing shops: Cadillac Mountain Sports, Cottage Street, Bar Harbor (207-288-2521); Acadia Mountain Guides, Main Street, Bar Harbor (207-288-8186).

Supplies: Bar Harbor.

Camping: Two national park campgrounds: Black Woods (207-288-3274) and Sea Wall (207-244-3600); contact Bar Harbor Chamber of Commerce (*www.bar harborinfo.com*) about the many private campgrounds.

Websites: *www.nerock.com.*

BIBLIOGRAPHY

Butterfield, Jeffrey. *Acadia: A Climber's Guide.* Portland, Maine: Maine Vertical, 2002.

Cummins, Clint. *Lake Willoughby Ice Climbs: A Few Climbing Yarns.* Cambridge, Mass.: Harvard Mountaineering, 1979.

Handren, Jerry. *A Rock Climbing Guide to Cathedral and Whitehorse Ledges.* Bishop, Calif.: Vertical Brain, 1996.

Harlin, John III. *The Climber's Guide to North America.* Volume 3, *East Coast Rock Climbs.* Denver, Colo.: Chockstone Press, 1986.

Lewis, S. Peter, and Rick Wilcox. *An Ice Climber's Guide to Northern New England.* 3d ed. Conway, N.H.: TMC Books, 2003.

Mellor, Don. *Climbing in the Adirondacks.* Lake George, N.Y.: Adirondack Mountain Club, 2001.

Nichols, Ken. *Hooked on Ragged.* N.p.: Self-published, 1997.

Schneider, Paul. *The Adirondacks, A History of America's First Wilderness.* New York: Henry Holt, 1997.

Viljanen, Patrik. *The Local's Guide to Smugglers' Notch.* Jeffersonville, Vt.: The Duke of Jeffersonville, Inc., 1999.

Waterman, Laura, and Guy Waterman. *Yankee Rock and Ice: A History of Climbing in the Northeastern United States.* Mechanicsburg, Pa.: Stackpole Books, 1993.

Webster, Edward R. *Rock Climbs in the White Mountains of New Hampshire.* 3d ed. (East Volume). Eldorado Springs, Colo.: Mountain Imagery, 1996.

Williams, Dick. *Shawangunk Rock Climbs.* New York: American Alpine Club, 1991.

———. *The Gunks Select.* High Falls, N.Y.: Vulgarian Press, 1996.

INDEX

ABOUT THE AUTHORS

Dave Horowitz. Photo by Jennifer East

S. Peter Lewis. Photo by Karen Lewis

Dave Horowitz is a climbing guide with the New York climbing school of Eastern Mountain Sports, guiding clients up technical rock climbs. He has nine years of climbing experience and has climbed in at least fifteen states, plus South America; he is also certified in Wilderness Advanced First Aid. His writings have been published in national magazines, including *Rock & Ice.* He lives in Rosendale, New York.

S. Peter Lewis has been a rock climber since 1976, an ice climber since 1979, and a professional mountain guide since 1983. He has climbed in almost every major climbing area in the Northeast and is an expert on the area's climbing history. From 1994 to 1999, Lewis was the executive director of the American Mountain Guides Association. Lewis also has been a freelance writer and photographer specializing in adventure sports since 1983. He has written dozens of articles, published hundreds of photographs, and been featured in two profiles, in *Outdoor Photographer* and *New Hampshire Profiles.* Lewis also has worked as a newspaper reporter and has won journalism and photography awards. He has authored or coauthored six books on climbing, including *Climbing: From Gym to Crag,* published by The Mountaineers Books in 2000. He researched, edited, designed, and marketed with Rick Wilcox a self-published book, the second edition of *An Ice Climber's Guide to Northern New England,* in 1992, and has just finished the third edition of the guide, released in early 2003. He currently works for TMC (Too Many Cats) Books in Conway, New Hampshire. He lives in Bridgton, Maine, with his wife and two children.

THE MOUNTAINEERS, founded in 1906, is a nonprofit outdoor activity and conservation club, whose mission is "to explore, study, preserve, and enjoy the natural beauty of the outdoors. . . . " Based in Seattle, Washington, the club is now the third-largest such organization in the United States, with seven branches throughout Washington State.

The Mountaineers sponsors both classes and year-round outdoor activities in the Pacific Northwest, which include hiking, mountain climbing, ski-touring, snowshoeing, bicycling, camping, kayaking and canoeing, nature study, sailing, and adventure travel. The club's conservation division supports environmental causes through educational activities, sponsoring legislation, and presenting informational programs. All club activities are led by skilled, experienced volunteers, who are dedicated to promoting safe and responsible enjoyment and preservation of the outdoors.

If you would like to participate in these organized outdoor activities or the club's programs, consider a membership in The Mountaineers. For information and an application, write or call The Mountaineers, Club Headquarters, 300 Third Avenue West, Seattle, Washington 98119; 206-284-6310.

The Mountaineers Books, an active, nonprofit publishing program of the club, produces guidebooks, instructional texts, historical works, natural history guides, and works on environmental conservation. All books produced by The Mountaineers Books fulfill the club's mission.

Send or call for our catalog of more than 450 outdoor titles:

The Mountaineers Books
1001 SW Klickitat Way, Suite 201
Seattle, WA 98134
800-553-4453
mbooks@mountaineers.org
www.mountaineersbooks.org

OTHER TITLES YOU MIGHT ENJOY FROM THE MOUNTAINEERS BOOKS

**Mountaineering:
The Freedom of the Hills,**
The Mountaineers

**Climbing: From Gym
to Crag,** *S. Peter Lewis &
Dan Cauthorn*

**Ice & Mixed Climbing:
Modern Technique,**
Will Gadd

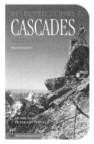

Climbing: Training for Peak Performance,
Clyde Soles

Climbing: Expedition Planning, *Clyde Soles &
Phil Powers*

OTHER TITLES IN THE SELECTED CLIMBS SERIES:

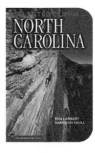

**Selected Climbs in the Cascades:
Volumes I & II,** *Jim Nelson & Peter Potterfield*

Selected Climbs in North Carolina,
Yon Lambert & Harrison Shull

OTHER REGIONAL CLIMBING GUIDES:

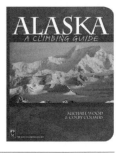

Washington Ice: A Climbing Guide,
Jason D. Martin & Alex Krawarik

Alaska: A Climbing Guide,
Mike Wood & Colby Coombs

Available at fine bookstores and outdoor stores, by phone at
800-553-4453 or on the Web at *www.mountaineersbooks.org*

THE MOUNTAINEERS BOOKS